Inclusion on Purpose

Inclusion on Purpose

An Intersectional Approach to Creating a Culture of Belonging at Work

Ruchika Tulshyan

Foreword by Ijeoma Oluo

The MIT Press

Cambridge, Massachusetts | London, England

The MIT Press would like to thank the anonymous peer reviewers who provided comments on drafts of this book. The generous work of academic experts is essential for establishing the authority and quality of our publications. We acknowledge with gratitude the contributions of these otherwise uncredited readers.

This book was set in Stone Serif and Stone Sans by Westchester Publishing Services. Printed and bound in the United States of America.

Library of Congress Cataloging-in-Publication Data

Names: Tulshyan, Ruchika, author.
Title: Inclusion on purpose : an intersectional approach to creating a culture
    of belonging at work / Ruchika Tulshyan ; foreword by Ijeoma Oluo.
Description: Cambridge, Massachusetts : The MIT Press, 2022. | Includes
    bibliographical references and index. | Summary: "A guide for organizations
    to improve their diversity, equity, and inclusion efforts, focusing specifically
    on the experiences of women of color"—Provided by publisher.
Identifiers: LCCN 2021015858 | ISBN 9780262046558 (hardcover)
Subjects: LCSH: Diversity in the workplace—Case studies. |
    Minority women—Employment. | Women's rights.
Classification: LCC HF5549.5.M5 T85 2022 | DDC 658.3008—dc23
LC record available at https://lccn.loc.gov/2021015858

10 9 8 7 6 5 4 3 2

To women of color everywhere, especially S and R. I am, because you are.
To all our champions in the journey, especially P, S, and V.
Om tat sat.

Contents

Foreword

Ijeoma Oluo

I will always remember the advice my mom gave me before starting my first real job as a young adult. She offered up a bunch of the expected basics: always be five minutes early, make friends by being helpful, don't gossip. I rolled my eyes through a lot of it as many young people do when their parents are trying to share their wisdom with them. My eyes glazed over as I, big on attitude in my early twenties, had already decided that having a successful career would be as easy for me as being successful in school had been.

"And most important," my mother concluded, voice raising to bring back my attention, "no matter what happens, NEVER go to HR."

Wait—what?

Did I hear that right? Was my mom telling me to not bring work issues to the people you are supposed to bring work issues to?

She explained that her experience of her years in the workforce and the experiences of her peers had made it clear that even if sexual harassment in the workplace was bad, even if racism from your coworkers or boss was bad, none of it was as bad as getting labeled a "troublemaker" by going to HR. Bringing your grievances to HR not only did little to end the harassment that the complainant was facing, it also would kill any chances of advancement.

"HR doesn't work for you," my mom said, "They work for the company. They aren't paid to make sure that there aren't any problems for you; they are paid to make sure there aren't any problems for the CEO. When you complain, you become a problem."

As I sat through the company initiation training over the next few days I became convinced that my mom was being overdramatic or her advice was out of date and out of sync with modern workplaces. Friendly Human Resources professionals clicked "play" on VHS players that showed films on how to avoid being a sexual harasser, how to not make racist jokes. The HR manager handed out thick packets that outlined the company's anti-harassment policies. We all had to sign them.

Surely, this was a place where any issues of racism or sexism would be swiftly dealt with.

I was assigned to my first work team in data entry. I sat in my very first cubicle, right outside my manager's office. I was eager to prove my worth, taking on extra tasks and trying to perform my work as quickly and accurately as possible. I tried to show that I had a good personality by occasionally telling my boss a funny little anecdote or work-appropriate joke.

The first time I told my boss a funny story, she turned to one of my coworkers, an older white man who had been with the company for years and said, "Isn't she just like Ebony?"

He nodded and laughed lightly in recognition.

Ebony must have been funny.

Then my boss walked by my cubicle one day while I was eating my lunch.

"Just like Ebony," she commented. My coworker chuckled again.

Another day I was asking her a question about an account I was working on and she interrupted me halfway through to say to my coworker, "Man, isn't she just like Ebony?"

It took me a while to realize that Ebony was just Black.

But, my boss had liked Ebony, so she liked me, too. I quickly became a favorite. I was given chances to show my potential in extra work projects that were offered my way. I was invited to take lunch in her office and catch her up on all the team gossip.

One day we were eating lunch and a woman from one of the neighboring teams walked by. She was a Black woman who had been at the company for a few months longer than I. There were very few Black people at the company, so we all had made it a point to know each other. I really liked her. She was a hard worker and always willing to help answer any questions I had. She had a great sense of humor. But as she walked by the office she looked positively miserable.

My boss looked at her and shook her head. "I can't believe she did that," she said, her voice full of disappointment and a tinge of betrayal.

"What did she DO?," I asked, expecting some scandalous gossip.

"She went to HR," my boss explained. "I know things were bad for her on her team, but she could have found another way. It's over for her now. She's never going to get a promotion; she's never going to get another special project. She might as well quit. She's on the shit list."

The shit list wasn't metaphorical. It was an actual list that our division manager, a white woman, kept in a notebook on her desk. It was literally titled "shit list," and on it she kept a list of names of people who had "wronged" her and she had vowed to make miserable. Occasionally, when she felt that people weren't fearing her enough to give her the respect she felt she deserved, she would show the list to enough people to get everyone talking about it again. You could get on the shit list for making her look bad in a meeting by being unprepared, or by being too prepared and making her look unprepared, or for buddying up with her work enemy (the other division manager). Going to HR, even with problems of racist harassment, would make her look bad once word reached her superiors—and would land you on the shit list for life.

There were many Black women on the shit list.

Over the years I learned that my ability to earn the money I needed to feed my family meant that I was going to have to ignore everyday racist and sexist insults, large and small. I have been the brunt of racist jokes. I've had managers reach over and touch my hair in the middle of office meetings. I've been groped and kissed in work elevators by men I hardly knew and gave no consent to. I've been talked down to and passed over.

And I did not go to HR once.

Why? Because I saw that, just as I witnessed in my first job, my mother was right. Time and time again, women and people of color who dared ask for a work environment free from harassment or discrimination were punished. Not all were actually added to a "shit list" but they might as well have been. Nobody seemed to pay for the audacity of expecting to be treated with respect as much as Black women were.

We tried to hold each other up in these hostile environments, but one by one we'd be picked off—our careers would stall and we'd move to another company; our doctors would tell us that the stress was killing us, and we'd quit and go back to school in hopes that another degree would give us a better chance of being respected when we reentered the work force; we'd get fired. In every team I worked on, if I wasn't the only Black woman, I eventually would be, and then eventually I wouldn't be there either, as I'd move to another company in the hopes of finding a safer place to spend the majority of my days.

Finally, after about fifteen years of this cycle, I left altogether to dedicate my time to writing on systemic racism and sexism in the United States. I had no plan and no savings. I did not believe that the world of freelance writing was going to lead to immediate respect and recognition, but I did know that I couldn't walk into another office building and leave half of myself at the door for one more day.

The writing industry is no less racist or sexist than just about any other industry in the United States—and don't get me started on the publishing industry. But free from the toxicity of sexist and racist corporate culture, I was able to build a strong career for myself with the help and mentorship of many amazing women, especially women of color. I eventually wrote my first book, *So You Want to Talk about Race*, which became a national best seller.

I was able to find a space for my work to grow toward my potential. I have found my place to shine and it has given me a career more rewarding than I could ever have imagined. My success has been built not only through my hard work and talent but also through my privilege, and a whole lotta luck. Not many of the talented Black women I worked with over the years were so lucky.

I had written *So You Want to Talk about Race* as a tool to help people address issues of racism in their everyday life: their schools, their churches, their families, and yes—their workplaces. Soon, my book was in workplaces around the country and I was suddenly asked to speak at corporations to share opinions that would have gotten me fired if I had worked there.

I would give a talk on my book and then I would almost always be asked the same question: what can we do to make our company more antiracist?

I'm a systems thinker. My work is almost exclusively concerned with ending systemic oppression. I do not believe that there is a capitalist solution to racism. And I do not believe that when companies ask me "what can we do to be more antiracist?" they are not looking to end lucrative business partnerships with entities that exploit or oppress populations of color. They are not looking to make sure that all of their contractors are paying living wages. They are not looking to investigate their environmental impact on vulnerable populations. But . . . I still tell them that they should, just in case.

The truth is, a world free of white supremacist patriarchy is a world truly revolutionized—one that I don't even think we can fully imagine. To free ourselves we must question each and every system we are in—even those that we cannot divorce ourselves from yet. I explain this. I ask each attendee to my talk to believe that it is possible, and to push for that new future.

And then I give some tips for how to make these spaces, these imperfect, often oppressive spaces, better for now.

I started writing because I was a Black woman whose life was being slowly and quietly drained away in a racist and sexist world. I started writing because I believe that Black Lives Matter and I, a Black woman, matter.

When I visit these corporate spaces, knowing that the revolution I want to see likely won't happen anytime soon, I also see the faces of so many people who matter. Women of color who are working and struggling in work environments so similar to the ones that I struggled in for years. Every one of those women deserves a safe and healthy place to work and the opportunity to work to her full potential and be recognized for doing so.

We must not only dream big but also work big. We must fight oppressive systems and build new, better ones in their place. And we also must fight within our systems for every marginalized person within them, who cannot wait for revolution, who deserve safety and dignity now.

I do this work because I believe what the white supremacist patriarchy does not want me to believe—that every woman of color in this country is of undeniable, undiminishable worth and unlimited potential. If you have the privilege and responsibility for helping shape the workspaces that women of color are or will be working in, I hope that you believe this, too. If you do, this book will help you turn that belief into an environment that give women of color the space and resources to discover her potential. There is revolution in that, and there is revolution in tying our companies and our corporate culture to that. And it's the only way that our corporations are going to be relevant in the new world that I know we can build one day.

We will be doomed to failure if we continue to stick to the idea that we can prosper as corporations—or even nations—while excluding entire segments of our population from that prosperity. We will be doomed to failure as long as we continue to think that the next great idea will always and only come from the privileged white men whom we have always turned to.

But I know, with every fiber of my being, that wherever we insist on centering those who have been most marginalized and over-looked, we cannot fail. It is the surest path to success (even if it has hills and twists and turns) and it is one that I hope we are finally brave enough to embark upon. No matter where we end up, a path where we walk in our faith in women of color is one that will always take us to a better place.

Introduction:
Inclusion on Purpose

My mission to highlight the experiences of women of color in the workplace was born out of many broken hearts and tears.

Not mine. Or I should say, not *only* mine.

Week on week, sometimes even hour on hour, I would meet professional women of color globally who would lay stories of broken dreams, thwarted aspirations, and thinly veiled discrimination at my feet.

Stories like my best friend's, a Singaporean Indian advertising executive who would get routinely patronized by her white female, British boss. My Black female colleague who was told by a former employer not to bring up the discrimination she faced with human resources (HR) because "who do you think you are, Michelle Obama?" The Latinx CEO who was asked to serve coffee to the white men around the table at her first board meeting. My Somali American student whose dreams of becoming a news anchor were dashed when she was told, "Nobody wants to see a woman in a hijab reporting the news." The Black trans celebrity I heard speak with regret about how she felt forced to laugh along at transphobic jokes to fit in with her colleagues. The Korean American executive who hid her sexuality from her peers in France, worried she would be seen as less worthy of leadership material because she was "young, Asian, and gay." The East Asian technology entrepreneur who was advised that she should cut her hair if she wanted to raise money from investors for her dating start-up because her long hair made her "too attractive" to be taken seriously. Even the stories of celebrity women of color like Michelle Obama, Serena Williams, and Salma Hayek, who have all spoken up about experiencing racial discrimination on some of the world's most prominent stages.

No one seemed immune from experiencing it.

As a diversity, equity, and inclusion (DEI) adviser, I would often serve as confidante to women of color as they shared the most poignant details of being excluded and marginalized at their organizations, largely off the record, with no hope for recourse or change. Sometimes, even later in the same day, I would meet organization leaders—mostly, Western white men and women—who would tell me they were determined to create a more equitable and inclusive workplace for their employees. That they wanted to prioritize it, but frequently they didn't know where to start.

I couldn't help but wonder, what was causing this mismatch?

Why Inclusion on Purpose

You're reading this book, so I don't need to tell you to believe in the business case for diversity and inclusion.

Fortunately, it's not up for debate. McKinsey research finds that fully engaging women in the United States would add $4.3 trillion annually to the US economy by 2025. Global gender equity would add $12 trillion to the global economy by 2025.[1] Working alongside people from different backgrounds makes us smarter, more innovative, and hardworking, according to University of California, Berkeley, research.[2]

The *why* is largely an accepted fact: including people of diverse and underestimated backgrounds in the workplace is both the right and profitable thing to do. What isn't largely understood or accepted is the *how*. If we believe in inclusion morally, ethically, and as a way to drive profitability and productivity, then why are we so terrible at it?

Because we don't realize—or don't want to accept—that inclusion isn't an inborn trait. It takes awareness, intention, and regular practice. We are too quick to blame women as a group for lacking ambition or talent rather than examine how biased systems perpetuate inequality.

No country has achieved complete gender equality in the workplace—not in terms of political representation, corporate leadership, pay equity, or equal opportunities to advance in the workforce. By some measures, we're over two hundred years away from global gender parity.[3] Yet the prevailing narrative tells women to negotiate, strategize, and advocate better to fix gender inequality. Absent from the conversation is the role of institutional gender bias in perpetuating the inequality and the role of people with power to dismantle these systems so that women can thrive.

This mismatch spurred my passion to write a counternarrative to business executive Sheryl Sandberg's notion that women needed to "lean in," advocated in her 2013 book of the same title. My 2015 book *The Diversity Advantage* was intended to help company leaders develop research-based strategies to advance gender equality at every level of the workplace—recruitment, retention, and advancement.[4] Since it was published, I've found that institutional changes like corporate diversity programs designed for women are only part of the puzzle. Strategies must be intersectional; to be effective, they must prioritize the advancement of women of color, who carry the two largest and most visible marginalized identities in the workplace. Without an intersectional approach, changes to support women's advancement are incomplete at best, and at worst, inadvertently create cultures where women of color are deeply discriminated against—often while white women ascend.

As I write this, the world is recovering from a devastating global pandemic, which disproportionately drove women of color out of the US labor force.[5] Black and Latinx women specifically were more likely to be working in jobs that made them particularly vulnerable to the pandemic, compared to white women who were able to work from home.[6] The impact of race and structural inequality cannot be unlinked from this crisis. When I was writing this book, "Black Lives Matter" protests were dominating headlines the world over. As the book is in production, violence and hate crimes against Asian Americans are at an all-time high and more East Asian American women I know have expressed fear of being out in public than in the decade I have lived in this country. Yet most societies are still reluctant to address race in the workplace even though racism is the biggest source of inequality in modern workplaces and tackling it head-on should be a key leadership priority. The contemporary interpretation of "diversity" has largely meant aiming for gender balance—which has led to the progress of white and other dominant-group women—rather than addressing the historical oppression of communities of color in Western workplaces.

I write this book because with my global experience—as a Singaporean of Indian origin who studied and worked in the United Kingdom and India, and is now living in the United States—it's clear to me that elevating women of color continues to be the most pressing issue in workplaces the world over.

The reasons why are threefold:

1. *White supremacy is pervasive.* Unequivocally, white people are associated with progress and wealth. Further, in almost all workplaces, white people are at an advantage, no matter where they are in the world, even in countries where there is paltry representation of them. White expats or nonwhite locals who assimilate with or display more proximity to whiteness, such as lighter skin color, Western education, culture, or accents, are typically more likely to advance than comparable peers without this proximity to whiteness.

2. *Anti-Blackness is pervasive.* Black people experience discrimination or disadvantage, even in countries where they are in the majority. One just need look at South Africa, ravaged by colonialism and decades of state-sanctioned racism, where the mostly white top 10 percent of South Africans hold 70 percent of the country's wealth, compared with the bottom 60 percent, which is mostly Black and has ten times less, according to the World Bank.[7]

3. *The intersection between gender and race/ethnicity uniquely impacts women.* While women all over the world are at a disadvantage in society and workplaces compared with men, the intersection between gender and race is a key differentiator between women's experiences. Taking an intersectional lens to equality becomes paramount because racism deeply compounds the bias women of color experience.

In addition to being a moral outrage, racism is an economic catastrophe. Citigroup data estimate that $16 trillion was erased from the US GDP between 2000 and 2020 due to racial discrimination.[8] If racial inequality was addressed immediately in the United States through the equitable distribution of wages, education, housing, and investment to Black people in the United States, $5 trillion could be added to the US economy over the next five years. *That's trillion with a t.*

I join a growing number of DEI practitioners in urging leaders to center antiracism in all diversity efforts. This book will illustrate how much the intersection of race and gender impact women of color. I continually challenge leaders to name racism, and walk toward the discomfort of addressing it even if it feels unfamiliar or challenging. Racism is the false belief that race determines the capabilities and traits of a community. Racial differences are used to justify the superiority or inferiority of one race over another, through racist beliefs, actions, or systems. We see racism impact workplaces the world over.

Before we go further, I want to define some key terms that will be used often in this book. "Diversity" refers to seeking the equal or greater representation of underrepresented, historically marginal-ized people, especially women of color. I do not use "diverse" as an adjective to describe a person of color as that framing centers white people as the default. Instead, I'll be specific where possible, such as "we are seeking to hire more Black/Latinx/Indian people," or "peo-ple of color" not "diverse people."

"Equity," which must be central to all diversity and inclusion efforts, refers to identifying and dismantling systemic barriers to the representation and inclusion of women, people of color, and people from other historically marginalized communities. Recruiting and meaningfully advancing women of color requires them to have a seat at decision-making tables, not just bringing them in at lower levels, which is why equity should be top of mind for the inclusive leader. "Inclusion" refers to the actions taken to represent, welcome, and value people from historically underestimated, marginalized com-munities such as women of color. Inclusive workplaces encourage women of color to bring their whole, authentic selves to work with-out fear of being excluded or discriminated against.

"Diversity is being invited to the party, inclusion is being asked to dance," Vernā Myers, vice president of of inclusion strategy at Net-flix, is frequently quoted saying. I like to add, "Equity is being part of the planning committee."

Collectively, I refer to this as DEI. One of the key barriers to work-place DEI is workplace bias, or the unfair preference for or preju-dice against a group, due to preconceived ideas about the group's capabilities. Workplace bias can show up in several ways including discouraging marginalized employees from being their authentic selves, exclusion from opportunities or social gatherings, or making racist or discriminatory comments as "jokes" while expecting oth-ers to laugh it off. I now intentionally limit the use of "unconscious bias" in my work because it is too often used to justify repeated harmful behaviors or prejudices because they were not perpetuated consciously, without considering the impact on the person harmed.

Why Women of Color?

First, women of color (nonwhite women) are the largest majority of women around the world. Second, their representation is rapidly growing in Western workplaces; women of color will be the majority of working women in the United States by 2050.[9] In fact, 2019 marked the first year in the United States where the majority of the new entrants to the workplace were nonwhite, spurred by an uptick in women of color entering the workforce.[10] Third, their experience in the workplace is deeply impacted by the overlap between their race and gender, especially when compared with white women or men of color, whose dominant identity (white or male) usually safeguards them from many women of color's negative experiences.

This is the argument that Kimberlé Crenshaw made in 1989, when she used the term "intersectionality" to specifically focus on the negative experiences that Black women were having in US workplaces.[11]

More than thirty years later, the law professor's framing is even more relevant. Crenshaw describes intersectionality as "a prism, for seeing the way in which various forms of inequality often operate together and exacerbate each other. We tend to talk about race inequality as separate from inequality based on gender, class, sexuality or immigrant status. What's often missing is how some people are subject to all of these, and the experience is not just the sum of its parts."[12]

When only white women ascend to the highest corporate leadership positions, we must identify the barriers that prevent *all* women from rising up the ranks. Without centering *women of color's* experiences when designing workplace inclusion policies, you're likely to miss important nuances that would benefit more employees. Researchers on organizational behavior and intersectionality have long found that women of color experience distinct, more negative challenges in the workplace than their white male, white female, and male of color counterparts.[13] These challenges range from getting jobs, to remaining stuck in lower-paid and lower-status jobs, to lack of access to leadership positions, to being considered less competent, less charismatic, or less deserving of advancement opportunities. Given that the vast majority of women of color are in low-wage jobs in the United States, the United Kingdom, and other Western countries, without inclusion on purpose, there is slim potential for them to advance. In non-Western countries, different matrices of division are applied to ensure women of particular socioeconomic classes, races, religions, or social castes are unable to progress at the same rate as other women.

That's a shame, because facing repeated bias and racism is driving out talented, ambitious women from corporate workplaces. Fifty percent of women of color surveyed by Working Mother Media in early 2020 in the United States were considering leaving their corporate careers within the next two years. This same study found that they're 25 percent more likely than their white women counterparts to aspire to senior leadership roles, so it is not for lack of ambition or a desire to "opt out" of leadership.[14]

I have spoken to women-focused companies' employee resource groups (ERGs) or at women's leadership conferences on how to communicate more effectively. In many cases, I'm the first speaker to bring up that women of color frequently experience more pushback when they negotiate or advocate for themselves as compared to white women, and that most negotiation advice is futile until we address workplace bias.

Afterward, women of color come up to me to thank me—because, they say, most other speakers would give these audiences advice that would work for white women to progress, but not women of color. For example, if you have been stereotyped as "angry" (as research shows that Black women are) or "submissive" (as research shows that Asian women are), then negotiating could actually be counterproductive to your advancement.

When we center the experience of women of color, we are likely to create cultures that benefit women *and* men, people of color *and* white people. And that intersectionality of race and gender must remain at the fore when we are working on habits and behaviors to be more inclusive.

Of course, no two women of color have the same experience, even if they have the same racial or ethnic identities. More important, there's deep variance between how different women of color (already an imperfect categorization in itself) are treated at work. In the United States, for instance, Black, Latinx, and Indigenous women experience some of the gravest discrimination, in terms of access to job opportunities, wage equity, and navigating deeply harmful workplace stereotypes including a lack of perceived competence. On the other hand, research shows that some Asian and Asian American women have better access to job opportunities as well as even higher wage equity than their white female counterparts, but navigate stereotypes of being perceived as competent yet lacking in leadership qualities. Therefore, they often have lower advancement opportunities than white women when controlling for education and experience.

This nuance is key to the premise of this book because no one ethnic group's experience can characterize the experience of all women of color at work. It is impossible to do. Other influences are also crucial to how women of color experience the workplace: education, socioeconomic status, immigration journey, health, and so on. But the research confirms one fact across all women of color at work: the intersection of gender and race is likely to profoundly impact their experience of being included and supported in the workplace. Women of color are not monolithic, but they all find themselves navigating (different, but largely negative) stereotypes in the workplace. It is not their problem to fix, and no "overcoming imposter syndrome" workshop or "confidence conference" can solve decades-long inequality.

That's why leaders must take action.

Making Our Workplaces Whole

How can we make meaningful progress to undo systems of harm? The answer is active, deliberate action—inclusion on purpose. I am convinced that inclusion is the most important leadership trait today. If we define leadership as the ability to influence and inspire others to action, we'll notice that for far too long, we have lauded white male leaders for grooming, inspiring, and propelling the next generation of leaders like them. We need to change this paradigm urgently so that *everyone* with ambition, skill, and potential can succeed.

I've met thousands of people around the world in my consulting and speaking, and I've learned one thing about bias in the workplace: usually it's not perpetuated on purpose. I deeply, truly believe that most leaders don't want to discriminate, inflict pain on others, or create a miserable environment for their peers. But as this book explores, inclusion doesn't just happen unconsciously. We're hardwired to prefer people like ourselves and feel most comfortable interacting with sameness. In stressful environments (like most workplaces), we're bound to default to what—and who—we're used to.

Our brain receives eleven million pieces of information per second. To cope with massive amounts of information, we often rely on mental shortcuts, called heuristics. Heuristics are useful to ensure that we don't need to learn how to brush our teeth again every morning, but also result in us defaulting to making judgments about people different than us. They're why many of us fall prey to stereotypes and prejudices that we have as a result of social conditioning, media narratives, and the biases held by those who shaped us. We frequently take exclusionary actions because of these prejudices.

Instead, inclusion on purpose requires awareness, a growth mindset, and intentionality. The good news is that inclusive behavior can be cultivated; I've developed it in myself, and it has now become part of my daily practice. If you are a cis, straight white man reading this, it is not your *fault* that you are overrepresented in the workplace or that people will not second-guess your abilities. It is your responsibility, though, to understand how people with marginalized identities are often held back at work because they face biases that your privilege has allowed you to be immune from. It is also your responsibility to recognize that just because you have not experienced discrimination, that doesn't mean it doesn't exist. You have the power to use your privilege to help create more equitable outcomes for those around you.

In fact, the more privilege you have, the more work you can do to fix broken systems. At its core, I believe in the power of inclusion as the only path to making our fundamentally broken workplaces whole.

Going beyond Race and Gender

Centering the experiences of women of color who carry other marginalized identities in related inclusion efforts is key too. If you're designing policies to better serve employees with disabilities, ensure that you are also collecting input from women of color with disabilities. If you want to show solidarity with your lesbian, gay, bisexual, trans, or queer (LGBTQ) employees, do not *only* engage white or male LGBTQ employees as the spokespeople for the group. I have unfortunately seen this happen far too much in progressive corporate efforts.

When we start by centering women of color who have other marginalized identities, we are more likely to include a much wider set of people. It is the greatest possibility that we have to include everyone in a complex and nuanced world.

Intersectional leadership demands that we see employees as their "whole selves"—and understand that there are barriers that especially hold back women of color from advancing when they are authentically themselves. If leadership is about motivating, influencing, and advancing your people to excellence, then intersectional inclusion shows us that we're not truly including women of color if we don't seek to empathize with their challenges. A woman of color who is facing exclusion in her day-to-day interactions at work cannot be fully engaged at work, let alone motivated toward excellence, until that issue is addressed.

Lack of caregiving support and the prevailing global gender expectations about women's caregiving responsibilities continue to be a major barriers to their participation as well as success at work.[15] We saw this gender inequality writ large during the COVID-19 pandemic.[16] Even in nonpandemic times, women everywhere are impacted by the lack of workplace and societal support to better distribute their caregiving responsibilities so that they can advance. For many women of color, working outside the home was never a choice, and not much consideration was given to the challenges that they faced to balance these responsibilities. Of course, women of color have the most to gain from better policies. Yet any serious discussion in the public discourse about women balancing work and caregiving has largely been driven by white women's demands. Even now, in the absence of governmental and societal support, the imperfect solutions to strike a balance still mainly favor richer, largely white women in the West who have long relied on the caregiving labor of women of color to enable them to enter the workforce in the first place.[17] Because that topic is so large in itself, I will be focusing this book primarily on workplace issues distinct from the larger question of creating greater work/life balance for women of color.

But I will say this: most workplaces were built by cisgender, straight white men who had typically minimal caregiving duties and did not face the same biases as the diverse employee base of today. Isn't it time we reimagine practices of workplaces built in the 1930s?

Setting the Expectations on Terminology

A note on using the term "women": I am inclusive of trans women. I acknowledge that the discussion of "men" and "women" in this book leaves unsaid the experiences of gender nonbinary people. In most cases, my recommendations can be used to create cultures of inclusion for people of color across all genders, although there is still additional work to be done to make workplaces inclusive of a spectrum of gender identities.

I use "women of color" broadly, acknowledging that it is a flawed and incomplete term, but the one that is most relevant to my work as it stands. I endeavor to be more accurate by naming exactly which demographic I'm referring to when I can—Black, Asian, Latinx, or Native or Indigenous women. Some of the research that I cite in this book explicitly relates to a specific racial or ethnic identity, and other research broadly analyzes women of color. *Women of color* is a political and social identity. It's a powerful one, one that has historically been underestimated. My use of it highlights that in the workplace, the intersection of a person's racial and gender identity can materially impact their access to high-paying, high status jobs, career advancement, mentorship, sponsorship and ultimately, decision-making and leadership opportunities.

Race is a social construct, not a biological one, but I see value in using "person of color" to describe how a person's social and political characterization as *non*white will impact their experience in the workplace and society. While the term is imprecise as well, it is useful to broadly compare and contrast the experience of communities of color in society with those of white people. More practitioners now also use "BIPOC" to center Black and Indigenous People of Color, but this is largely relevant in Western contexts, so I still use people of color in my efforts to be more globally relevant. I refer to white people to racially describe people of northern European descent, although the classification of who can call themselves white has contracted and expanded throughout history to include some and exclude others. I frequently seek to examine the impact of whiteness as a social construct, especially as it relates to workplace professionalism, rather than focusing on the individual actions of white people.

I'll be noting "Black women" when referring to people who identify ethnically, culturally, and socially as Black. I'll write "Asian women" when referring to research around the experience of Asian women, although I have deeply struggled with this categorization as a Singaporean of Indian origin and as I am learning how much other intersections, such as socioeconomic class, immigration journeys, and educational opportunities, impact the professional outcomes for Asian women. Indeed, Indian and Chinese Americans reflect some of the highest-income groups in the United States, and Burmese and Nepalese Americans are among the lowest—and yet we categorize all four as Asian. A similar lack of nuance is often found in describing women from Latin America, where the number of richly diverse countries, cultures, and ethnic origins can never be fully captured in one word, but I will use "Latinx" when referring to this demographic. While I focus on the identities of women of color chiefly represented in the United States, the experiences and challenges can broadly be applied to women of nondominant ethnicities anywhere in the world. I explore the global context more deeply in chapter 10.

When referring to individual stories of women in the book, I will write their race or ethnicity in the way that they feel most comfortable being identified, with the gender pronouns that they have shared with me. Some names have been anonymized at the teller's request to protect their identity, in which case I have used pseudonyms chosen by them.

How to Use This Book

Use the stories in this book to identify what cultures of exclusion look like and take small but impactful actions to create a culture of inclusion on purpose. Inclusion doesn't have to be expensive or take up too much time. You just need to be willing to do the work. With practice, it can become a way of life.

Creating inclusive work cultures is a combination of how the individual leader approaches the workplace, with institutional practices to ensure that inclusion is everyone's experience, not just the result of actions taken by an individual manager. As such, this book is structured in two parts.

The first part focuses on the individual—why the belief that everyone starts at a level playing field is dangerous, and how we can develop a deeper understanding of the ways that privilege and intersectionality show up at work. Much of your individual progress in developing inclusive leadership behaviors is dependent on having a growth mindset geared toward inclusion along with cultivating awareness and empathy. Learn about the particularly challenging workplace circumstances that women of color have to navigate, from being considered less capable or committed to being seen as less of an organizational culture fit. Read the latest research on how you can advocate for women of color to progress. Then develop the actions that you can take individually in order to drive change, using the BRIDGE framework, which I detail in chapter 2.

The second part revolves around how to create equitable organizations that are run by inclusive leaders. Consistent inclusion depends on creating the right institutional structures—from better hiring practices, to running inclusive meetings, to creating cultures of psychological safety within teams. The ADAPT framework gives leaders a place to start on taking a holistic approach to creating psychologically safe, inclusive environments for women of color. This work is not easy, nor is it close to being fail-safe.

It matters less how many times you fall down, rather that you get back up each time and try harder. It could make the biggest difference between being a manager who's stuck in the past or becoming an innovative leader of the future.

The choice is yours.

I

Individual Behaviors
to Drive Inclusion on Purpose

You have the power to make change. You have the power to be inclusive on purpose to women of color in the workplace. These chapters look at the power of our personal mindsets, behaviors, and actions that can drive inclusion regardless of our position within an organization—from recognizing and understanding our privilege, to using that influence to create opportunities and cultures of equity as well as belonging for all.

1

How to See Past Privilege

It is not our differences that divide us. It is our inability to
recognize, accept, and celebrate those differences.

—Audre Lorde

I grew up subscribing to the ideals of meritocracy. I was born in
Singapore, a tiny island-city-state that moved from being a developing country to a financial hub within two decades, founded on
the principle of "if you work hard enough, your gender, skin color,
and socioeconomic status won't matter." It's why I worked hard all
through school (OK, part of it was that I also feared disappointing my
immigrant mother!), attended a top university in London, and then
went to the world's most recognized graduate school for a master's
in journalism. I took a simplistic view of the world: if you work hard
and are smart enough, you could overcome the chips that were
stacked against you on a societal level.

Then I entered the workforce. I was a journalist for recognizable
media outlets—*Forbes*, *Time*, and *Bloomberg*. Again, I held fast to the
belief that hard work, determination, and perseverance were all that
I needed to get ahead. In 2013, I made a transition to the technology
industry in a fast-growing, soon-to-be-public company at that time.

For the first time, I saw gender and racial bias in full form. Not to say that I hadn't encountered it before, but it was cloaked in other ways; for example, at one newspaper, my editors said that my breaking news story had to go on the second page because they didn't want to upset the famously temperamental male journalist who wanted his story to take up the whole front page. I acquiesced, but quietly seethed.

In the technology industry, I saw extremely bad behavior. A colleague shared a harrowing incident of sexual harassment from a male leader; a C-suite leader's entry-level, all-white millennial, female team were referred to as his "harem"; man after man was hired to the executive level while women flanked the junior ranks, and the few women in senior leadership were all white; and white women were invited to the "in-group" while I was firmly shut out.

Experiencing bias and discrimination on a daily basis, not seeing role models like me, and being excluded from work meetings and social gatherings all took a toll on me. I began second-guessing myself and my right to be in my job, despite having ample qualifications to be there. I didn't enter the workforce believing that I would be discriminated against (part of my privilege), but it became clear when I realized there wasn't room for a leader who looked like me.

My own views on meritocracy changed after my experience. It spurred me to advocate for inclusive workplaces as my life's work. Now I know for sure that the imposter syndrome I felt then wasn't my fault. Jodi-Ann Burey and I explored how imposter syndrome has less to do with individual women's failures and more to do with experiencing institutional bias:

> The impact of systemic racism, classism, xenophobia, and other biases was categorically absent when the concept of imposter syndrome was developed . . . [which] puts the blame on individuals, without accounting for the historical and cultural contexts that are foundational to how it manifests in both women of color and white women. Imposter syndrome directs our view toward fixing women at work instead of fixing the places where women work.[1]

Recognizing and Acknowledging My Own
Privilege Was Step One

I offer my own story because it's important to know that we can all learn and grow. No matter your background, the time you grew up in, or your own personal experience, you can learn to identify bias and work to undo it, whether you have experienced it or not.

I've learned that there's a lot of good intention out there when we say "diversity and inclusion," but our societies and workplaces often operate on the principle that if we mean well, then even the worst of behaviors can be excused. It's why most well-meaning people get so defensive when you call them discriminatory. There are few phrases that would get someone more angry than if you called their behavior racist or misogynist. Many people will retort with some version of, "But I don't see color" or "I didn't say that because you're a woman."

This is precisely the moment when I ask leaders or managers to stop and examine their privilege. If you have never had to "see" color, then you're most certainly in the racial majority. There's no person of color I know who does not have to consider how their skin color or racial identity will impact the way they're perceived. If you have never had to worry about your safety when walking home late at night or how you will be perceived in the workplace because of your gender identity, you are most certainly a white man. Examining privilege can make many people defensive, as racial or gender privilege are not earned through actions but instead by the coincidences of birth.

"Asking you to acknowledge your privilege does not minimize your personal hardship and suffering. It does not make your pain any less legitimate if you acknowledge someone else's pain, which, by chance or birth, you find yourself free of. When it comes to white privilege, having it does not make your life easy, but understanding it can make you realize why some people's lives are harder than they should be," as organizational psychologist John Amaechi explains in the *Financial Times*.[2]

Overcoming Defensiveness and Acknowledging Our Privilege

I understand the defensiveness to examining privilege. I really do.

For too long, I had it too. But I had to confront my own privilege first to have any hope of making any meaningful change toward inclusion. I was born with many chips stacked in my favor; I had socioeconomic privilege so that I never had to incur debt of any kind. I come from an overall supportive environment and don't have any underlying health conditions. I have had excellent education from world-recognized institutions—fully paid for by my family—and that has helped me build a great network. When I suffered in a toxic work environment, I had the privilege to walk away from a lucrative job because my spouse had, and still does, a high-earning job and health insurance. For millions of people in the United States whose health care is tied to their jobs, this is simply not an option. Most of all, while I've incurred some anti-immigrant and racist sentiments, I've never been in a situation where I feared for my life, unlike many Black, Indigenous, East Asian, and Latinx people in the United States. So that's quite a lot of privilege already.

Along with confronting this previously unacknowledged privilege, I had to undo my belief that my success was only a result of how hard I worked to get to there. While I was aware that societal bias and discrimination existed, I thought that I would be immune from it by working hard enough.

That started changing, of course, when I experienced the workplace discrimination that I previously mentioned. But what meaningfully helped me begin my exploration into cultivating inclusive behaviors at work was listening intently, without defensiveness or jumping in with my own experiences, to the stories of *other* people who had been marginalized at work. And listening to believe, not to respond, question, or disprove that they had experienced bias.

Some of these biases are hard to identify. Research shows all women, especially women of color, are expected to constantly reestablish their presence and authority at work. This is known as prove-it-again bias.[3] One study by the Society of Women Engineers found "that 61 percent of women reported having to prove themselves repeatedly to get the same levels of respect and recognition as their colleagues" compared to 35 percent of white men reporting the same.[4]

Over the years, constantly facing prove-it-again bias becomes soul crushing for women of color. Like being asked to reestablish their credentials in meetings, or having ideas ignored in meetings until they're repeated by white men or women, or being denied promotion or tenure despite being overqualified for the opportunity. Every woman of color I spoke to for this book could name multiple instances of facing these biases.

I can deeply understand why prove-it-again bias or similar ones might be hard or uncomfortable to acknowledge. If you believe everyone enters the workplace with a largely level playing field, especially if their credentials are equal, it can seem wholly unsavory to think that bias may be at play, particularly if it doesn't match your experience.

That's why to be purposefully inclusive, we must step outside of what our personal experiences at work have been and seek different perspectives to help guide us in the right direction.

It's not easy, but it's critical.

Use This Framing

As a professor, I strive to create spaces in my classroom where all students feel welcome and safe. While being uncomfortable is par for the course in any meaningful dialogue on addressing inequity, I am against proposing the inclusion of women of color at the expense of excluding or demeaning white people or men. That's why I begin these classes by reminding my students that we are going to discuss overcoming exclusionary *systems*. I also urge them to lay down individual defenses—and remind them that even if they're white, male, heterosexual, and financially privileged, it doesn't mean that we want them to be shamed about their privilege or that we're attacking them because of these identities. My focus is always on understanding and dismantling systems of oppression rather than blaming individuals.

Here's how I describe this framing:

"The problem isn't men, it's patriarchy.

The problem isn't white people, it's white supremacy.

The problem isn't straight people, it's homophobia.

Recognize systems of oppression before letting individual defensiveness stop you from dismantling them."

My purpose in using this framing is twofold. One, it helps people with influence and privilege shed individual defensiveness against engaging in this important work of recognizing oppression along with their own role in dismantling systems built on inequities. Second, it allows people with privilege to develop empathy with communities that have been oppressed by others, perhaps even their own.

This framing is relevant in our quest to create inclusive workplaces because it helps leaders understand how individual acts of bias and exclusion play out in the larger context of systems of oppression. We all carry biases that are seeded, shaped, and strengthened by the society that we live in. Chief among them is racism. Until we fully understand and accept our complicity in upholding racist systems, we will never be able to build a fully inclusive workplace.

Here's the hardest sentence I've had to write in this book: I'm racist and benefit from upholding racist systems.

To take one of many small, significant examples, as an Asian woman of color, I am often compared with non-Asian women of color in the workplace. I've been lauded by white colleagues for being a "good" woman of color and directly compared favorably with other women of color, usually Black women, for my cultural norms, which means I don't always question authority or am quieter in meetings. I've received professional opportunities because I benefit from the stereotype of being a "model minority," where I'm viewed as polite, intelligent, and submissive, thereby allowing me to prosper in white supremacist systems.[5]

I benefit from upholding racist systems by not always challenging my white peers about why I am rewarded or even selected over my Black, Latinx, or Indigenous peers at work.

I had racist beliefs that a workplace was adequately diverse and inclusive, even if only white and Asian people were represented and able to advance, like when I worked in technology. I now know better; without adequate Black, Latinx, and Indigenous representation, we can never be fully diverse or inclusive. Once again: *I am both racist and benefit from upholding racist systems.*

If more of us could say this phrase out loud, and examine and accept it, we would all likely be a lot more inclusive in both society at large and especially our workplaces. Acknowledging ourselves as racist or accepting racism as a concept is deeply uncomfortable for most people, and I can empathize. Our brutal histories—of European colonization, slavery, and wars against communities of color—are racist, and of course we want to separate ourselves from that. We are *good* people, after all, with *good* intentions.

But as much as Nazism and the Ku Klux Klan embody racism, we also co-opt and normalize racist behavior when we don't question our current systems, in which, say, the average white college dropout is still wealthier than a Black person with a college degree in the United States.[6]

Simply being a person of color does not make you immune from the benefits of racist systems. So pervasive is the system that it can benefit people of color in nuanced ways too, frequently rewarding those who are considered more proximate to whiteness, while punishing those who are deemed further away from it. Some examples include English-speaking immigrants who can successfully code-switch to assimilate as well as lighter-skinned Asian, Black, or Latinx people. This book demonstrates how white people, including white women, have benefited from racist workplaces. You also will learn how many Asians and Asian Americans have benefited from racist systems, and how for many Black, Latinx, and Indigenous communities globally, those racist systems have been set up at the expense of their progress.

Historian and race scholar Ibram X. Kendi posits that in every moment, we have a choice to take racist or antiracist actions. Kendi guides us to learn that it is only through taking deliberate and consistent action to undo racism in society that we can work toward a future where everyone is free from racism. The opposite of being racist is not not-racist, he emphasizes; it's being *antiracist.* "Many people are very, in many ways, closed-minded or even defensive, especially when they're charged with being racist. In many ways, we're taught to close up and to feel as if we're being attacked and to sort of not confess and not admit when we're being racist," he says in an interview with NPR.[7]

There are incredible resources that detail the history of anti-Black racism and how the legacy of institutionalized racism has cast a long shadow over every facet of contemporary life. For more information on anti-Black racism in the United States, I recommend best sellers like Ijeoma Oluo's *So You Want to Talk about Race,* Isabel Wilkerson's *Caste,* and Kendi's *How to Be an Antiracist.* Literature specifically related to undoing anti-Black racism is crucial to read in tandem with this book.

Without fully understanding how deeply entrenched racism is in all our systems—and our own role in dismantling these systems to be more equitable—we are nowhere closer to cultivating inclusive leadership so as to create workplaces for all.

Undoing Homogeneous Social Circles in the United States

Making connections with a diverse social group is central to inclusion in purpose. As a non-American, one of the most troubling observations that I've had since living in the United States is how segregated many cities within this country are.

A lack of diversity in the average white person's social network has far-reaching consequences on inclusion in the workplace. A 2013 Public Religion Research Institute study found that 21 percent of people in the United States reported "never or seldom" interacting with someone of a different race or ethnicity. And even among those who did frequently interact with someone of a different racial or ethnic background, three-quarters said that those interactions happened at the workplace. Less than half said that these cross-racial interactions happened in friendship circles.[8]

This matters deeply when we consider the importance of empathy and awareness in creating inclusive behaviors. Even when leaders have attended a racially diverse school or live in a multiethnic city, many of their views are still largely shaped by those who look like them because interactions with people of color are "cursory" for the majority of US whites, according to an article in the *Atlantic*.[9]

One significant barrier to creating an inclusive workplace is that many in the majority lack the cultural intelligence to work with peers of different backgrounds. Without experience with interacting with people from different backgrounds, it becomes easy to fall back on stereotypes or preconditioned biases. Leaders might not have developed the lens to view the world through others' eyes, particularly the employees who may experience marginalization or discrimination. This is precisely why it is so important to gather a variety of perspectives, especially focusing on the experiences of women of color at the organization. Your decisions may only benefit people who have experienced the workplace from your lens, but if your decisions impact a larger group of people, their needs also must be served by your decision.

Once we acknowledge that most people struggle to relate to others from different backgrounds, the danger of a homogeneous high-level leadership team becomes clear. McKinsey data show that white men fill 64 percent *more* of the C-suite roles in US corporations than do women of color.[10] This unequal representation deeply impacts company culture and poses a challenge to inclusive leadership.

A broad definition of company culture that I like is from Singaporean entrepreneur Oswald Yeo, who says that a company's culture relies on "who you reward, punish, and tolerate."[11] Often these decisions about hiring, advancing, keeping problematic people on, and firing others in many companies are made without much transparency. We've been taught to believe that in meritocratic cultures, the best people are hired and promoted. Without examining structurally biased systems and leaders who aren't inclusive on purpose, we risk perpetuating the false narrative that white men keep advancing in corporations because they are the best leaders for the job.

Not all bias faced by women of color is intentional discrimination. We shouldn't let a lack of intention, however, distract us from the detrimental impact of such bias on women of color. That is why leaders cannot look away when it happens or refuse to address it in themselves.

Some practices may even seem innocuous to men and white employees, but end up unintentionally excluding women of color, who are least likely to be in a leadership position to influence company culture in the first place. In the United States, networking events centered around alcohol are commonplace and acceptable, but don't include everyone. A number of the women of color whom I interviewed mentioned that while they saw male colleagues regularly drinking alcohol at company events, and sometimes even at their work desks, it was never clear to them whether drinking at work was acceptable for women of color. For women who don't consume alcohol, or who are from cultures that forbid it, a strong dilemma emerges: Do I attend the company networking event because it's good for my career, or do I skip it because it makes me uncomfortable or clashes with my beliefs?

Here's an example of how work cultures can be redesigned to be inclusive on purpose. Leaders must consider the experience of a variety of employees, not just men. And not just white women either. When I confer with white women or even immigrants to the United States from western European countries, the discomfort is absent. Of course, not *every woman of color* does not drink alcohol, and some white men don't drink too. Finding alternatives for corporate socializing at the bar may even benefit, for instance, white men who are teetotalers.

Does that mean that companies should do away with events at bars? Not necessarily. But being inclusive on purpose would ensure alcohol-fueled events aren't the de facto option for networking with colleagues. There should be networking and gathering opportunities that exist outside these happy hours. This is an illustration of a well-meaning aspect of company culture that can end up excluding others. Networking events centered around alcohol are prevalent throughout corporate life in the United States because the leaders who create and uphold company culture are rarely from underestimated backgrounds.

Then there are aspects of a company's environment that deliberately harm women, especially women of color, who often incur the largest costs associated with speaking up against discrimination. The #MeToo movement exposed multiple instances of a (almost always) white man who was rewarded or tolerated, despite having serious allegations of sexual harassment or assault against female employees. Examples include that *NBC News* allegedly paid multiple settlements to protect Matt Lauer, a former news anchor with multiple sexual misconduct claims against him, and Google paid two male executives accused of sexual misconduct $135 million to leave the company.[12] Meanwhile, a number of female employees who protested against the company's forced arbitration clause cited retaliation from the company for speaking up.[13] Put simply, we can get a glimpse into a company's culture when people accused of sexual harassment (largely, male and white) are rewarded or tolerated, while survivors are punished.

I use these examples of overt bias to highlight how even when investigations were conducted and wrongdoing was proven, companies sided with the perpetrators rather than the victims. What hope, then, do women of color have of justice in cases of harder-to-prove bias or discrimination?

White Women Don't Struggle with the Same Challenges as Women of Color at Work

That's why leaders must take time to personally understand what bias against women of color looks like. A study by McKinsey and LeanIn.org shows that women of color have the highest drop-off between entry-level jobs and the C-suite compared with white men, white women, and men of color in US corporations.[14] Specifically, 17 percent of women of color enter the workplace at the entry level and just 4 percent make it to the C-suite. By contrast, white men represent 36 percent of the entry level and are overrepresented at 68 percent in the C-suite. White women make up 31 percent of the entry-level workforce and comprise 18 percent of C-suite roles.

While for many years we called the barriers to women's career advancement the "glass ceiling," mounting evidence has shown that for women of color, it's a concrete ceiling, as coined by the global nonprofit Catalyst.[15] Many women of color whom I interviewed contend with constantly feeling hypervisible and invisible at the same time in their workplaces.

It is impossible as a leader to correct what you can't identify. To make meaningful progress, we must specifically seek out what exclusion looks like, and the experiences of women of color are key to guiding this inquiry. Then it's up to us to take the right steps to fix these issues—from advancing more women of color within the organization to taking personal actions to be more inclusive.

Examples of exclusion are not hard to find, although we may often be unaware of them unless we pay attention. One popular culture instance of the marked difference between how white women and women of color experience the workplace is from the US-based reality television show *America's Got Talent.* Actress Gabrielle Union served as a judge for the fourteenth season of the show, but in November 2019, reports emerged that Union, who is a Black woman, was allegedly fired for bringing up concerns of a toxic and racist work culture at the production, including being told that her hairstyles were "too Black" for the mainstream audience.[16]

Heidi Klum, a white woman who also judged the contest, contradicted Union's experience by publicly stating that she had not experienced a toxic work culture on the production: "I've only had an amazing experience. I can't speak for [Gabrielle]. I didn't experience the same thing. To me, everyone treats you with the utmost respect. I've never seen anything that was weird or hurtful."[17]

This incident is illustrative of how the same work environment can be inclusive to *some* women, but not to all. Union's experience directly related to her being a Black woman, so of course Klum was not impacted by the same bias. This is a clear case of why it's necessary for leaders who are inclusive on purpose to specifically seek out the experience of women of color to gauge how inclusive an environment *really* is.

We can't *only* rely on data because there's a lack of publicly available data on the workforce and leadership disaggregated by race and gender. That's why anecdotal evidence (stories) matter. Even in countries like the United States, where workplaces are legally allowed—and in many cases required—to collect it (unlike, for example, in France, where it is unconstitutional), many organizations refuse to publicly release data on the racial makeup of their work-force or pay.[18] The "color-blind" approach (everyone is equal here; we don't see race!) is harmful because it does not allow us to truly create inclusion and equity in the workplace. If we cannot name the problem, how can we tackle it? We may all believe in the ideal that race and gender shouldn't impact one's career advancement, but that approach ignores the very real challenges that women of color face to entering and advancing in the workplace. It is like saying, "Because we believe no one deserves cancer, we are not going to study its root cause." Turning away from these intersections, as we have been doing for decades, will only exacerbate the issue.

How Can You Start Using Your Privilege for Good?

I look to Oluo's sage advice on why those with the most social privilege are the most responsible for speaking up against injustice. Once you begin to identify biases and speak up about them even if your voice shakes at first, you can start practicing inclusion on purpose.

In an article for the *Establishment*, Oluo writes about how white people can use their white privilege to advocate for people of color:

> Your actions against racism carry less risk. You can ask your office why there are no managers of color and while you might get a dirty look and a little resentment, you probably won't get fired. . . . You can share articles and books written by people of color with your friends who normally only accept education from people who look like them. You can help ensure that the comfortable all-white enclaves that white people can retreat to when they need a break from 'identity politics' are not so comfortable. . . . You can make a measurable impact in the fight against racism if you are willing to take on the uncomfortable truths of your privilege.[19]

Use your privilege to identify and expose bias, safe in knowing that you have less to lose than a woman of color who speaks up.

Then use your privilege to create an environment where women of color aren't penalized for speaking up. Now more than ever before, as information becomes freely available thanks to its digital spread, leaders have an opportunity to reward inclusive behavior, coach exclusionary managers, and show no tolerance for toxic behaviors. It's more than the right time. As you read more of this book, do try to become aware of how your privilege may have prevented you from seeing the issues that I detail here. Commit to making change.

When more of us work to develop inclusion on purpose, we can all win.

■ ■ ■

KEY REFLECTIONS

1. Which advantages or privileges do you have, and how have they helped you navigate and advance in the workplace? Reflect on this statement: You may not have chosen to be born with the skin color, gender, or socioeconomic advantage that you have, but what's more important is how you use that privilege to advance those who may not have the same advantages as you.

2. Can you reflect on how racist systems and racism in society have benefited you? How have they harmed you?

3. Do you have a homogeneous social group? Are most people you interact with from the same race and ethnic background as you? Reflect how this fact impacts your view on your own experience in the workplace and your perception of how others experience the workplace.

4. Most practices in the workplace are not designed to be exclusionary, but they can end up being—like when the majority of

workplace social events revolve around alcohol, for example. Are there instances that you can think of in your own organization? What could some alternatives to those gatherings be that would include everyone?

5. What is one thing that you could do to take action today? Write it down here:

2

How to Develop
an Inclusion Mindset

You can start late, look different, be uncertain— and still
succeed.
    —Misty Copeland, principal dancer, American Ballet Theater

Jodi-Ann Burey received a frantic phone call from her manager to
attend a leadership team meeting scheduled for the next hour at the
fast-growing start-up that she had recently joined.

"And if you have any slides or anything you can show the management team on what you've been working on, please bring them
too," her manager said. Burey laughs without mirth at this part of
her recalling the incident, incredulous at the last-minute ask to come
prepared to a meeting with twenty leaders, including the company's
white female CEO.

"I was clearly added as an afterthought," she says, although she
was leading DEI efforts at the organization.

Burey was one of two people of color, and the only Black woman
in that oval conference room. Perhaps, she reflects, she should be
grateful that she was even invited.

"Even though I was surprised by the need to participate in this meeting at the last minute, I actually had all my slides ready."

As Burey began presenting her slides, the CEO started to look more and more agitated. Eventually, she verbally shot down and loudly reprimanded Burey in the meeting. She said that Burey's ideas weren't relevant to the company's work, while nitpicking on minor details.

"I was trying to contribute and be collaborative, but it felt so combative," Burey recalls.

The leader's hostile line of questioning continued for another thirty minutes, and it soon became apparent that the issue wasn't with what Burey was presenting or the quality of her work but instead with the perception that Burey wasn't competent at her job.

"I was really disturbed by why I was being picked on in that kind of way and so publicly. She was not hearing me, she was talking over me, and projecting this feeling of 'you're not supposed to be doing this,'" Burey notes.

As the leader's animosity toward her grew in the conference room, Burey's own brain started going into overdrive.

"Women of color often hold multiple conversations in our head at once," she describes. While trying to process the racism that she was experiencing, she understandably started getting upset at the injustice of having to deal with it. "Then there's all the things that you actually want to say, but you have to go through this checklist in your head of, 'If I say this, then that could happen . . . and if I say that, then this could happen.' You're trying to strategize what you should say to maintain your job and to try to de-escalate the situation, which is escalating for no reason."

When asked how it felt in the moment, she explains, "What do you do with all of that energy? It literally heats up your body. You know when your computer gets hot from having too many tabs open? I was processing too much information, and it was heating me up."

And the part that she still carries with her today, years later? No one else in the conference room stood up for her, although many privately expressed shock after the meeting was over at witnessing the showdown.

"Even a white person who has less power than me in the company could have said something to redirect the conversation. But what bothers me is that white people at my level or above didn't stand up for me . . . and these were the same people who were really open to me before the leader came in. When you have toxic leaders, everyone falls in line," she says.

"But when you're white, you have protection from consequence, and they should have spoken up for me."

While the CEO had hired Burey to head up diversity and inclusion at the company, Burey believes it was tokenism—a symbolic measure to assure investors that the leadership cared about inclusion. When faced with actual changes the company could make to be more inclusive, Burey found that the CEO was defensive and disinterested.

"Inclusion initiatives that don't have sufficient staff or financial resources behind them are harmful because they show that a company to some extent knows that there is an issue, but is unwilling to commit to real solutions that create the changes they say they're seeking," she observes.

Burey didn't stay at the organization for much longer. What started as an exciting new chapter in her life, dissolved quickly into multiple instances of being second-guessed and humiliated, receiving biased feedback, and eventually being rudely reprimanded by the CEO while her colleagues looked on in silence in the meeting described above.

When she finally quit, she felt desolate about what her career prospects would look like and how she could find a place to belong where her identity as a Black woman would be an asset, not a liability, to her career progress.

"It feels like you can't go anywhere and be safe and be great. It's a reminder that I can't be great . . . that I can't thrive or excel. And the pain of questioning: Where can I go to be great and grow? A place where I could contribute and mess up and do phenomenal work and get rewarded?"

The Leader's Inclusion Mindset

Burey's story is unfortunately common and experienced constantly by women of color. Erika Stallings, a Black woman, wrote for *New York* magazine's the Cut about how experiencing racism at work gave her post-traumatic stress disorder.[1] For many women of color, experiencing racism early and consistently can result in toxic stress, finds the Center for American Progress.[2] By the time they reach the workplace, many have experienced decades of bias and trauma, which is only exacerbated in exclusionary work environments.

So what is the answer? Is there a way for women of color to progress in majority-white environments? Burey's career has spanned a number of industries—from education to a global health nonprofit, technology start-up, and large retailer. While she faced more bias in majority-white environments than in racially diverse workplaces, she felt included at one majority-white employer previously.

The difference between the leaders at other organizations and this global health organization? The leader had an inclusion mindset.

Burey once brought up her concerns to him that their US-headquartered organization wasn't being racially and culturally inclusive enough considering it largely served sub-Saharan African countries. Rather than get defensive or hostile, the leader, a white man, listened. He acknowledged her concerns. Soon they were meeting monthly to work toward ensuring that the team's Africa-based operations would be involved in strategic decisions within the headquarters and engaging a more racially diverse staff in the United States too.

Some conversations between Burey and her former CEO got heated, but he always listened. He didn't expect her to have all the answers.

He was prepared to learn and put down his defenses. Together, they were able to make changes for the institution to become more inclusive that are still in place today.

He demonstrated an inclusion mindset.

To understand the inclusion mindset, let's first look to the seminal work of psychologist Carol Dweck. Her decades-old research on the "growth mindset" compared with the "fixed mindset," first explored in education settings, has become a celebrated approach to learning as well as growth, and has been adopted by innovative leaders across the world.

Dweck's research shows how the success of many people has less to do with talent or innate brilliance, and more to do with a mindset that embraces challenges and thrives in the face of adversity.

As she clarifies in an article for the *Harvard Business Review*, "Individuals who believe their talents can be developed (through hard work, good strategies, and input from others) have a growth mindset. They tend to achieve more than those with a more fixed mindset (those who believe their talents are innate gifts). This is because they worry less about looking smart and they put more energy into learning."[3]

Even without the explicit connection to workplace inclusion, research demonstrates that workplace cultures that value a growth mindset see greater trust, engagement, innovation, and ethical behavior.[4]

This approach, then, becomes relevant to successful inclusion efforts. When leaders employ the principles of cultivating a growth mindset to create equitable workplaces, they can develop an inclusion mindset. Conversely, if they approach inclusion with the mindset that they already know everything there is to know about this subject, they're likely to fall prey to biases and even becoming unwilling to learn from mistakes. If we tell ourselves, "I can't change because I'm a product of my time, and I was brought up in a culture that wasn't inclusive," then we are not cultivating an inclusion mindset.

The inclusion mindset depends on us to work hard, strategize, and seek input from others, especially those who have experienced exclusion and bias at work. Unfortunately, all too often we adopt a fixed mindset toward the challenges of inclusion because it seems like too large a hurdle to scale. Instead, we must believe that we can grow, learn, and adapt to include a rapidly changing, diversifying workforce.

As I write this, my toddler is learning to ride a bicycle in our neighborhood park. He has fallen down or nearly done so at least four times in the span of me typing one paragraph. His knee is bruised, and he's fearful of getting up again, but he does. I gently remind him that he has already improved so much since the first time he got on that bicycle. He now needs to push past the fear and failure of falling off the bike. Seeing children navigate tough yet necessary "firsts" makes me think about how much discomfort and pushing past fear are key to the learning beliefs that we all need to adopt in being inclusive on purpose.

Introducing the BRIDGE Framework

So where do we begin? I developed a memorable acronym—BRIDGE—to approach cultivating an inclusion mindset.

1. **B**e uncomfortable
2. **R**eflect (on what you don't know)
3. **I**nvite feedback
4. **D**efensiveness doesn't help
5. **G**row from your mistakes
6. **E**xpect that change takes time

Be Uncomfortable

First, expect and accept that you will be uncomfortable. A growth mindset demands it, as does an inclusion mindset. We must push past feelings of uncertainty, fear, discomfort, and frustration to create equity and justice everywhere, but especially in our workplaces.

The discomfort may show up in many ways and at unexpected times, from having to acknowledge your own privilege to investigating where you may have perpetuated bias in the past. You may feel uncomfortable while reading the stories in this book of exclusion and bias faced by the women of color. Or as you read the data on the progress of white men and women in US workplaces compared with women of color. Or even as you read some of the strategies that I recommend, thinking back to times that perhaps you weren't being inclusive. Embrace that discomfort. Sit with it. Be humble and willing to be imperfect. In fact, if you aren't facing some level of discomfort when it comes to learning about inclusion in the workplace, assume that you're not learning enough. Developing greater awareness of our own racism, prejudices, and biases is both extremely uncomfortable and absolutely necessary.

Reflect (on What You Don't Know)

Despite spending much of my career addressing bias and inclusion at work, I hope that I never think that I've mastered this field. Already, concentrating on my specific focus on women of color means that I have to make an extra effort to learn about the challenges faced by other marginalized communities. I have much to learn to fully understand the systemic barriers holding back others, such as people with disabilities, employees from the LGBTQ community, and neurodiverse employees. As most people do, I have gravitated toward investigating the experiences of people with my shared identities—woman and person of color.

This is precisely why it's so important to reflect on what you don't know. What don't you discern? What are the viewpoints of the communities (and remember, no community is a monolith) that you already are familiar with? Which perspectives are you missing that hold you back from being fully inclusive of others in communities that you aren't part of? An inclusion mindset demands us to examine these questions.

Some years ago, the CEO of a Fortune 500 corporation decided to begin searching for the company's inaugural chief diversity officer position. This Indian American CEO was a two-time public company founder and had recently sat in on a meeting convened by the company's Black ERG. He attended the meeting just to listen.

When he heard the stories of bias and racism particularly faced by his Black employees, he was shocked and saddened. He realized that his own experience as an Asian man did not fully equip him to understand what other employees of color were facing, especially the Black women whom he heard from that day. Listening to their experiences sparked in him a commitment to create a more inclusive environment. He rightly believed the charge should be led by a Black employee with a seat in the C-suite. Hence the search for the inaugural chief diversity officer, which the company began thoughtfully and with the full engagement of its race-based ERG, aware that its majority-white C-suite alone could not drive this hire. The company ended up hiring a woman of color.

Taking time to reflect on this is key to cultivating an inclusion mindset.

As you investigate this, reflect on which areas of exclusion and bias in the workplace you're familiar with already. You might identify as female and have experienced gender bias, or you may have disabilities or be LGBTQ. Where do you already have some awareness of bias and how to counteract it? Then reflect on which areas you haven't spent much time considering. What do you need to learn more about—and how will you go about doing this?

Invite Feedback

Seeking feedback on how you may have perpetuated bias or where the team you lead isn't being inclusive is one of the hardest things you will hear. It is not easy to hear critical feedback; it's even more challenging when you may hear that you've caused someone discomfort, challenge, or even pain.

Do it anyway. Inviting feedback and responding with a growth mindset can make all the difference between paying lip service to the idea of inclusion and practicing it in action.

If you're ready to engage, start by asking your direct reports, especially from underestimated backgrounds for honest feedback on your management style. I like to begin here because an effective manager-employee relationship is incumbent on effective feedback, so asking for it in this setting isn't out of the ordinary—or at least it shouldn't be. Even nonmanagers can ask for feedback, again prioritizing feedback from teammates from marginalized backgrounds.

For managers, I recommend stating transparently to your employee that you're seeking open and candid feedback on creating a culture of inclusion on the team. Emphasize and ensure that candor will not impact your employee's advancement or job at the company. If you can announce this in a group setting (say, at a larger team meeting), then you're setting the expectation up front that your employees can expect this line of questions in their one-on-one meetings.

Steer the conversation to glean feedback specifically on inclusion and belonging on the team.

Here are some questions to ask:

- Do you feel like you belong here? Why or why not?
- Was there a time when I made you feel included? What did I do to foster that?
- Was there a time when I could have done more to make you feel included? How?
- How can I create a more inclusive environment on this team?
- What would you like to see me committing to in order to create a more inclusive team environment?
- What could I do differently now and in the future?

Next, demonstrate that you have listened to the feedback by taking action. If you have received feedback that you often cut off women of color when they speak in meetings, then be sure to wait until your turn. If women of color say that they are not receiving professional development opportunities on the team, work to create them.

I recommend this approach to managers who have generally created a culture of inviting feedback and transparency on their teams. Unfortunately, not all organizations encourage and welcome feedback. In that case, and even in tandem with verbal feedback, I recommend using anonymous surveys to gather feedback on whether employees feel like they can bring their authentic selves to work. I emphasize this recommendation throughout the book. I urge you to gather demographic data, and look at the responses by gender and race. When working with companies that have brought me in to gather these data for the organization or specific team, I constantly note that women of color report feeling less included than their white male counterparts. This has rung true when I have collected quantitative (using a five-point Likert scale, where responses are ranked from "strongly agree" to "strongly disagree") as well as qualitative data (anecdotal evidence around bias and exclusion).

One area to be cautious about: this does get tricky within organizations that don't have a large representation of women of color. We must ensure that responses are not traced back to individuals. In this case, I always recommend working with a third-party researcher. I'll reiterate here that, as many instances in this book outline, women of color are often hypervisible and invisible simultaneously—so we must be careful that leaders do not collect data that would later jeopardize the careers of women of color. I can't stress this enough; if employees get punished for offering candid feedback, they won't provide it.

Over time, once you become more experienced with asking for this feedback, translate it to other areas of your workplace: your peers, customers, and even other people within the organization whom you may not interact with as regularly as your team. This practice will likely also help you recognize the areas you need to develop ("reflect on what you don't know").

I specifically do not recommend that white people solicit this feedback from women of color friends or have these conversations in social settings. It can create an uncomfortable dynamic that could jeopardize the friendship. And while being able to solicit candid feedback on inclusion is a hallmark of being an effective manager, in social settings it is unfair to expect the other party to take on the labor to educate you. Online and other resources exist specifically for this reason.

At work, remember that this is never a one-and-done check-in. In fact, the more regularly you can check in with your team about inclusion and belonging, the easier it will become. It will likely be uncomfortable the first time you do it, even if you do engage a third-party service, because regardless of how you collect the data, you will have to address them yourself. Circle back to the *B* in the BRIDGE framework. I never said that this would be comfortable!

Defensiveness Doesn't Help

Actionable feedback is a gift. Even if it makes you feel hurt, upset, or angry. Even if it makes you question whether you are a "good" or "bad" person—a judgment that invariably comes up when talking about sexism and racism. An inclusion mindset demands that we work through defensiveness—constantly and relentlessly.

Some years ago, I attended one of my first communication department meetings at Seattle University. What transpired in it confirmed my decision to teach there; it was clear that my colleagues valued inclusion and were demonstrating an inclusion mindset, even when the conversation got uncomfortable.

A white female faculty member brought up how she noticed the difference in how she was treated by undergraduate students when they called her by her first name compared with when she required them to call her "Dr." or "professor." In her experience, the former frequently resulted in her being slightly less respected by students. She also found that her student evaluations were negatively impacted when she didn't assert her authority.

I could see some of the white male professors in the room starting to shift in their seats, clearing their throats and looking down uncomfortably. A few said that they didn't notice this and preferred to be called by their first names; it created a better bond for them with students. Besides, why should we be discussing how they were referred to in their classrooms? Didn't they have the authority to run their own classrooms? I could sense their defensiveness.

Then our department chair, a white man, spoke up: "I know this is a personal topic and nobody is suggesting we mandate a policy on how students refer to you in your own classroom. But this is a discussion worth having. Personally, my students call me 'Chris,' and I do treat them as friends. That's because I know my white male privilege lets me do that."

The room went so silent that I could hear the air from the heaters whooshing through our building.

The four faculty of color exchanged glances—three women of color, and a Black, openly gay faculty member.

He went first: "I have to start the beginning of each new class with my résumé, and there's no way I could get away with being called anything but Dr."

"Agreed, I've recently moved to requiring students to call me 'professor' and I see a marked difference in how students interact with me in class," I added. One by one, the faculty of color in the room shared stories of how much harder we had to work to be considered worthy and competent by our majority-white students.

Research backs up the opportunity challenges that faculty of color face in the academy, like recruitment, tenure, and retention.[5] But I could see that for many of our white male peers, we faced challenges that they couldn't imagine, such as having to establish our authority to be considered worthy to teach by our students.

As the white male professors laid down their defenses, I could see that our stories were opening their eyes to a bias that they hadn't ever faced or considered. The inclusion mindset demonstrated by our department chair also had a part to play in ensuring that the conversation didn't devolve into defensiveness and finger-pointing.

At the end of the meeting, we concluded that while faculty would continue to decide how students would refer to them in their own classrooms, when referring to each other in front of students, or when introducing a student to another faculty member, we would use their title of Dr. or professor. We have carried on this practice to date.

It's easy to get defensive or hung up on requiring evidence when you hear stories of bias or discrimination. Just because it isn't your experience, it doesn't mean that it doesn't exist. We know institutional sexism and racism play a huge part in holding back women and people of color in the workplace. When we listen to their experiences without defensiveness, when we listen to learn and then act, we operate from an inclusion mindset.

Grow from Your Mistakes

Even with all my experience in working toward equity and inclusion, I don't always get it right, and indeed, 100 percent perfection is not an attainable goal. We should know that we will make mistakes. That is when the biggest opportunity for growth and learning arises. A willingness to keep learning from errors is linked to having an inclusion mindset.

There's a fascinating overlap between having a growth mindset and learning from mistakes. Psychologist Jason Moser found that when people with a growth mindset make mistakes, they're more likely to learn and grow from them.[6] In fact, his study on brain activity found that our synapses (the electric signals in our brain) literally fire differently after we've made a mistake, depending on our mindset. People with a growth mindset produced a bigger brain signal that was related to paying more attention to right a wrong once they realized that they made the mistake.

One of the responses commonly found in people with a growth mindset was a willingness to make things right—to learn and grow. In 2018, a Starbucks employee called the police on two Black customers who had done no wrong. The racist incident was rightly condemned by the media and customers. Rather than get defensive, justify the actions, or ignore the incident, Starbucks CEO Kevin Johnson publicly apologized while taking personal responsibility. "These two gentlemen did not deserve what happened, and we are accountable. I am accountable. . . . [Y]ou have my commitment, we will address this and we will be a better company for it," he said in a video published on the company's website.[7]

Starbucks' leadership has made noticeable strides in growing from this highly public mistake. With the apology, the company announced a series of long-term initiatives to address racism within Starbucks after gaining input from the community and antiracism experts.

Expect That Change Takes Time

Confronting biases can create a desire to take immediate action. You understand that you're going to be uncomfortable, you've reflected on what you've failed to see, and now you're ready to go! This is called action bias, and results in us rushing to move because we don't want to address the discomfort or shame that we may feel from learning these challenging topics. But without taking time to listen and learn, we're likely to only make minimal changes—at a minimum—not lasting ones.

I saw this during summer 2020, after the murder of George Floyd, an unarmed Black man, by a white policeman and the racial justice movement that came after. Many US organizations that rushed to have events to address racism in the workplace, but without expert facilitators, ended up putting an undue burden on Black employees and retraumatizing them. Many women of color told me that it was harmful to hear other employees sometimes ask, "Why are we doing this?" or "How is this relevant to our work?" because the organization had not taken the time to address why it was addressing racism. Many also didn't have any follow-up commitments that would improve the representation of Black employees or leaders. So all in all, many organizations' quick rush to action may have done more harm than good. Change takes time; it takes intention and listening.

"When I talk to leaders about the role of listening in being inclusive and demonstrating a growth mindset, they're often surprised by the idea that you have to be silent. That you have to pay attention to what's happening and how things are moving, because only then can you become a meaningful participant in the change," Amber Cabral, author of *Allies and Advocates*, tells me.

As Cabral eloquently sums up the connection between slowing down, listening, and then taking action, "There's a difference between someone running toward the tide because talking about justice and inclusion is trendy, and being the person who says, 'I want to understand my part [in exclusion], I want to understand how I am a party to the system connected to it,' and moving it forward, so that I get to have a say in changing its direction. You cannot have that if you don't listen."

I couldn't agree more.

A Picture That Speaks a Thousand Words on the Inclusion Mindset

I turn to an excellent visual created by Dr. Andrew M. Ibrahim, assistant professor of surgery, architecture, and urban planning at the

University of Michigan, titled "Becoming an Anti-Racist," inspired by Kendi's work. As Ibrahim states on his website, "It is impossible to work on 'Redesigning Healthcare' and 'Health in All Design' without the lens and context of race."[8] I believe that it is impossible to effectively include everyone in *any* field without the lens and context of race.

You will find that many of the elements I've detailed above overlap with the picture. Use the BRIDGE framework as you reflect on moving from the Fear Zone (prioritizing comfort and familiarity) to

the Learning Zone (inviting feedback and reflecting on what you don't see) to the Growth Zone (rejecting defensiveness and growing from mistakes). Ibrahim's Growth Zone circle will be especially useful as I explore effective action in later chapters, but its foundation depends on having a mindset geared toward inclusion.

An inclusion mindset also hinges on developing empathy for people unlike us. By reading the stories in this book, you are already learning to confront the fact that women of color face a number of barriers to progressing at work. In the next chapter, you will learn the important skill of being able to recognize and understand the challenges that we face in our professional lives. Working with an empathetic leader can change the trajectory of anyone's career, but especially if you come from a marginalized background.

■   ■   ■

KEY REFLECTIONS

1. Do you currently work for, or in the past worked with, a leader who demonstrated a growth mindset? How did that impact your career?

2. Which part of the BRIDGE framework (**be** uncomfortable, **re**flect [on what you don't know], **i**nvite feedback, **d**efensiveness doesn't help, **g**row from your mistakes, and **ex**pect that change takes time) seems in line with how you currently approach your work?

3. Do you often believe that you can't escape from stereotypes that you were conditioned to believe about people different than you? Why?

4. What are some beliefs about women of color at work that you've seen changing?

5. Who is someone you could invite feedback from on inclusion right now? How will you ensure that you're ready to listen, learn, and not become defensive if you hear something you don't like?

6. What is one thing you could do to take action today? Write it down here:

3

How to Develop Empathy as an Inclusive Leader

One child, one teacher, one book, one pen can change the world.
—Malala Yousafzai

Ayesha Syed wanted to be a journalist when she was young.

But her father insisted that she become a lawyer, too worried that her smart mouth would get her kidnapped, she says. Syed, whose name has been anonymized, finally agreed to go to law school, believing that working in a field that centered on justice would allow her to fight the good fight.

What she didn't expect was that her fight for justice would be against her bosses at the corporate litigation firm that she worked at in New York City.

On two separate occasions, Syed, who identifies as a South Asian Muslim American woman, was in a meeting where a partner in her law firm said in conversation, "All Muslims are terrorists."

"When I said to him, 'I'm Muslim,' everyone around me was shocked. They hadn't until then realized that I was Muslim, and it became clear to me they wouldn't have hired me if they realized that earlier," she explains.

What gets under her skin is how casually the partner made a racist comment. It was said in such a matter-of-fact way that Syed even
tried to convince herself that the incident wasn't as bad as what her
initial gut reaction indicated. Everyone in the room was a lawyer,
after all, fighting for justice.

"When you're in this field, you believe that when something goes
wrong you have the legal system to protect you. Eventually you realize there's something really wrong with this system and it wasn't built
to protect people like you," she says, referring to women of color.

Unfortunately, Islamophobia was so rampant at her former company that after finding out Syed was Muslim, another colleague said
to her, "Shouldn't you be blowing up places?" When she complained
to HR, it denied wrongdoing and told her that it was all in her head.
She also found that if she spoke up about certain topics, specifically
the Israel-Palestine conflict that was frequently discussed at the law
firm among colleagues, she would come under scrutiny and even
feared losing her job.

Shortly after, citing the 2008 financial crisis as a reason, the firm
systematically laid off all people of color, including Syed. "At the layoff conversation, I told the partners, 'I'm aware that this is racist—
only people of color are being let go—and my layoff is based on the
fact that I'm Muslim.'"

The partners in the room said, "Do you have a paper trail for that?"

Rather than acknowledge or deny wrongdoing, they were asking
whether Syed would be suing the firm.

"Of course, I would never be able to because I'm a younger attor-
ney who, if I sue a firm of this size, would never get another job again.
I just needed them to know that I knew what they were doing and
that it was wrong," she says.

Syed went on to have a successful career spanning the legal,
media, and start-up industries. But she finds that Islamophobia continues to go unchecked in most workplaces. She's been told "you
don't look like a Muslim," constantly gets mistaken for an assistant

despite being in leadership roles, and was denied advancement opportunities when she spoke up against anti-Black racism as a Muslim woman of color.

Syed notes that many women of color constantly toe the line between speaking up and staying silent against bias and racism to assimilate within or protect their jobs. Now that she leads her own team at a start-up, she believes that more managers must work harder to include women of color by developing greater empathy.

Many white leaders' lack of awareness and empathy with the experiences of women of color underpins the racism that Syed has witnessed in the workplace. What changes the equation, she finds, is when people shift viewing bias and racism from their own perspective to approach it from the vantage point of the person experiencing discrimination.

"I try to explain it from a perspective of trauma. Using the example that you may not be able to relate to racism, but you can relate to trauma. Now imagine if your life is based on this idea that you have to be fearful of the police or the criminal justice system or your boss and that's your day to day, imagine what that does to your body? And they can finally *start* to understand the experience of Black and brown women," she says.

If you have not had lived experiences of racism, it can be more comfortable to live in denial that it exists. That's precisely why we need more white people to sit with this discomfort, and investigate how racism impacts the lives and careers of people of color, particularly women of color. It's not easy, nor intuitive, but cultivating awareness and empathy is deeply important to inclusive leadership.

A Missing Piece of the Puzzle in the United States

Can you empathize with difference if you have largely lived a life surrounded by people like you, especially people from the same race?

It's a question that I've been trying to answer given that racial homogeneity plagues the lives of most people in the United States. White people say that 91 percent of their core social networks are comprised of other white people, and for many, the most interactions that they have with people of a different race are in the workplace, as I wrote about in chapter 1.[1]

By contrast, diversity—though not always inclusion—was a fact of my life growing up in Singapore. Even if the average Singaporean may not have always had close friends of different races, we have always been exposed to racially and ethnically diverse people in our neighborhoods, schools, and workplaces.

Through a number of deliberate and often-criticized government social policies in Singapore, it has become virtually impossible to limit your interactions only to people from the same race.[2] In 1989, Singapore enacted the Ethnic Integration Policy mandating that no government-subsidized housing could consist only of one racial group. Considering that the majority of Singaporeans live in government-subsidized housing, this has meant that the majority will interact on a daily basis with people of other races.

That is far from the case in the United States. Seeing such social separation among the racial groups was deeply surprising to me when I immigrated here in 2012 and remains a key reason I find that workplace inequities continue on in the United States. Of course, there's no denying that racism and xenophobia exist globally and in many workplaces. But when you don't have regular and close contact with different people, it's more challenging to empathize with experiences unlike your own or even be aware that they exist at all. That's why inclusion takes intention.

One key obstacle to inclusive leadership is a lack of inclusion empathy.

As you continue to read stories of exclusion faced by women of color in the workplace, I encourage you to stop and reflect on how you would feel if you were in that position, or someone who you loved deeply like a family member or friend was. How would it make you feel about yourself and your own abilities? How would you perceive your colleagues and managers if you routinely faced exclusion and bias from them?

You would feel *underestimated*. Being underestimated means being seen as less capable or important than you really are. You feel unseen and unrecognized for your full potential. The thread of being underestimated as a woman of color runs deep throughout this book, so for any leader who is focused on being truly inclusive, they must first be able to empathize with these feelings and the situation at hand. Only then can they identify and disrupt these situations as they arise in the future.

The intersection between gender and racial exclusion may not resonate with everyone, but everyone can remember a time when they were overlooked or felt like they didn't belong.

I have repeatedly looked to Arlan Hamilton's leadership on this. Hamilton is a gay Black woman who overcame homelessness to become a successful Silicon Valley venture capitalist. Her own experience of being underestimated fueled her commitment to invest intentionally in start up founders with incredible ideas who were passed over because they were underestimated by the largely white male investors who run the industry.

Hamilton urges leaders to call people of color "underestimated"— not underrepresented. This shift in nomenclature could be profound. If you consider someone underrepresented, you may rationalize that it is not in your hands to increase representation; they need to shift from being underrepresented to "represented." But if someone is under*estimated*, the onus now shifts to you, as the leader, to ensure that they are recognized for their full potential.

Why does this matter so much? Why should the inclusive leader need to understand and empathize with what it feels like to be underestimated or be the "only" in your workplace? Because being underestimated harms women of color. It takes a toll on their productivity as well as their financial, emotional, and physical health. It impacts their self-worth when they don't find others like them in the workplace.

Empathizing with Feeling like a "Token"

Data on what it's like to be the only woman at work were first collected by Rosabeth Moss Kanter, the first woman to become a tenured professor at Harvard Business School. In 1977, Kanter studied how women (not categorized by race or ethnicity) experienced male-dominant workplaces. She found that token women felt highly visible and their actions would be perceived as representative of how *all* women would perform in those roles. She also found that while women felt their presence was easily recognizable, they would have to work extra hard to have their achievements recognized, and at times they would have to downplay or even hide their achievements to not outshine the men in their organization. Kanter concluded that being a token, the only one from a social group or one of the very few, has a "dramatic" impact on a person's career, and it tends to be negative.[3] Over forty years later and multiple studies after Kanter's initial publication, academics have found that tokenism acutely and negatively impacts women's and people of color's careers.[4]

When an employee is part of a social demographic comprising less than 15 percent of the overall organization's makeup, it can have negative consequences on the employee's well-being and productivity. "Our review showed that tokens have higher levels of depression and stress. They're more likely to experience discrimination and sexual harassment than women and racial minorities who are working in more balanced environments. Research shows people are less satisfied and less committed at their jobs if they're tokens. Companies should be concerned about this," said researcher Marla Baskerville Watkins.[5]

Feeling tokenized can dampen the spirits of even the most enthusiastic employee, especially when it's combined with constantly experiencing other discriminatory behavior. Sage Ke'alohilani Quiamno, a woman who identifies as Native Hawaiian, says that she was told she felt like the token "other" from the first day of her public relations job at a large Seattle-based technology company.

"At three o'clock on my first day of work, a white male colleague comes up to me and says, 'I've been looking at you all day. . . . What are you? And that reminder of being told I'm so different from everyone else pretty much set the tone for the rest of my career there."

Quiamno comments that combined with the general nerves that one would typically expect in a new job in a new city (she had just moved from Honolulu to Seattle), the constant questioning of her background—she was asked questions like when did Hawai'i get electricity and how come she looked Asian if she was Indigenous—kept reminding her that she was not part of the group. Her department barely had any nonwhite people. No leaders were people of color.

Then in one of her first one-on-one meetings with her manager, she was told that she was "intimidating." She describes herself as "physically small" but "someone who always speaks up when I have ideas, because my ancestors were part of the original labor movement in Hawai'i, and I was taught to stand up for myself and others."

Combined with being constantly reminded of her "unusual" cultural background, Quiamno was disheartened by the feedback about her style of speaking, which didn't impact her productivity or deliverables.

"When I was called intimidating for the first time, I internalized right then that I needed to start being small. I started being quiet. I didn't want anybody to see me. And so I made myself smaller to make others feel like they were in control or so that maybe they would felt better about managing me."

That wasn't the last time that she received this feedback. As she moved around to different industries and organizations, always managed by white leaders, Quiamno says feedback about her appearance, culture, and style of speaking persisted. Eventually, she left the corporate world to become an entrepreneur.

Developing Empathy Could Teach Us Why Exclusionary Behaviors Are Harmful

Some of the interactions that Quiamno had with her colleagues may appear well intentioned due to genuine curiosity or ignorance about her background. I've been told to overlook seemingly benign statements about my English-speaking abilities or accept compliments about my "unusual-sounding name." But comments highlighting our differences are always harmful to women of color.

These seemingly innocuous remarks, steeped in the fact that many leaders with privilege may never have encountered this type of discriminatory behavior, are never acceptable. In the field, some scholars call them "microaggressions," a term coined in the 1970s by Harvard University professor Chester Pierce to describe the subtle, everyday ways that Black people experienced discrimination from their white counterparts. In 2007, counseling psychologist Derald Wing Sue's use of the term brought it back into public consciousness when he described microaggressions as "the everyday slights, indignities, put downs and insults that people of color, women, LGBT populations or those who are marginalized experience in their day-to-day interactions with people."[6]

Some scholars now don't use the term at all; in fact, Kendi writes in his *How to Be an Antiracist*, "I do not use 'microaggression' anymore. I detest the post-racial platform that supported its sudden popularity. I detest its component parts—'micro' and 'aggression.' A persistent daily low hum of racist abuse is not minor. I use the term 'abuse' because aggression is not as exacting a term."[7]

While I prefer the term "exclusionary behaviors" over "microaggressions," the inclusive leader must recognize these, whichever term they encounter. We all know that it is unacceptable to call a team member a racial slur, but some people may not always understand why it is also harmful to encounter more subtle exclusionary behaviors. When I get commended for my perfect English, this may seem like a compliment to a white person, but for me it is a reminder that I must constantly be on guard to prove my English-speaking abilities or that I can fit into an English-speaking workplace. When her white peers questioned Quiamno about electricity on the island, they were pointing out that people like her were expected to be less advanced than them. Their questions signaled that they didn't think she belonged there.

Even if expressing surprise at someone's ability to do their job well may feel like a compliment to you, it is important to empathize with the impact on someone who has been made to feel like an outcast their whole lives. Exclusionary behaviors remind the other person that they weren't expected to belong or are being stereotyped as being "less than" because of their identities.

A manager who finds themselves easily represented in the workforce may not understand why exclusionary behaviors can negatively impact women of color's progress. A white person may think that they are giving a compliment that they themselves wouldn't mind receiving. But calling a person of color "articulate" is a microaggression rooted in the racist belief that people of color are not expected to be articulate. The fact that so many are unaware of why this (and other similar "compliments") constitute a microaggression is only further proof of the need for white as well as other people with privilege to develop awareness and empathy. It may be easy for a white man to laugh off jokes about his hometown or skin color, but that isn't even remotely similar to expecting someone like Syed, who we met earlier, to laugh off derogatory comments about Muslims, who have experienced terrible discrimination and violence the world over.

As I previously noted when citing Kendi, there is a growing movement in the DEI field to rethink whether microaggressions

are truly "micro" given that the effect of encountering them repeatedly over the course of a woman of color's career can cause diminished self-worth, hamper career growth, and even cause mental
health challenges.[8] Plus, minimizing their impact to protect the
biased person's feelings—centering their intentions over the impact
on the recipients—isn't fair. My take is that while we work toward a
bias-free workplace, those who are inclusive on purpose will take it as
a learning opportunity and not do it again. If someone tells you that
a statement you made was biased or a microaggression, apologize
sincerely, seek to understand why it may have been harmful (sometimes they may tell you, and at other times it's up to you to do your
own homework), and then refrain from doing it again.

Am I advocating for not being curious or asking colleagues questions about themselves? Absolutely not. But there's a time and place
to have conversations about identity, especially in the workplace.
Going up to someone on their first day at work to ask "what are you"
isn't the right approach; it's a dehumanizing way to express curiosity about someone's background. Even if you ask it in a more tact-
ful way, though, conversations about identities and backgrounds
in the middle of a work meeting, or marching over to a colleague's
desk to inquire, have a different tenor than at a casual networking
event or over a work lunch. The former relates, "I can't work with
you until we have a random conversation where I demand that you
answer my questions." The latter communicates, "I'm genuinely
curious and interested in you, and want to take some time to get to
know you. I'm also inviting your questions about me."

Recognizing this difference requires cultivating empathy, especially if you wouldn't be bothered by a comment like this—likely
because your experience in the majority wouldn't make anyone
question your background, ability, right to be there, or competence.

The women of color whom I interviewed often felt most excluded
when they received subtle comments or gestures from peers that were
exclusionary and harmful because they reinforced that they didn't

belong there. Hardest of all is when the offending party didn't even realize why what they said was problematic.

As *New York Times* best-selling author Kiley Reid says in a podcast, "I've experienced racism in my life that has scared me. . . . I remember once I had people yell at me from their car and call me an alien, but I have to admit the times I really think about are those little moments, like where I was walking in a white neighborhood and I had someone say 'excuse me, are you lost?' and I think those just stick with you more because . . . when you think you belong, but very quickly you realize that *other* people think you don't belong."[9]

To get to the heart of creating an inclusive workplace, we must lead with empathy. Managers who are white must seek to understand what their counterparts of color, particularly women of color, are feeling and facing. Most of all, they must be willing to set aside their own perception of the situation to really listen, seek to understand, and empathize with what their employee is telling them.

How to Develop Empathy That Relates to Inclusion

Empathy is extremely hard to quantify, but most of us can remember a time when we were treated with empathy at work. I turn to the definition of it as "the ability to sense other people's emotions, coupled with the ability to imagine what someone else might be thinking or feeling," according to Greater Good Science Center at the University of California at Berkeley. The center developed a twenty-eight-question quiz to help people measure empathy, which can be a useful self-assessment.[10] Scores on the test are rated along two dimensions: affective and cognitive empathy.

Affective empathy relates to the ability to sense others' emotional states. While this can be positive in wanting to help out when someone is distressed, one drawback of affective empathy is it can hamper people from offering effective support to the person in distress because they experience personal distress from seeing suffering.

Cognitive empathy relates to the ability to take on other people's perspectives, which helps us communicate and negotiate more effectively in personal and professional relationships, and may also make us less likely to rely on stereotypes when trying to understand others' behavior.

Inclusive leaders must cultivate cognitive empathy. Cognitive empathy demands that we don't automatically assume that others experience the workplace in the same way we do. Instead, they believe that there is nuance to how peers are experiencing the workplace, especially based on their identity and how they are perceived, frequently dependent on the stereotypes associated with those identities. When we take time to understand the larger context of inequity in the workplace, particularly against women of color, we can cultivate inclusion empathy.

A different component of empathy, which scientists call "empathic concern," is essentially *compassion*: Do we feel concerned about how someone else is feeling, and can we understand what our role is in making them feel better? Compassion is deeply necessary for us to harness inclusion empathy; it is empathy in action. Cultivating all the three dimensions of empathy, awareness, and action together are key in helping us develop a more inclusive work environment.

The good news is that empathetic leaders who create empathetic organizations also benefit from greater employee trust and engagement. An empathetic organization "treats others how they would like to be treated," according to Jon Shanahan, whose company researched this in a 2018 survey.[11]

This study found that 60 percent of the employees surveyed would take a pay cut to work for an empathetic company. Ninety-five percent of these employees said that they would stay longer with an organization that could empathize with their needs, and

81 percent reported that they'd be willing to work extended hours for an empathetic employer. The study's authors did caution that leaders must not take a "one-size-fits-all" approach to empathy.[12] While their focus was on understanding the different needs of a multigenerational workforce, I absolutely find that relevant to the intersection of race and gender. Understanding the needs of white women at work doesn't necessarily mean you will be empathetic to the needs of women of color, who as we know, do not constitute a monolithic identity in the first place.

When leaders are overwhelmingly men and white people, empathy is both a necessary yet elusive trait. That's because power and empathy have an inverse relationship: the more power you have, the less empathetic you are likely to be. Stanford psychologist and author Jamil Zaki says people who have historically been underrepresented or marginalized are more likely to practice their ability to understand other people and their suffering because they recognize the importance of needing others.[13] Privileged people often don't need to rely on others to progress and so they are less likely to try to empathize with others. Some may even be reluctant to take responsibility for dismantling systems that cause others harm because this would mean that they would need to recognize their part in perpetrating and benefiting from these systems.

Zaki also emphasizes that while most people view empathy as an inborn trait (and have a fixed mindset about it), in reality it can be cultivated with practice.

We can't expect empathy to last, and many of the issues we see of racism and inequality in society are not just problems of empathy but rather structural inequality, says Zaki in an interview with NPR. "But one thing that I think we can do is use the empathic momentum we have to make sure that we're creating policies that put Black and brown voices in positions of leadership and in high-profile positions in our culture, because one way to practice empathy is to hear from people who are different from you on a regular basis."[14]

Below are research-backed ideas from the Greater Good Science Center on how to cultivate empathetic leadership. With a focus on listening, awareness building, and compassion for others, we can work toward being more inclusive, empathetic leaders.

Practice Active Listening

I want to reiterate the benefit of understanding other's perspectives and feelings without defensiveness, as explored previously in the BRIDGE framework. Engaging in active listening with a mind toward empathy and inclusion means that you listen to your peer's words without interrupting them, with careful attention to their verbal, facial, and body language cues. It can also help to periodically repeat back what you've heard them say and clarify that you've understood their perspectives correctly.

When you're having a conversation with a peer from a different background, silencing cell phones, closing laptop screens, and putting away all communication devices to make eye contact with your colleague is important in practicing active listening. Work to moderate your own facial expressions to ensure that you're not communicating disbelief or disgust, particularly if someone is sharing a view that is different from yours.

Ensure that you're not preparing a mental rebuttal while they're speaking. Rather, seek to validate their feelings. If a woman of color says it was a microaggression when you told her that she's articulate, your role is to hear her out. Active listening can go a long way in building empathy.

Seek Shared Experiences and Commonality

This is a tricky point to navigate because indeed we are all human beings and have many similar experiences. Yet research shows that many of our experiences, especially at work, can be incumbent on a range of factors including our visible and invisible identities. For example, I often hear from white women that being a woman in male-dominated workplaces is so difficult that the shared identity of being female means that we must have had similar experiences. There are similarities, but not sameness.

In a former technology job, my department had many white women employees, but I was the only woman of color for much of my time there. My experience of being a woman of color was distinctly different than theirs. Most of the white women were invited to social gatherings or meetings that I was excluded from. While we may have all experienced the sexism prevalent at the organization, I was the only one in my department who had experienced sexism *and* racial exclusion. So when I attempted to explain my experiences to the few white women who were trying to empathize with my experiences, I frequently said, "It feels like the sexism that I know you can understand, but it's compounded in ways that you may not be able to understand, but I hope you can seek to empathize how sexism is compounded for women of color."

Most of us are deeply motivated by wanting to be valued, recognized, and appreciated at work. And while contexts may differ, most have experienced emotions like fear, joy, sadness, worry, and anger. If we can find these connection points that make us uniquely human, we have a great chance of empathizing with someone different than us.

In my workshops, I sometimes begin the day with a social identity icebreaker called identity mapping.

In a simple version of the exercise, I ask each person to draw a large circle and large square next to each other on a piece of paper. In the circle, I ask them to write their visible identities that they bring to work. For me, I usually write:

1. Female
2. Woman of color
3. Millennial

4. Indian

5. Tall

6. Wears scarves

In the square, I ask them to write their invisible identities that they bring to the workplace. For me, that is:

1. Mother

2. Extrovert

3. Immigrant

4. Speaks three languages

5. Social justice minded

I then ask them to share their identity maps with someone on the team who is similar to them. While this prompt is deliberately vague, people instinctively pair up with a team member of the same race, gender, and/or national identity.

Next, I ask them to share their identity maps with someone "very" different from them. And in this case, people instinctively partner up with someone of a different race, gender, or nationality.

When I ask people to reflect on the experience of sharing their identity maps with the two different partners, invariably people find that they have a richer discussion on shared experiences with people quite visibly different than them versus those they connected with just over their shared visible identities. When I ran this workshop at a 150-person technology conference in San Francisco, a white man from Australia shared that when he partnered up with a Black woman from the United States, he thought that they would have little in common. But they found some profound similarities that impacted their "work selves" including that they were both parents, had both lost their own parents at a young age, and had both grown up impoverished. The man then said he planned to stay in close contact with his global team member and wanted to get to know her better, although it was the first time they'd met.

Research demonstrates that finding these common shared identities can help us be more empathetic and collaborative, while overcoming fear and distrust. Finding common ground related to values that shape who you are and how you want to show up in the world yields a richer dimension of connection than our physical attributes. Tough life experiences that shape us, such as losing a parent at a young age or growing up in an impoverished environment, are just as out of our control as most of our physical attributes, yet they can profoundly shape us and our leadership. They can help create deeper connections than bonding simply over physical attributes. Even when the nature of those experiences differ, a meaningful connection and empathy can be formed just over the shared experience of survival and resilience.

Read Fiction

"The shortest distance between two people is a story," says activist Patti Digh.

Reading fiction or watching a film that portrays a life very different from ours can help build empathy. When we can temporarily step out of what's familiar and immerse ourselves in the shoes of someone different from us, it can have a strong impact on how empathetic we feel toward others. Research also suggests that we can be better attuned to the social and emotional lives of others by consuming fiction.

When it comes to building your own muscle on empathy through fiction, there is no shortage of prizewinning literature, film, or theater that can help you. I will always recommend seeking out art from people from underestimated backgrounds to fully be able to convey what it's like to step into someone else's shoes. I was an avid reader as a child, and often got lost in bookstores or libraries, much to my mother's chagrin. But as a child in Singapore, a country with less than four million people when I was growing up, I felt like I wasn't adequately exposed to the vastness of the world. Fiction became a necessary lifeline, and I could find myself empathizing with someone wholly different from me.

Professionals sometimes overindex on turning to business or management books to become better leaders. Often, the empathy we require can be cultivated by learning from the experiences of fictional characters. We feel less defensive when a story is fictionalized, but we can also experience a greater depth of understanding about the situation through the details, contexts, and descriptions that can be lacking in nonfiction. Remember to seek out content by authors who look different than you—no matter what type of fiction you seek. Most important, seek out authors who represent the group that is being covered; for example, when you read books by Black authors writing Black characters or characters with disabilities created by authors who have them, you're far more likely to get a more complete and true picture.

These are some questions to reflect on as you seek to build empathy with experiences unlike your own:

1. How does the protagonist or protagonists highlight perspectives that I haven't considered before and experiences different from mine?

2. What are the similarities between how they approached a situation and how I would have done so? What are the differences between my approach and the protagonist's?

3. How does this character's social identity—race, ethnicity, gender, socioeconomic background, and so on—impact their lives?

4. How do other characters perceive the protagonist because of their social identity?

5. What can I learn about the challenges that others who carry these identities face?

6. How can I use my privilege and influence to better advocate for people I work with who may be facing challenges like the ones detailed in the story?

There is no magic wand that can ensure anyone develops empathy, particularly later in life. This is why I like to encourage white parents with young children to ensure that their children form friendships with friends from different backgrounds and read a range of books featuring a diversity of protagonists by a diverse set of writers.

We must practice this too. As Zaki stresses, empathy can be developed with practice and can also atrophy if not used. The more influence and power that we have in society, and by extension, in the workplace, the more we risk being less empathetic to the plight of others. But do not let individual defensiveness—the idea that we didn't choose to have privilege—hold you back in your desire to cultivate empathy and inclusion. We must recognize that we have the responsibility as privileged individuals to dismantle larger systems of oppression, which we can only fully comprehend when we can empathize with how it impacts those most affected by it.

When we spend time seeking to understand the perspective of others, particularly women of color, and try to walk in their shoes, we are able to better include and advance them. The key is not just to empathize but use that empathy to spur action as well. Being inclusive on purpose is not about passive learning or empathy just because but rather using it to spur active advocacy for change.

■　■　■

KEY REFLECTIONS

1. The three areas of empathy are: affective (how easily can you feel another person's emotions), cognitive (can you understand and empathize with perspectives that may not be like yours), and empathic concern (how easily do you get concerned about another person's challenges). Which of these, if any, come naturally to you, and are there dimensions you could improve on?

2. Have you experienced or witnessed exclusionary behaviors (also known as microaggressions) in the workplace? What can you do differently the next time you notice it?

3. Is there someone you work with who has different social identities than you (race, gender, sexuality, etc.), but that you have other things in common with? What are those commonalities, and how did you discover them?

4. Is it easy for you to find fiction books where the protagonists have the same social identities as you? If so, how can you expand the texts that you read to develop more empathy with people different from you? If not, which texts have you found most useful in detailing your experience in the world?

5. What is one thing that you could do to take action today? Write it down here:

4

Shine the Light,
Then Get out of the Way

Your crown has been bought and paid for. Put it on your head
and wear it.

—Dr. Maya Angelou

Laura Gómez was excited for her upcoming meeting with a successful start-up founder and machine learning expert. She had a good
feeling about this connection; he was going out of his way to meet
at her office on a quiet part of Stanford University's campus—a
coworking space for Latinx entrepreneurs.

An angel investor had introduced her to Amit (not his real name)
as Gómez was looking for a cofounder and chief technical officer to
join her new technology start-up, Atipica. It was 2015, and while technology focused on workplace diversity and inclusion was nascent,
Gómez was convinced that she had a brilliant idea to democratize the
technology industry, especially so that more underestimated technologists like herself could gain entry.

Gómez showed the Indian American man in front of her the
product prototype that she had built using artificial intelligence
and machine learning to create more diversity in hiring. Often,

technology recruiters are required to fill open roles as quickly as possible and so they default to hiring from a stereotypical archetype: white, male, prior technology experience, and with a degree from the same handful of colleges. Gómez, who had worked at Twitter and YouTube before becoming a start-up founder, knew that people like her—children of Mexican immigrants who grew up in lower-income households—were often passed over by technology recruiters. Due to bias, their technical brilliance was routinely underestimated. She wanted to create technology to ensure that recruiters didn't skip over résumés from underestimated applicants who would otherwise have been hired.

Amit remained silent but engaged throughout their conversation. At the end of it, he politely thanked Gómez for her time and said that while her prototype was interesting, he needed more time to think about his next career move. She didn't think much of it and was looking forward to staying in touch. Numerous meetings with potential investors, customers, employees, and even cofounders were all part of the start-up life. But she was hopeful: if Amit joined her business, they could leverage his expertise and connections to build Atipica into the next unicorn, the Silicon Valley term for a company that is valued at a billion dollars or more. She continued building Atipica as a solo founder.

Eighteen months later, Gómez got a call from an interested investor who read that she had raised $2 million in her seed funding round. She said that she wasn't taking any more investment, but would reconnect with him when she was raising more money.

"By the way, I just invested $5 million in another HR Tech company that sounds very similar to yours. I can't tell you more details because it's in stealth mode, but the founder's name is Amit."

Gómez's heart sank. As she investigated further, she realized that Amit stole her idea and was building a competitor using her exact prototype.

Amit continued to sneakily send over his investors and advisers to "check in" on Gómez to see how much more she had built of her product since their last conversation. Unbeknownst to Gómez, as she shared her pitch deck, recent designs, and ideas with some of these investors in good faith, they were being given to Amit. Her customers even confirmed that the design of Amit's product was similar to hers. There were too many overlaps to be coincidental.

While she held a patent for her idea, he was far too influential, wealthy, and connected for Gómez to take him to court. Amit had raised $5 million before even launching his company, while Gómez worked doggedly to raise every cent of the $2 million she had, only after she had built a viable product with paying customers.

Even her own lawyers and advisers told her not to pursue legal action—it would not be worth the financial and emotional anguish. Silicon Valley was the ultimate boy's club, where connections mattered more than competence, they said. For women of color, particularly for people like Gómez who had entered the industry without connections, there was no way forward.

She soldiered on for three more years before closing Atipica in early 2020. Amit's company continues to flourish. At last count it had raised $45 million.

Reflecting on Gómez's shocking experience, what stands out to me is not the behavior of Amit—who is clearly a bad actor—but rather the complicity of the people around him, even when they knew that he was stealing Gómez's idea. As Martin Luther King, Jr., said, "In the end, we will remember not the words of our enemies, but the silence of our friends."

If you're reading this far, the message isn't just don't be like Amit, although for the record, please don't be like Amit and steal a woman of color's idea to then pass it off as your own.

Instead, reflect on when you might have ignored wrongdoing or even been complicit in upholding a powerful, privileged person just because they were influential. I urge you to reflect on how you can use your influence to create opportunities for women of color to surface great ideas, advocate for these great ideas to flourish, and most important, get duly recognized and rewarded for them. In Gómez's case, investors and other people with privilege should have stood up for her and challenged Amit. They should have used their network to ensure that Gómez's company continued to shine and she was credited for being the trailblazer that she is. At the very least, they could have expressed their dismay and stopped supporting Amit. Left without options, too many women of color are forced to concede their power and brilliance. It doesn't have to be this way.

Crucially, being inclusive on purpose doesn't mean seeking an award for propelling women of color ahead.

Learn to make room for women of color to shine, give credit, and then get out of the way.

Why Credit Matters

Giving and taking credit is a tough subject to speak up about, let alone write about in a book. The prevailing cultural narrative around the world is to be humble, that no task is too small, and when you work hard, the satisfaction of a job well done should be reward enough. And if you keep working hard, you'll be recognized. I've seen the concept of karma, which I grew up with as a religious concept in my Hindu household, take flight in a big way out west. A plethora of inspirational messages tell us to "trust our karma" and believe that we will be rewarded for good work.

But what happens if you never end up receiving credit—or worse, someone else does for your idea? What if you are left in stasis, while your white male peers continue to advance in your organization and get plum opportunities to prove their worth? How important is credit if your contributions are often unrecognized or considered insignificant? Worst of all, what if you're so underestimated that you aren't even thought to produce good ideas?

All the above has been true for women of color at some point. Often, they're denied the opportunity to do the work that is recognized and celebrated in an organization. While it deviates from industry to industry, we instinctively know what this looks like. Researchers call it glamour work, or "work [that] gets you noticed by higher-ups, gives you the opportunity to stretch your skills with a new challenge, and can lead to your next promotion. It's the project for a major client, the opportunity to build out a new team, or the chance to represent the company at an industry conference," says feminist legal scholar Joan C. Williams, whose research shows how women and people of color—especially women of color—are unfairly assigned work that keeps workplaces running smoothly, but doesn't lead to advancement or a raise. It's what she calls "office housework."[1] By contrast, men and white people are more likely to get glamour work.

A number of influential white men and some white women tell me that they never planned to be leaders, were frequently just tapped to lead unexpectedly, or had a connection who recommended them for glamour work. I can understand why this narrative of "you will get your dues even if you don't ask for them" is so attractive for people for whom opportunity and related credit comes unasked. Keep your head down, do the work, and opportunities for glamour work and credit will follow.

When women (specifically, white women) weren't getting glamour work opportunities to progress, the overarching narrative was that women weren't asking for them or were even actively rejecting opportunities to progress due to their own imposter syndrome. This was the message of Sandberg's *Lean In*. Unfortunately, "lean in" doesn't work. In fact, behavioral scientists conducted an experiment to assess the impact on women when they listened to messages from *Lean In* and found that these women thought it was their responsibility to fix structural inequality. The researchers concluded that the book's narrative could cause victim blaming, where individual women were blamed for not being able to progress at work, not the structural barriers that prevented any women from advancing.[2] For women of color who navigate tropes that they're angry, hysterical, or submissive, there's often no way to lean in and be rewarded.

What does work? Dismantling structural bias. I'll talk about how to do that in part II. On an individual level, however, leaders and managers must intentionally select women, especially women of color, for plum assignments so that they have a fair shot of being recognized for a job well done. Side note: I could write a whole other book about why I believe women's feelings of imposter syndrome have less to do with any internal deficit and more to do with the sexism and racism they encounter at work. My collaborator Jodi-Ann Burey and I concluded in the previously mentioned well-read *Harvard Business Review* article that, "Imposter syndrome directs our view toward fixing women at work instead of fixing the places where women work."[3] Suffice to say, when women of color get the credit they deserve, we are much likely to see this narrative desist.

In short, opportunities to advance matter. Getting credit does too. In tandem, both matter greatly to advancing women of color.

White men and women largely get the advancement opportunities and credit. While a gap exists even in the recognition that white women receive compared with white men, white women are still more likely to be in high-visibility positions compared with women of color.

Using Your Privilege to Advance Women of Color

For people who knowingly or unknowingly get credit for their brilliance, who know their social identities will largely afford them opportunities to progress and prosper, there is a chance to use their privilege for good. How can they use that influence to be more inclusive toward women of color? For that, I draw inspiration from Ella Fitzgerald and Marilyn Monroe.

Fitzgerald, the US jazz singer, is a global musical icon dubbed "the Queen of Jazz." But she very nearly did not reach the celebrity status that she is now famous for. In the 1950s, Fitzgerald tried to get a booking to sing at the well-known Hollywood jazz club Mocambo (where Frank Sinatra made his Los Angeles debut in 1943), but was denied the stage. Music historians say this was likely due to a combination of her being a Black woman and because she wasn't considered glamorous enough to perform there.

When Monroe heard about it, she personally called the owner of the club and said that she wanted Fitzgerald booked immediately, and in exchange, Monroe would appear at the front table of the club every night of her performance.

"The owner said yes, and Marilyn was there, front table, every night. The press went overboard. After that, I never had to play a small jazz club again. She was an unusual woman—a little ahead of her times. And she didn't know it," Fitzgerald reportedly said in an interview.

What's significant is that Monroe did not seek to book her own performance and invite Fitzgerald onto the stage with her. She sat in the crowd, allowing Fitzgerald to shine. Monroe's celebrity status would have overshadowed Fitzgerald and likely not have resulted in much advancement opportunity for Fitzgerald. Instead, Monroe used her influence to advocate for Fitzgerald alone to prosper. She made room and then got out of the way.

Below are some ways that you can do the same.

Run Inclusive Meetings

Meetings are a fact of office life that we can't seem to shake. During the coronavirus pandemic, the physical office went away, but research shows that most office workers had to attend more meetings than in prepandemic days.[4]

We know that meetings are here to stay, and done right, they're an important way to connect with each other and make decisions. When meetings aren't designed to be inclusive, however, they often end up excluding women of color.

If you're a manager who leads many meetings, there's ample opportunity for you to be inclusive on purpose. The first step is to take stock of who usually leads meetings, who gets to present at them, and who is celebrated as innovative and productive during them. In most cases, this is a white person. Being inclusive on purpose requires leaders to seek opportunities to create room for women of color.

Designate a facilitator for every meeting, ideally the leader, who ensures that everyone has equal speaking time. Research shows that men speak more frequently and for longer durations in meetings than women.[5] Women—of all races and ethnicities—are also more likely to be interrupted than men, even in online meetings.[6] This is even true in the highest offices, such as when female US Supreme Court justices are likely to be interrupted at more than twice the rate of their male counterparts.[7]

So interrupt the interrupters. Anyone, especially you, can interrupt people who interrupt women of color when they speak at a meeting. Some ways to do this politely are to say:

- "I think she hasn't finished"
- "I'd really like to hear her point of view first"
- "Please wait your turn"
- "Please don't interrupt the current speaker"

What's fascinating is that the first few times that people do this—awkward as it may be—the dynamics of meetings start to shift and soon it becomes the norm to wait your turn to speak. The opposite, interruptions normalize interruptions, is also true.

If you see that a woman of color's idea is not being heard, try another tactic.

Repeat and then get out of the way.

Many women can attest that often when they state an idea, it's ignored, but when a man repeats it, it's revered and applauded. When it happens in corporate spaces, astronomer and professor Nicole Gugliucci calls it "hepeating."[8] Meritocracy convinces us that like cream, brilliance rises to the top. But in reality, it depends on who delivers the message. The phenomenon of hepeating shows us that men are frequently viewed as brilliant and leader-like—the ones with the good ideas, while women supposedly don't have good ideas.

Women of color experience an even more acute form of invisibility. They often find that their ideas aren't heard until they're repeated by a man *or* white person. If you find that you don't have trouble getting attention in meetings, but the woman of color next to you does, you can repeat the idea (even if you don't identify as a man) and then get out of the way.

One woman of color whom I interviewed, Kiara, experienced this firsthand. In a former job, her white male manager took her aside before a meeting and said, "I have something to say at this meeting. Don't interrupt me, just trust me." Her manager went on to present a great idea that Kiara had. Every time that Kiara presented the idea before, her boss noticed that the team would shoot it down. Yet when her manager was done presenting the idea, the whole team applauded at the brilliant pitch that he had made.

He then turned to Kiara and said, "It's her idea, but all of you don't listen to her. Please applaud her and direct all questions to her. I'm just the messenger, but she's the visionary."

In this case, he turned the idea of hepeating on its head to make room for her idea and then got out of the way.

Pass the Mic to Amplify

Become aware of who is considered a visionary and who is seen as a follower. Once you intentionally observe, you will notice that it's largely white people and men who are given the floor to air ideas or ask questions.

One of my clients had a meeting-heavy culture, where big presentations were routinely made by the team to key stakeholders. When we assessed who got to present at their last four large meetings, it was always the white male team leaders. It became clear that the glamour work and recognition wasn't being distributed to the women and women of color on the team, even though they were typically working closer to customers on the ground and could answer strategic questions too. When preparing for the next meeting, the leader decided to assign a woman of color to present to the team. No surprise, as she gained visibility with key stakeholders, she was tapped for higher-visibility projects.

The leader made room and then got out of the way.

Yet the onus is not only on leaders; even colleagues of women of color can practice allyship in the moment. Whenever possible, call on women of color in meetings or other settings to share their ideas, especially if you are facilitating the gathering. Avoid tokenizing behavior, however, or just taking this action as a symbolic gesture to signal that you're including women of color in the moment. You also need to engage with the ideas that women of color share and create opportunities for them to put their ideas into action beyond the meeting.

Yamiche Alcindor, the US White House correspondent for PBS News, has often been at the receiving end of racism and sexism as a Black woman covering the Donald Trump–led US presidential administration. On August 4, 2020, at the height of the coronavirus pandemic, White House press secretary Kayleigh McEnany refused to let Alcindor ask a question. Seeing this, a *Boston Globe* reporter who was present, Jess Bidgood, raised her hand to ask a question, and when summoned, passed her turn over to Alcindor to let her ask the press secretary her question. Bidgood realized that her own privilege as a white woman would likely ensure that she was called on by the white woman onstage. So she used her position to get the mic and then passed it on to a woman of color.

Another way of ensuring that women of color get due opportunity and credit is "amplification," a technique used by the female staffers of President Barack Obama. The *Washington Post* reported that women staffers would usually have their ideas taken without credit by male staffers or ignored in meetings. So the women banded together to amplify each other's voices; "after one woman offered an idea, if it wasn't acknowledged, another woman would repeat it and give her colleague credit for suggesting it."[9]

If you often see that a woman of color's ideas are ignored or unacknowledged in meetings, and you hold rank by seniority or white male privilege, amplification can be an effective tool to include women of color. Some useful prompts are:

- "I want to pause and acknowledge this great idea that Priya just brought up"
- "Keisha, that's a great idea to . . ."
- "I love Miriam's suggestion to . . ."
- "Building on Tania's excellent suggestion to . . . , I propose . . ."

When we address these exclusionary behaviors intentionally, we can create a workplace environment that includes women of color.

Sponsor Women of Color for High-Visibility Projects and Roles

The existing research shows that high-visibility projects disproportionately are led and staffed by men. A Catalyst study on projects assigned to high-potential employees found that men's projects had double the budget and triple the head count compared to projects led by women. Just 22 percent of the women's project budgets exceeded $10 million, compared with 30 percent of the men's. Most troubling of all, one-third of men reported that their assignments got significant attention from the C-suite compared with only a quarter of women saying the same.[10] No comparable research has been done specifically on women of color and critical assignments, but we know that women of color face a concrete ceiling to leadership, likely exacerbated by a lack of opportunity to fully demonstrate their capabilities.

When women are tapped to lead these plum assignments, they're disproportionately white women. While white women face an invisible glass ceiling to advance in corporate careers, for women of color, it's frequently an entirely impenetrable concrete ceiling, compounded by years of being denied opportunities to lead and advance.

This is where your personal action becomes necessary. Recommend women of color for high-visibility assignments and roles. Take the time to cultivate relationships with various high-potential employees in your organization, not just the ones who are the same race or gender as you, particularly if you identify as white and male. Gauge the career ambitions of these employees so that when it's time to make decisions on how to staff these projects or roles, you will have a diverse array of names. Then intentionally recommend women of color with the same vigor that you would a protégé with the same social identities as you.

Erin Okuno, executive director of the Southeast Seattle Education Coalition, has spent much of her career advocating for closing education gaps for students of color in Seattle. Early in her career, she realized that the stereotypes of her Asian identity—being perceived as acquiescent, smart, but submissive—allowed her into spaces that other women of color, particularly Black women, weren't invited to. Okuno has since become a powerful force in the traditionally all-white rooms where decisions about Seattle's public education system are made.

"I know I have Asian privilege that allows me into many spaces others may not have access to. I can enter certain conversations and spaces where other people of color may not be able to, like getting onto task forces," she says. "If I see really juicy opportunities, I think hard about whom to reach out to and flag it for them."

Okuno once received an influential fellowship, and when it came time for next year's applications, she reached out specifically to a Black female friend to apply. She coached the woman during the interview process, and was candid about the positives and negatives of the experience, including the benefits to her career.

Her friend narrowly missed getting it the year after, but Okuno insisted that she try again the following year and recommended her name again to the selection committee. That year, the Black woman got the fellowship.

A career sponsor is someone who uses their social capital to advance someone else's career. They will leverage their influence to open the doors for their protégé by recommending them for glamour work opportunities. Research shows that while women have more mentors than men—people they can have casual conversations with about their career—men have more sponsors.

Three-quarters of senior leaders pick protégés who look like them, according to Center for Talent Innovation (now called Coqual), and considering that the majority of corporate leaders are white men, many women of color don't get sponsored for career-making glamour work.[11]

While institutional sponsorship programs exist in efforts to advance women—I've even written about them before in my last book as showing early promise to create a path forward for women to advance—the real change begins when leaders individually make the commitment and take personal action to sponsor high-performing women of color.

In 1997, technology executive Denise Reese, a Black woman, was recruited by OpenNetwork Technologies, a software development company. While Reese had a related certification, her background did not include identity management, the company's main offering. OpenNetwork's vice president of sales, Shane Whitlatch, hired her as an inside account manager anyway, believing in her potential to grow in and excel at the role as a salesperson—and that she'd learn about identity management on the job.

"It took me a few months to find my rhythm, but I eventually became a top performer. Shane and subsequently OpenNetwork's CEO, Kurt Long, took me under their wing and taught me the finer points of solutions selling," she says.

A few years later, as the two white male leaders continued to sponsor her by ensuring that she received stretch assignments and new opportunities to shine, Reese was assigned to the international team, and in 2002, was asked to relocate to the United Kingdom to help build the company's business in Europe.

"Shane and Kurt's belief in my abilities coupled with adequate training and career development opportunities set the stage for my transition to work internationally. My move to the United Kingdom was a game changer both personally and professionally," she notes. Twenty-three years later, she says that "none of this would have happened had Shane not taken a chance on me."

Reese's experience of being sponsored is rare because all too often, it is the potential of white men and women that is recognized. Women of color do not need special accommodations to excel (not even close); what we need is the unwavering belief in our potential to succeed and being offered opportunities to prove our capabilities, like our white counterparts.

This is why change can begin with one person (you) sponsoring one woman of color for one opportunity. Individual acts of inclusion can spark a movement for change.

When Okuno, the education specialist, realized that her individual acts of recommending women of color for high-profile opportunities in education was paying off, she decided it was time to institutionalize her efforts at scale. She wanted to ensure that women of color weren't just involved in one-off high-visibility projects but also would become decision makers and leaders.

One night in 2018, Okuno was at a gathering with other women of color and the conversation turned to how to elevate even more women of color, particularly Black, Latinx, and Indigenous women of color, in political leadership in Washington State. It was the birth of a committee to recruit, fundraise for, and endorse women of color to run for as well as get elected to school board seats.

A casual dinner of committed individuals became a concrete and systemic effort to promote women of color in leadership roles. Within one year, seven women of color ran for school board seats in Washington State and three were elected. Okuno and her friends are already gearing up for the next election cycle, when she can continue sponsoring aspiring women of color political candidates.

Public Speaking Opportunities

From media appearances to conference and panel opportunities, men and white people are more likely to be offered a platform as experts. One study found 69 percent of conference speakers globally are male, thus raising their visibility as leaders and experts.[12]

Here's an opportunity to change the ratio intentionally: seek out women of color to be speakers if you're organizing a conference or recommend them as commentators if media approaches you.

The first time I was recommended by a white woman friend to keynote a Fortune 500 company's talent event, I was frozen with fear. It was a gigantic opportunity, but when I saw the lineup, all the other speakers at the three-day conference were white men and women. My friend could have volunteered herself as a speaker; after all, it was a lucrative and high-visibility opportunity. But instead she made room for me and got out of the way.

That presentation remains a key building block for me in elevating my expertise as a public speaker.

A few other important notes. Don't just enlist women of color to speak about diversity issues, especially if that is not their expertise. I have built much of my career speaking about DEI because that's my skill set, but I am always thrilled to see women of color cited as experts on literally any other subject—from astronomy to medicine to politics. I often dream of when my own speaking on DEI could become obsolete because inclusive workplaces become the default, not the exception. What would I present on next? The possibilities are endless!

I frequently get both conference speaking and media commentary opportunities. I will always recommend other women of color, especially Black, Indigenous, and Latinx women, to the people who ask me for suggestions. That's an actionable way for me to use my privilege to make room for others. None of us can be successful without the other.

Redistribute Office Housework

Part of the change comes from us taking personal responsibility to ensure that women of color get the glamour work and are credited for it. In terms of the other part, to be truly inclusive on purpose, we must ensure that they don't get saddled with the polar opposite: office housework.

As discussed earlier, office housework refers to routine administrative tasks to keep the organization running smoothly. They are a necessary chore in most organizations that don't have a dedicated individual to do them. Short of hiring someone dedicated to helping order lunches, taking meeting notes, smoothing over client miscommunications, or serving on committees that don't advance one's career, there's only one way to ensure that women of color don't get burdened with this work.

Audit who does the office housework today in your workplace and then equitably redistribute it. Measure what work in your workplace has to be done for things to run smoothly—from taking meeting notes, organizing birthday/retirement celebrations, ordering lunches, and serving on committees. Where possible, then create a rotating system so that different people are responsible for these tasks and it doesn't default to women of color.

Be intentional. Where tasks can't be easily rotated, such as mentoring a junior employee for a longer period of time, find ways to recognize the employee taking on this task, particularly in performance reviews and even with financial compensation.

Ben Reuler, executive director of the nonprofit Seattle Works, says that he's tried yet another strategy to equalize office housework: have men take meeting notes and explicitly acknowledge office housework that's upcoming. "It's now commonplace at Seattle Works to acknowledge 'office housework' and approach it with a gender and racial equity lens, from room reservations and catering orders to virtual meeting invitations and tech administration," he explains. This means that less onerous tasks like reserving meeting rooms are not off-loaded onto junior staff and instead are managed by leaders. Tasks that need to be done repeatedly are rotated throughout the team.

As a white man, he notes that he has the privilege of not having to worry whether doing office housework would be held against him because when men perform administrative tasks at work, it's at worst perceived neutrally and more likely perceived as positive, not unlike when fathers take on caregiving responsibilities of their own children. In contrast, women's career growth—especially women of color— may be diminished because they are more likely to have their work taken for granted and be underestimated, he says.

"Redistributing office housework is one part of changing toxic work cultures that I've probably been complicit in perpetuating throughout my career. It's really a win-win situation in every possible way."

Some organizations will hire an administrative assistant or office manager who may find themselves at the receiving end of all office housework tasks, well beyond the scope of what they were hired to do. In the United States, the likelihood of a woman of color being hired in this position is high. When a woman of color is hired into an administrative role, auditing office housework becomes even more necessary or otherwise she may inadvertently get saddled with work that she wasn't hired to do. Ensure that there is a detailed scope of work for her to complete, and all else must be intentionally rotated among other team members. And just because a woman of color was hired into an administrative role, it doesn't mean that she may not have other career goals. Could you sponsor her to shine in other ways such as through stretch assignments?

For this chapter, instead of key reflections, I've created a checklist for you to audit opportunities to make room and then get out of the way.

■   ■   ■

CHECKLIST

☐ Are there a diversity of people represented at this meeting? Are women of color represented?

☐ Who is presenting at or leading this meeting? Could a woman of color lead or present?

☐ Does this high-visibility project have at least one woman of color as part of it? If not, who should be part of it?

☐ Do women of color repeatedly get interrupted or have their ideas repeated by men who get the credit? How can I intervene?

☐ What proportion of the speakers on this panel or conference are women of color? Can it be higher?

☐ Are people getting paid (financially or otherwise) to take on a task or extra work? Are women of color getting equally compensated?

☐ Am I sponsoring any women of color professionally?

☐ Who do I personally consider role models of leadership? Is there diversity in that—and are women of color represented in my models of leadership?

☐ Is the office housework being distributed equitably? If not, how could it be?

☐ If I am involved in hiring or promotion decisions, when have I last advocated for a woman of color?

What is one thing you could do to take action today? Write it down here:

II

Organizational Behaviors to Drive Inclusion on Purpose

Now that you have learned the power of personal intentions and actions to drive change, the following chapters focus on manager actions combined with institutional processes to recruit, retain, and advance women of color in the workplace. From more equitable hiring practices to creating psychological safety for women of color, individual action propelled forward by equitable institutional practices can create inclusive workplaces for all.

5

Your Role in Creating Inclusive Hiring Practices

Too often, we tell people to be inclusive without really showing them what that looks like.

—Bo Young Lee

Tiffany Tate was eagerly awaiting the phone call informing her that she had gotten the job as career center director at a recognized college.

Not only was she qualified—overqualified, in fact—as a college career development expert with two degrees, her interviews with the university's hiring team had gone exceptionally well. The team was selling the role to *her*; she had spent ample hours in the interview process including having dinner with the team that she was sure she would be working with.

Tate was excited to move to a beautiful part of North Carolina with her then two-year-old daughter. The role would give her a growth opportunity, she would manage a significant budget, and the person she would be reporting to had bonded with her over the fact that they graduated from the same college.

It was all laughs and smiles. The fact that the twelve people who had interviewed her were all white was par for the course in Tate's experience in North Carolina. As a Black woman, she had learned to navigate being the *only* at work.

When the hiring manager called back, she had all but packed her bags. She was ready. "Tiffany, I really hate to call you with this. It was such a tough decision. The search committee struggled with it, and it came down to you and one other person. And they just felt like the other candidate was a better fit. I'm sorry," he said.

The blood drummed in her ears. Did she hear correctly? But she quickly collected herself, dusting off the disappointment.

"OK, well, can you offer any feedback?" she inquired. "Can you share what would make me a better fit for this role?"

He responded, "No, I just want you to know you asked all the right questions. I don't have any feedback, I want you to keep being who you are. I love your transparency. You are obviously very skilled at what you do."

It's been five years since that day, but Tate remembers those words perfectly.

She wonders, "Weird! I'm not a good fit, but they're telling me to continue being the way that I am. That doesn't make any sense."

When a hiring manager can't offer constructive feedback, despite a candidate having all the experience and certifications, despite them being able to demonstrate skill in navigating institutional leadership and customers—students in Tate's case—it's a red flag. Considering that she had all the pedigree and all the best references, but was then told she wouldn't fit the culture of the institution, she couldn't ignore the only noticeable difference she had with everyone on the selection committee and eventually the person they hired: her identity as a Black woman.

"I felt defeated," she says.

Don't Hire for Culture Fit

Hiring for culture fit is among the most widespread and exclusionary hiring practices today. When you're hiring for a fit—given that most companies in Western countries are led by white men—by default, you're hiring for sameness. "Culture fit" is an unspoken code that people have around what's acceptable and what's not within an organization, or even in society.

It reminds me of when I first moved to the United States as an adult in my twenties. When people encountered my unfamiliar name, they frequently asked if there was an easier or shorter way to say it. Depending on the situation, I would come up with an Anglo-Saxon nickname (like Rachel). If I had to interact with them often, say at work, I'd let them call me Ria, removing most of my name to make it easier for them to write or read it.

As I grew older, I got more comfortable with telling people I didn't have a shorter name and that Ruchika was the only version I would respond to. But even then, for years later, I wouldn't correct them if they mispronounced it. A common mispronunciation still is for Westerners to call me "Roo-sheek-ah" instead of "Roo-cheek-ah" (like it's spelled). Now I'll correct people and remind them until they get it right. In the past, I was so eager to fit into the culture—both what I considered US culture as well as assimilating into the workplace culture. Now I see that my biggest asset is the difference that I *add* to the culture.

Rather than focusing on culture *fit*, organization leaders must concentrate on culture *add* to be inclusive. A plethora of research shows that harnessing the power of diverse teams leads to better outcomes, such as less groupthink, more innovative solutions, and overall more profitability.[1] My favorite data point, though, is how culture add can lead to justice and fairness.

Tufts University psychologist Samuel Sommers created a mock jury experiment with two hundred adults. Some juries were racially mixed with white and Black jurors, and some were all white. After watching a video trial of a Black defendant facing charges of sexual assault, the juries were first to submit their own verdict of guilty or not guilty, and then deliberate as a group. Even prior to deliberation, the mixed juries were nearly 10 percent less likely to presume that the defendant was guilty, compared with the all-white juries. During deliberation, the racially diverse juries had a more thorough consideration of the evidence and deliberated on average for longer, making less factual errors and being more open to discussing the role of racism in the process.[2] In general, even though there may be more debate, or what psychologists call "interpersonal conflict," when teams are diverse, the benefits of better outcomes far outweigh the drawbacks.

When teams prioritize hiring a candidate who would be a culture add rather than a culture fit, they're more likely to benefit from out-of-the-box thinking and better outcomes.

Yet the language of who is a culture fit persists—and one survey of global organization found 84 percent of recruiters look for it in their selection process.[3]

Think back to the last time that you talked about someone being a fit or not. The more trouble you have articulating why a candidate is not a culture fit, the more likely your judgment is biased. Instead, seek to hire people you don't already have represented, whether by race and gender, educational background and experience, country of origin and languages spoken, or other identities.

Tate, whom we met earlier, is a hiring expert with over a decade of career development experience. She advises her clients to move away from an outdated model of assessing how much you "like" a candidate to how well could they do their jobs.

"The old culture fit model relied on deciding whether to hire someone if you thought you could be stuck in an airport or blizzard with them. It's a bizarre metric—and riddled with biases, because you would likely choose to be stuck in an airport in a blizzard with someone who looks like you," she says. But that isn't the best assessment of who would best perform a job on your team.

Hiring practices that revolve around assessing for culture fit result in bias. One such example? Black women are earning college degrees at record numbers, but remain underrepresented and underpaid in corporate workplaces, with low access to leadership opportunities, as most workplaces still hire for a fit with Eurocentric culture norms.[4]

Structural racism cannot be dismantled overnight, but declaring that your workplace is no longer seeking a culture fit for new roles and disrupting peers when they reject a candidate for not being a culture fit is a quick win. So is creating a workplace environment where diversity and inclusion are valued, and culture add is celebrated.

Ensure that your organization prioritizes the hiring of a diverse range of employees, especially women of color. This is not just HR's job; it is every manager's responsibility.

As for Tate? She's since founded a company where she coaches clients to navigate the recruiting process, and advises countless leadership teams and boards on hiring and retention best practices.

During these interactions, she advises her clients to inquire of interviewees, "How will you add to the culture on our team?"

Everyone Loves to Hate HR, but Inclusion Isn't (Only) Its Job

I hear complaints about ineffective HR departments regularly in my consulting. Managers moan about how HR recruiters aren't sending over more underestimated candidates. Job seekers tell me that thanks to bad HR practices, they feel like their application disappears into a black box. Company leaders tell me that I should talk to HR if a company isn't measuring well on diversity and inclusion metrics.

Employees tell me that HR is often the biggest blocker when they're seeking insights into whether they're getting paid equally.

Everyone loves to hate on HR.

That's unfortunate and unfair. Over the years, I've advised a number of HR leaders on how to create more inclusive organizations, and indeed, some have demonstrated self-awareness and a growth mindset, while others get defensive and block recommendations for progress.

But the reason that HR doesn't do a good job of creating inclusive work environments is because it's not just *HR's* job. Inclusion certainly should be part of its job description, but in actual fact, it should be everyone's responsibility at a company—inclusive hiring, most of all.

I saw a leader taking responsibility for this firsthand when I was engaged as a consultant by John Paul in 2018. Paul, whose name has been anonymized, had just been hired to lead a global health organization's multiyear investment in the ultimate goal of eradicating a disease that kills millions of children worldwide.

I was nervous during my first meeting with him, feeling the gravity of his team's work. I said to him, "Your work is so meaningful, it literally saves the lives of millions of children." He looked straight at me and said, "Without your help to build a diverse and inclusive team, I don't see how we will be able to fully reach our goal to eradicate this disease from the world."

I had to pause, because while I deeply believe in my work in inclusion, there are many disheartening days. There are also many people who don't acknowledge these issues, largely because they are so wedded to the ideals of meritocracy, or if they do see the problems, they don't believe them to be a priority or their responsibility to fix. But here was a world-renowned disease expert who was able to connect the value of my work directly to his mission. It was among the more validating moments that I've had in this work.

Paul had inherited a leadership team that was all white and male, like himself. For years, the leadership team had been largely homogeneous, save for a few white women who had left before he was hired. No people of color had been on the leadership team, at least in recent memory. He recognized that to tackle a disease that disproportionately impacts non-Western countries, he would need a leadership team that was innovative, would think outside the box, and be representative of a variety of viewpoints. Disease eradication in developing countries is particularly challenging. It's not just a scientific problem to solve but also one that requires cultural context, from navigating resource-poor infrastructure, governmental regulations, and gender and religious norms, to integrating solutions with local customs and norms.

Paul was looking to hire three new leaders on his team and was determined that they would not be more of the same. Together, we shifted the typical focus of hiring for culture fit to hiring for culture add. We were looking for capabilities, strengths, and indeed backgrounds that were markedly different from those already represented on the team.

Paul isn't in HR, but his role as a hiring manager and team leader centered on inclusive hiring practices made all the difference. He recognized the need for adding to the culture of the team, not finding more people like him. He took personal responsibility to make change.

At any established company, it's no surprise that leaders like Paul receive pushback for adding extra steps to the hiring process. Often, the hiring process has been "tried and true" for a number of decades; referrals are prioritized, and people are so busy that adding any extra or new steps is met with understandable hesitation. The need for filling roles quickly is prioritized over an equitable process. That's precisely when it's most critical, however, for hiring managers to insist on reducing bias in the process and make the business case for how, even if additional funding or time is needed, creating an equitable hiring process will deliver better results in the long run. Emphasizing the need for inclusion on purpose, Paul used his leadership privilege to push for what he considered most important to his team's long-term success.

With regard to the three leadership hires, Paul specifically refused to consider a homogeneous slate of candidates sent by the company's recruiters, thus delaying the process until he had qualified women and people of color to interview. He sought candidate referrals from a diverse slate of people. When I reminded him of how much our own identities impact our network and preferences, he understood that sourcing referrals from a network of white men would largely yield white male candidates. So he sought referrals from more people of color in his network.

Once Paul had begun interviewing candidates for the three highly specialized roles, one of his choices said that she was interested in the role but could not relocate. While more organizations have started exploring remote leadership hires since the COVID-19 pandemic, at the time of this search, the team had little precedent of hiring US-based leaders who would not operate from its headquarters. Yet Paul knew that this candidate was so extraordinary and would, as a welcome bonus, ensure that he met the diversity priorities he had set. So he made an exception and hired her, setting a new precedent for the team on remote working—a year before the entire team was forced to work remotely anyway.

We make exceptions all the time for those in the majority groups yet hesitate to make them for candidates from underestimated backgrounds. Have you ever been hiring for a job and received an application from someone looking to switch industries? Or perhaps received a referral from a friend for a candidate who doesn't fully meet the job qualifications? In those cases, research shows that affinity bias (forming a connection with someone based on shared identities, like the same gender, race, and educational backgrounds) would make a hiring manager generally more willing to hire a candidate like them.[5] To be inclusive on purpose, hiring managers must become aware of the ways that bias might prevent them from extending opportunities to women of color who would be able to transfer skills or expertise from a different role and bring value to the organization.

How to Reduce Bias in Hiring

In most cases, the idea of culture fit stems from affinity bias.[6] It makes sense that we would believe people with shared identities would be easier and more fun to work with. Unfortunately, this approach to hiring people like us means that we leave people out who don't share the same affinities as us. Uncomfortable as it is to admit, affinity bias is rampant in our workplaces today. When leaders try to justify why every single member of their leadership team is white (because no qualified people of color made it through their rigorous processes, is what I frequently hear), I push back and say, "Either you believe only white people are qualified enough to lead . . . or there was some bias in the process that left out people of color. Which is most likely?"

For my clients, I've created "reducing bias in hiring" guidelines, which take an immersive and well-rounded look into the hiring processes of most companies. You can find the entire checklist at the end of the chapter, but I'll walk you through the three key areas where barriers to equitable hiring show up:

1. Candidate search
2. The interview
3. The job offer and follow-up after hiring

Inclusive Candidate Searches

The job listing itself can often create barriers to inclusion. It's an area that many don't think about. Take job listings that state a mandatory need for college graduates. I've been urging more employers to assess whether every job requires a college degree or would a pro-spective candidate be able to learn necessary skills on the job. A 2017 Harvard Business School study found that six million job list-ings in the United States require a candidate with a college degree, when in actual fact the job could be or currently is being done by a high school graduate.[7] Communities of color face disproportionate challenges to obtaining a college degree. As the first in my family to apply for and attend a four-year college, I can attest that not having access to information like how to apply to college or what standard-ized testing is can deter capable students from applying for a degree.

In the United States, a deep racial disparity exists in college gradua-tion rates; 51.5 percent of Black and Latinx students graduate college compared with 70 percent of white students.[8] The gap begins early. Neighborhoods that are majority white have significantly better-resourced K–12 public or private schools, while communities of color are usually assigned to less resourced public schools. Issues like the lack of nonwhite teachers in the school system as well as that Black and Latinx students are disproportionately more likely to be disci-plined than white students and experience noninclusive school envi-ronments all contribute to the fact that many communities of color are left behind in accessing college. So does the selective and opaque nature of admission to top colleges—thereby often leaving out appli-cants of color. At Harvard University, 42 percent of white admits are children of prior graduates, big donors, faculty, or athletes. Three-quarters of them wouldn't be accepted on academic merit alone, according to a 2019 study called "Legacy and Athlete Preferences at Harvard."[9] I would like to see hiring managers push against the idea that only an applicant from a brand-name college can fulfill the job criteria. Understand that the higher education system today is fraught with discrimination based on race and ethnicity, gender, who has access to better college prep classes, and who can afford college.

Furthermore, any hiring manager prioritizing inclusion on purpose would ensure that when a listing states a college degree requirement, the job really does require it. Instead, I recommend listing out skills that would be required to complete the work that we today too easily default to "college degree required" as a shorthand, such as familiarity with Microsoft Office, proven ability to meet deadlines, ability to communicate clearly in writing, or capacity to demonstrate ideas in meetings.

It's also important to make your application process as transparent and explicit as possible, and inform the candidates about what every step will look like. We easily assume that everyone starts on the same page (meritocracy again!) and has the same information on what a typical hiring process entails. That's simply not true. For example, I didn't know that in the United States, you're supposed to negotiate a salary with a recruiter, not a hiring manager, as is typical in Asian countries. Other disadvantages could be when candidates are unfamiliar with the fact that there are multiple rounds in an interview or how long an interview should last.

To be inclusive on purpose, be up front about the process. Telling all candidates that "you will have three rounds of interviews with three different managers at the company, and the salary band is as stated in the listing. We expect to make the hire within three weeks" is much fairer than the typical process today where only people who know the rules of the game win. Most often in the United States, these are white people who are most likely to have family members and friends already in the professional workforce.

I also advise employers to prioritize diversity in a candidate pool too. Refuse to review résumés or move to the interview phase unless there is a diverse representation of backgrounds. In fact, press pause unless at least 50 percent of the candidates are from nonwhite, non-US, non-male backgrounds. Even if you're sourcing from a recruiter (internal or external), this stipulation ensures that you're purposefully creating a diverse pool—racial, gender, ethnic, and so on—to draw from.

Again, one of the most maddening statements I hear is that there aren't enough qualified applicants from underrepresented backgrounds applying. If qualified underestimated applicants aren't applying, it's the organization's responsibility to seek them out and encourage them to apply. Advertise jobs in a variety of places, especially industry affinity groups (e.g., Black Girls Code or the Asian American Journalists Association). Make time to build relationships in professional affinity networks, even if you aren't from that community. Warm employee referrals matter greatly; one-third of US employees landed the job they're currently in because of an employee referral, writes Lydia Frank in the *Harvard Business Review*. Affinity bias in how we form our networks negatively impacts equitable hiring. Even with everything else held constant—from job title to industry to location—female and applicants of color were much less likely to get referred to a job, compared with their white male counterparts. Women of color were the most disadvantaged by employee referrals; they were 35 percent less likely to get a referral, while white women were only 12 percent less likely to receive a referral, Frank reported.[10]

While doing away with referrals altogether may not be a viable option every time, I recommend not relying heavily on them. Certainly, do not make referrals the *only* way that you hire. When I ask my network for referrals, I ensure that I solicit responses from a diverse group of individuals *and* specifically state in my referral request that I'm prioritizing people from underestimated backgrounds, like my client Paul did.

Inclusive Interviews

A homogeneous interview panel and group of people making a hiring decision are less likely to pick someone different. When a hiring process doesn't include women of color, we are less likely to be called for an interview or offered the job.[11] Multiple studies show that job applicants with non-Anglo-Saxon names are discriminated against during the job search process.[12] If your company has a practice of having multiple people make a hiring decision, ensure that there's diversity in the backgrounds of people calling the shots.

Assemble a diverse interview loop to create an inclusive interview experience for a candidate from an underestimated background. Encountering all-white and male interview loops was always a daunting experience for me, and made me question whether I would truly belong in previous jobs. Conversations that I've had with other women of color support this. A number of companies, including Intel, Accenture, and Cisco, now require diverse interview slates for new hires. Intel especially has reported promising results. According to data published in *Working Mother* magazine, in two years, Intel's new hires who were women or people of color rose 13 percent between 2014 and 2016.[13]

Next I recommend that each interview debrief should begin with the question, "Where could bias be showing up in this decision?" It sounds uncomfortable, and it can be, but naming biases is necessary to practice inclusion on purpose during hiring.

This also illustrates how and why hiring in an inclusive manner is everyone's responsibility. The first few times it may feel silly, like saying, "Bias is showing up here because the candidate was wearing red and that's my favorite color." But over time, you can start to pinpoint patterns that can create exclusion, such as a propensity to hire people who went to your college, smiled in the interview (research shows that we expect women to smile and showcase a sunny disposition because of our gender biases, but don't expect the same from men), or remind you of your younger self.[14]

I recommend making this part of the process—explicitly asking this question—because you are more likely to weed out biases that are so subtle, they rarely come up otherwise. For example, not all countries value the small talk and overt enthusiasm that is expected during job interviews in the United States, yet we so frequently make hiring decisions on these "gut feelings" of liking a candidate rather than a standardized process. One study at Stanford

University found that hiring managers were biased toward candidates who showed emotions during interviews as opposed to those who appeared calm and collected. So they were more likely to offer jobs to European Americans who had been socialized to display enthusiasm at job interviews instead of Hong Kong Chinese job applicants who had not.[15]

Through this exercise of explicitly naming biases, one client noticed how many of their hiring decisions were made by choosing "who they would be most likely to go for a beer with." Valuing social connections, which we often form based on our identities and backgrounds, over job competence is a key reason why hiring bias is so insidious as well as pervasive.

This is a particular barrier to hiring women of color, who are typically underrepresented in the workplace, especially beyond entry-level roles. If you're a white man, would you be more inclined to go for a beer with another man like you or a woman of color? Even if it makes you uncomfortable to admit, affinity bias tells us that you're most likely to choose the white guy. While affinity bias in itself may not be nefarious, the decisions you make as a result of it usually exclude women of color.

That's why it's so important to actively identify where bias may be showing up in your hiring process. When you're assuming that you're biased—and we all are—then that leaves more honesty to assess a candidate whose background you may have preconceived stereotypes about.

During job interviews, it's critical to be as objective as possible, but we also must be proactive in recognizing and reducing our biases. If a white male candidate is judged favorably for demonstrating a passion for his work, but a Black woman is not, then the only way that we could solve this is by naming and acknowledging it.

Create more structured interview processes to reduce the subjectivity that often informs hiring decisions. This takes more work up front, but later on is more likely to safeguard against decisions that are rationalized by statements like "I don't know why I liked the candidate . . . I just did." Create a standard list of questions that each interviewer will ask and decide on a corresponding interview score-card for each question, ideally with a numerical rating scale. Decide in advance whether each question is weighted equally or are there certain skills that are more necessary to the role. Determining this in advance is crucial because bias could emerge if you end up weighting the factors that candidates in the dominant majority (white male) scored well in more heavily so as to give them the edge.

After the interviews are completed, reconvene as an interview group as soon as possible. We have an overreliance on first impressions rather than facts to make decisions. If you wait a long time to discuss candidates, it's more likely that you will default to these first impressions versus their qualifications. Next, articulate decisions out loud. When we are required to explain our reasoning, or listen to others' thoughts, we can typically catch our own bias in action or even ask for more information if we hear our colleagues making biased judgments. For instance, you might ask, "Did you mean that she appeared passionate or was she truly angry?" When hiring teams prompt a conversation on bias by asking, "Where could bias show up in our decision today?" they're more likely to disrupt bias by naming where and how it shows up.

If you're reading this and groaning at the extra steps that I'm recommending, let me pause and say, I understand. Adding more processes isn't my definition of fun either. And yet if this level of detail is counter to the way that your team normally interviews, it may explain why it's hard to achieve the results of creating the diverse and inclusive workplace that you're aiming for. When we rely on our gut without prioritizing inclusion on purpose, we're more likely to fall prey to our biases. Having the checks and balances in place can prevent us from making these errors, and thus yield the outcomes that we're seeking.

Salary Transparency and Inclusive Job Offers

Information about the salary range stated up front can reduce the unintentional creation of a pay gap. Depending on how your organization handles salary conversations, a recruiter will either discuss this with a candidate before the interview or pay will be discussed once a hiring decision is made. The earlier this conversation is had, the better.

While more states in the United States are making it illegal to ask for a candidate's salary history, it is still a wide practice in other states and around the world. This often means that if a candidate was being paid poorly in a past job, they frequently get stuck in a cycle of lower pay because they don't have insight into what the job should really pay. Asking for past pay data continues the inequality that likely started long before a woman of color even got to your organization. Instead, operate from the principle that you will pay what the job commands, not a variable rate that changes based on a candidate's past salary. Of course, you must ensure that the salary you're offering is in line with the current market rate. I've laid out a much deeper dive into pay inequity in the next chapter, but doing away with salary negotiations—or expecting women of color to demand a higher salary or "level up" to the market rate—is unfair and noninclusive. Rather, focus on transparency.

When Inclusion Matters More Than Pay

One woman I know, Sarah, is a highly skilled software developer, sought after not only because of her incredible talent but because as a Latinx woman she also checks off many US companies' diversity boxes. She recently was headhunted and successfully interviewed for a lucrative job with a technology giant, yet she turned it down. It would have raised her current salary by at least 20 percent if she had moved.

When asked the reason for staying put after the rigorous hiring process, she said that she was turned off by the company's apparent lack of inclusive culture. "Everyone talked about how they were 'all work, no play' and were bragging about how they worked such long hours," she told me. "It sounded like the typical 'bro' culture in tech, not one that would be inclusive to working parents, or in general, someone like me that values time outside work. Plus I was the only Latina around for miles . . . and I passed by at least a hundred people there."

Research supports the "why" behind Sarah's decision. Talented individuals deeply value and prioritize managers who create inclusive workplaces. In fact, inclusive behaviors far outweigh other company benefits for millennials, the largest demographic in the US workplace today. A Deloitte study found that 39 percent of millennials would leave their current employer for a more inclusive one, and 80 percent of millennial employees say that inclusion is important when choosing a new employer. The same study found that for many millennials, a company-wide corporate diversity and inclusion program was less important than inclusive behaviors demonstrated by their peers and leaders.[16]

Inclusion on purpose matters now and will continue to become more fundamental in the future of work.

I could imagine that the hiring team must have been surprised by Sarah's (who happens to be a millennial) refusal to join this recognizable brand that was offering her a significant pay raise. If its leaders were my client (they're not, but I hope that they're reading this), I would direct them to the last point in my inclusive hiring guidelines: follow-up with candidates who didn't accept a successful job offer about their reason for declining.

Understand what's keeping qualified women of color from joining your organization and then work on fixing it. More job seekers are actively looking for clues to indicate that the company's culture would be inclusive to them. As a working mother, if interviewers keep talking about an "always available" work environment, I know that I wouldn't belong there. If the current employees keep talking about happy hours as the way to network, I probably wouldn't fit in there if I didn't drink alcohol. Of course, I'm not suggesting that interviewers fake an inclusive work environment but instead recognize the meaningful and long-term work ahead to create a more inclusive culture. Learning what these barriers are is the first step. Remember that the job interview process runs both ways; the candidate is assessing whether the employer would be right for them too.

I did warn you that inclusion on purpose is not a comfortable and easy thing to do. If it was, it would be ubiquitous. As we work on developing an inclusion mindset and step out of our comfort zone to confront problems, we're more likely to proactively cultivate solutions steeped in equity and inclusion.

Does This Really Work?

By focusing on inclusive hiring Paul's team went from an all-white, all-male leadership team to one that is gender-balanced and the hiring of the first leader of color, in 18 months.

The buck should never stop with HR. Anyone in the company looking to hire more equitably can take these actions, from an entrepreneur hiring their first employee, a team evaluating working with an external vendor, or managers in a large corporation looking to hire for hundreds of new roles.

Everyone can choose inclusion on purpose, because it's not just HR's responsibility. Below are some hiring guidelines developed by Candour, my inclusion strategy firm.[17]

Candour's Inclusive Hiring Guidelines

Candidate search

Recommendations	How this can help mitigate bias
Make the hiring process transparent and inform candidates about the process. State all the information required to apply, how many interviews to expect, tests that may be administered, timelines on when to expect a follow-up from the organization, salary range, and whether the salary and benefits are open to negotiation.	Not all candidates receive the same information about the job search process, particularly people from different countries and candidates from underestimated backgrounds. Seek to eliminate bias by creating a level playing field so that all candidates know what to expect, especially if they are not already con nected to someone at the organization. Additionally, stating salary specifics up front reduces the likelihood of unintentionally creating a pay gap as well as the risk for women and people of color, who are more likely to face backlash for negotiating.
Request candidate referrals from a diverse group of people.	It widens the pool of potential candidates rather than engaging the same type of candidates each time.
Reach out to ERGs, professional groups for people of color, LGBTQ, and so on. Advertise with such groups.	It widens the pool of potential candidates.
Include an authentic equal opportunity statement.	The best candidates of all backgrounds are more likely to apply when an equal opportunity state-ment is included.
Refrain from using words in job listings that have been shown to negatively impact women and people from underrepresented groups as well as discourage them from applying. Where possible, emphasize skills and experience over professional degrees.	By removing words that indicate certain people do not belong, it increases the likelihood that a wide variety of candidates will find the job appealing. Examples of words to *avoid* in job listings: *rockstar, ninja, hacker, guru, manage, build, aggressive, fearless, independent, analytic, and assertive.* Examples of words to *use* in job listings: *create, dedicated, responsible, conscientious, and sociable.*

(*continued*)

Candidate search (continued)

Recommendations	How this can help mitigate bias
Include growth mindset words and avoid fixed mindset words in job listings.	Jobs where women are hired are twice as likely to contain growth mindset language, according to research from Textio. These jobs also fill faster. Examples of words to *use* in job listings: *learn new things, commitment to improvement, and highly determined.* Examples of words to *avoid* in job listings: *high performer, genius, uniquely talented, and overachiever.*
Create a preinterview hiring scorecard to evaluate the applicants, particularly if different team members are reviewing the résumés and making decisions on who to interview.	This reduces the impact of bias by comparing candidates on measurable scores rather than relying on memory.
Only review résumés or move to interviews when there is a diverse representation of backgrounds. Refuse to interview unless at least 50 percent of the candidates are from nonwhite, non-US, nonmale backgrounds.	A diverse slate of candidates can lead to a more equitable hiring outcome, but just having one candidate from an underrepresented background has shown not to lead to change.
Bonus: Anonymize gender- and racial-specific data when looking at résumés, where possible.	By anonymizing this information, bias about the perceived competence of a candidate is minimized.

Interview

Recommendations	How this can help mitigate bias
Have a diverse interview loop and avoid panel interviews.	A homogeneity of interviewees can indicate to candidates that diversity is not valued on the team. Panel interviews can reinforce hiring for culture fit over culture add.
Create structured interviews, asking each candidate the same questions. Create corresponding interview scorecard for each question, with a rating scale (such as one through five). Determine whether questions will be weighted the same or if some are more important.	This mitigates affinity bias.

Interview (continued)

Recommendations	How this can help mitigate bias
During interviews, ask the same questions in the same order, every time.	This mitigates affinity bias or an interview process where the candidates are judged on different criteria.
Score interviews right away.	By not relying on memory, bias is reduced because we're more likely to remember feelings and affinity rather than specific answers.
Refrain from asking questions or having conversations about culture fit or criteria (both official and in discussions) around culture fit. Seek to bring culture add—people who are different and will add diversity to your team.	If you're seeking to diversify your organization, why hire for sameness?
When discussing candidates in a group, start with the question, "Where could there be bias in this decision?"	Making a group aware that biases may exist in decision-making is more likely to help draw out the biases and seek to rectify them.
Using the interview scorecard, compare all the candidates one line item at a time, similar to how academics grade exams.	This reduces bias by ensuring that all candidates are judged equally.
Articulate your decisions out loud.	This reduces bias in decision-making and also helps catch potential biases in action.
Bonus: Consider audition-style challenges for the first round of interviews in which candidates are asked to solve a challenge, but you can't see any demographic information about them.	A tool for mitigating bias, this audition style allows for the demonstration of skill without indicators of race, gender, and other factors.

Job offer and follow-up

Recommendations	How this can help mitigate bias
Refrain from asking salary history/ expectations.	Women, people of color, and others historically are paid less. Lower past salaries can hinder them from reaching parity even later in careers
Ensure that salary offers are made fairly and in line with other comparable salaries.	Women, people of color, and others are historically paid less.
Follow up with candidates who didn't accept successful job offers about their reasons for declining them.	Uncover what about the hiring process or culture may have deterred high-potential, underestimated candidates.

What is one thing that you could do to take action today? Write it down here:

6

Pay Women of Color Equally for Equal Work

The only thing that separates women of color from anyone else is opportunity.

—Viola Davis

Piya Singh (a pseudonym) is making less money than her white male counterpart for doing the same work. Tom has less educational qualifications and experience in the department that they are both working in at their US-based technology company.

Singh, who identifies as Indian and Canadian, was hired in 2019 to market the company's reputation as a diverse and inclusive employer. The role and pay were significantly lower than what her qualifications should have garnered. But as a Canadian immigrant, she had been out of work for over two years while waiting for her right-to-work documentation to process in the United States. So she accepted a job offer that she was less than happy with and was told that she wouldn't be able to negotiate a higher salary.

Soon after she joined the company, Singh realized that she had been brought in at lower level than other people with similar experience. She noticed that everyone in her department above her was white.

When she compared her career trajectory with Tom's, she became disheartened. "He was brought in at a higher level and since then has been promoted. I've been told I'm not eligible for a promotion for at least a few more years," she says.

At the beginning of the coronavirus pandemic in March 2020, the company started moving its US employees to a virtual work environment. Singh and Tom were told that their responsibilities would be combined since much of the in-office responsibilities that they had would be eliminated for the foreseeable future. This meant that despite being hired in different capacities, at different levels and with different pay, both ended up doing the exact same work.

"The pandemic forced us to break down our deliverables month by month for the next year. We cycle back and forth every month, doing the exact same work," she explains. "But he's at a higher level than me. And he's getting paid more than me. And that of course leads to him being able to make more decisions than me."

When Singh brought up the pay and level discrepancies, her white female manager defended Tom's seniority. "My manager said that she knows him more than me and she's more familiar with his work so therefore she trusts him more."

Singh was surprised by her manager's blatant favoritism for her colleague.

"She did say she's working on it, but that was a big red flag for me. For anybody to even admit that they have this bias and think it's OK. She should have said, 'We all have biases, and they need to be corrected.' Instead, she was defending that the reason why he is trusted and paid more than me is because she's more familiar with him."

Singh also raised the concern that other women of color in her department were consistently hired into the company at lower levels than white men and women, even if they had more experience. "I brought up that I had done statistical analysis on pay and role gaps by race and gender, and noticed that women of color, like myself, were at lower levels and making lower pay than our white male and female colleagues. And most women of color were also more educated. . . . [My manager] told me, 'Yes, this is something we know is a problem.' And that's it. That was the beginning of the end of the conversation."

The irony of experiencing and witnessing pay disparity while being tasked with building the company's reputation as an inclusive employer is not lost on her. But she's stuck. She and her husband are financially supporting their extended family as well as raising a young child in an expensive urban city in the United States. Looking for a new job as an immigrant woman of color during a pandemic has proven challenging too. So she stays on in a job where she's undervalued and underpaid.

Singh's is one of many stories that I heard in interviews. Most often, when women of color brought up pay disparities to their organizations, they were met with resistance. In some cases, they were penalized for being ungrateful, difficult, or troublemakers.

"I don't do what I do for money," Singh tells me. "But it's unjust that someone gets paid more because a manager is more *familiar* with them, because they're white and male," she emphasizes.

Money Makes the World Go 'Round

In a capitalist society, wealth—money earned and accumulated—is a powerful measure of worth. So it's a logical assumption to make that when women of color are repeatedly underpaid for equal work, we believe women of color's contributions are worth *less*.

Pay inequality continues to be a rampant issue around the world; women make a global average of seventy-seven cents to their male counterparts in the same role. By the United Nations' estimates, it would take seventy years just to close the gender income gap if we immediately started to pay men and women equally.[1]

When we drill into the data, the picture is bleak. Women of color are conspicuously absent from senior management roles in global organizations and overrepresented in lower-paying jobs, especially childcare. The people with the most wealth, access to the best education, and opportunities to rise in organizations, and whose earnings aren't impacted by parental status, all have one thing in common. They're almost always white and male.

Taking an intersectional lens to the data in the United States presents an even more nuanced picture. For every dollar that a white man earns:

1. Asian women make eighty-five cents
2. White women make seventy-seven cents
3. Black women make sixty-one cents
4. Native American women make fifty-seven cents
5. Latinx women make fifty-four cents[2]

I've previously discussed how the categorization of Asian is too large and incomplete to capture an accurate portrayal of all Asian women's experiences. While some Asian women are often well represented in higher-wage jobs, when you control for their educational and work experience, they make less money than white men and Asian men with the same or even less human capital.

Scholars Lilian Gomory Wu and Wei Jing tracked the progress of Asian women in US science, technology, engineering, and mathematics (STEM) corporations for three decades, and found that Asian women's pay in STEM fields lags behind not only men but also white women and other women of color. According to their experience and education, Asian women should be more represented at the highest leadership positions, yet they are typically stuck in non-managerial, nonfaculty, or nontenured academic positions.[3] Again, this is where nuance is necessary; we can't just look at Asian women in relatively high-paying jobs compared with other women of color and believe that they're immune from bias.

As Wu and Jing conclude,

With so many entering the workforce, it is easy to assume that Asian women are progressing nicely and that they can be found at the highest levels of STEM industry, academics, and government institutions. The data tell a different story. . . . [There] is a double bind for Asian women, facing both a *bamboo ceiling* because of Asian stereotyping and a *glass ceiling* because of implicit gender bias. The scarcity of Asian women in upper management and leadership positions merits greater attention.[4]

Conducting an actual pay audit in an organization lies in the domain of HR, and I'll address that as a critical step for the *organization* to be inclusive on purpose. But there are a variety of steps that individual managers can take before we get to institutional practices like instituting pay equity policies.

Understand How Racial Disparities Feed the Pay Gap

Women of color, especially Black, Latinx, Indigenous, and Native American women in the United States, experience compounding barriers to receiving fair pay. I've seen employers explain gender and racial wage gaps by factors that shouldn't matter when two people are performing the exact same tasks, such as which college they went to, which organization they came from, or their prior salary history. Yet the past routinely impacts a woman of color's present earnings.

Let's just take educational disparities by race. I've previously cited data to show how the average Black and Latinx student in the United States lacks educational opportunities due to systemic racism. Unfortunately, this continues on well into the workplace.

When a Black or Latinx woman who attended a less prestigious college enters the workforce, they could have all the skills to perform the work at hand exceptionally, but will most likely be offered a lower starting salary than a comparative graduate from a top-tier college. It becomes more necessary to take an intersectional lens to the college premium or the belief that college education is a path for social mobility for all. A study by the Urban Institute found that going to college raised white women's earnings by 26.1 percent, but only by 18.9 percent for Black women.[5] "In America, it's better to be born wealthy—which often means white—than to be born smart," states an *Axios* article investigating educational inequality in US public schools. This is not just a US issue; the socioeconomic achievement gap impacts lower-income communities—usually ones that have experienced racial, ethnic, and/or religious marginalization—worldwide.[6]

Wage inequality for women of color can begin early, and it carries forward to which jobs they are considered qualified for and the salary that's offered to them. It extends onward to the fact women of color are left out of high-visibility projects or other opportunities to showcase their potential. All these factors compound to result in women of color being blocked from ascending to the highest-paying roles.

Managers must take time (*really* make an effort) to understand the barriers faced by women of color to educational and advancement opportunities. Only then can they examine how these societal biases play into preventing women of color from entering and advancing into higher-paying jobs.

Many people may assume that an employee who graduated from a top college deserves higher pay than one who graduated from a lesser-known institution, or did not complete or even attend college. Yet given what we now understand about disparities in educational attainment, as I illuminated in previous chapters, it is time to let go of that harmful assumption. Tying pay to the educational institution that a person attended is just another way of perpetuating a racist system where white men are paid more than women of color. In fact, according to the National Center for Education Statistics, Black women earned more degrees than any other racial group.[7]

The concept that everyone who advances in the workplace does so because they were entirely self-reliant and motivated is not only detrimental to the progress of women of color but also false. Women of color face persistent biases about their capabilities, so even when they do demonstrate grit, they're underestimated. We know mentorship and sponsorship are critical components of success regardless of race, and women of color are the least likely to receive it. Managers must familiarize themselves with these challenges so that they can advocate for their employees of color.

Talk about Money, Even If It's Uncomfortable

Years ago, I met a white woman, Cara, for coffee and buttery croissants at Semillon—my favorite Parisian-inspired bakery. Right opposite my office, Semillon Bakery was one of the few establishments in the area owned by a woman of color (although it has since closed as a result of the COVID-19 pandemic).

Cara and I were both advising the same organization as inclusion consultants, but we were retained by different leaders within the institution. When she told me the hourly rate that she was commanding, I nearly choked on my croissant. It was exactly double what I was charging for the same work.

I set my own hourly consulting rates, and when I conferred with other women of color who are in my industry, my rate was in line with their fees. This organization, however, chose not to reveal that it was paying other consultants double my rate for the same work. This is why pay transparency is a critical part of being inclusive on purpose.

Had Cara not told me her fee, which she felt was the right thing to do as someone with white privilege, I would never have known. I would have gone on undercharging. I finished my croissant, marched back to my office, and promptly emailed my client that I had learned about the fee disparity. The client ended up paying me the same amount after I brought it up, thereby indicating to me that they could have afforded to do so from the beginning.

As I reflect back on this experience, the reasons for the fee disparity are many. First, many women of color undercharge because they receive pushback when they command the same fees as white experts. In 2020, white female antiracism expert Robin DiAngelo was paid 70 percent more than Black expert speaker Austin Channing Brown for speaking at the University of Wisconsin, despite both being represented by the same speaker agency.[8] Indeed, I have had prospects tell me that my consulting fee is too high, but later learned that they worked with white inclusion strategists who command more than me. Second, women of color often don't know exactly how much white people are being paid. It's a black box. In fact, 68 percent of people surveyed in the United States said that they'd rather talk about their weight than money, and some experts say that people would prefer talking about sex than their salaries.[9]

Until white people, especially white men, transparently share rates, women of color will not know the fair market rate for a role.

If your privilege will safeguard you from suffering a hit to your reputation for bringing up this taboo topic, then it's incumbent on you to do so. Where possible, be transparent about what you're making, what your budget allows you to pay, or how much money you paid in the past for similar services. Inequality proliferates in the darkness. It's the lack of information about who is making what that allows companies to pay people differently, even if they don't intend to discriminate.

The greatest way to advocate for women of color is to share your numbers. If all managers could plainly state numbers, such transparency would create inclusion at scale.

But it's not just in hiring conversations that these numbers matter; transparency as much as possible in other facets involving money is key to being inclusive on purpose too. When negotiating a speaker fee in 2017, I learned that the fee that I had originally planned to ask for was *five times lower* than the white male speaker with comparable experience. Once the organizer shared the other speaker's fee, I felt more comfortable asking for the full fee that my experience should command.

When I asked for the numbers, I was taking a risk; the organizer could have viewed my request as unprofessional or that I didn't have a standard rate. He could have declined to share the fee of the other speaker, citing confidentiality. He could have decided not to work with me just for asking—and I'll get to how much negotiation can negatively impact a woman of color's prospects soon. I'm glad I asked and that the other party shared, thus deviating from common practice. But having him state his organization's budget (it had the budget to pay me equally) up front would have ensured that I would be paid fairly regardless of whether I inquired.

When you are in a position to work with vendors, including speakers or consultants, state your budget up front. And please do not ask professional speakers to speak for free. You would not expect your catering company to provide refreshments for your event for free, nor would you expect the light and sound technicians to supply their services uncompensated. So why expect that of conference speakers?

Even in salary conversations with your team, you have an opportunity to be inclusive on purpose; if you manage a woman of color who is about to be promoted, you can and should compare the new salary that you are offering with others in the same role. When pay practices during promotions go unchecked, women of color frequently have the most to lose. So we need managers to intentionally seek out these numbers and share them transparently.

How Women of Color Are Underpaid

In June 2020, a viral social media hashtag #PublishingPaidMe revealed just how inequitable pay can be when we aren't transparent with numbers.

L. L. McKinney, a Black woman author of young adult books, urged other writers to share their advance numbers—the money that publishers pay authors to write their books. As one would expect, first-time authors get lower advances as they don't have a proven track record of selling books, while renowned authors can get seven-figure advances.

The disparities between women of color and white authors' advances were staggering.

Two-time National Book Award winner Jesmyn Ward, a Black woman, tweeted that she had to "wrestle" her way to a $100,000 advance after winning prestigious awards. By contrast, Chip Cheek, a white man author, tweeted that he received an $800,000 advance for his *debut* and even noted "shock" on seeing Ward's advance after her established track record.

"I, a totally unknown white woman with one viral article, got an advance that was more than double what Roxane Gay got for her highest advance," tweeted Mandy Len Catron, who received $400,000 for her first book. Eminent Black, queer female author Gay received an advance of $15,000 for her celebrated essay collection *Bad Feminist*, which became a *New York Times* best seller.

Publishing advances illustrate how those who are given more money are expected to perform better, and more important, are given the resources to succeed.

As Constance Grady wrote in *Vox* in relation to the #Publishing PaidMe campaign,

> An advance doesn't just determine how much money an author is getting for a book up front. It also reflects how much money the publisher plans to invest into the book elsewhere, again based on how well they believe it will sell. A book that is projected to sell 100,000 copies gets its author a higher advance than a book that is projected to sell 10,000 copies, and it also gets a higher budget for marketing and publicity. . . . So, in the end, an advance becomes something of a self-fulfilling prophecy. When publishers are confident enough in a book to pay the author a healthy advance,

they are also going to be putting significant money into the book's marketing budget, which generally means the book is more likely to sell well. When publishers think a book is likely to have soft sales, they'll pay the author a small advance and put less money into publicizing it—which, in turn, means fewer readers will ever hear about the book and it's less likely to sell.[10]

It's disappointing to see the racism in action; when we analyze the data, we see that books by people of color that received lower advances have gone on to become national best sellers, but they were being underestimated the whole time. Imagine what could have happened if they received the same belief in their potential that their white counterparts did from the start—the high advances as well as top-notch marketing and publicity?

This "self-fulfilling prophecy" noted by Grady can be applied to any industry. Many women's and especially women of color's contributions are underestimated. Companies believe that they aren't the ones worth "betting on" for longevity and leadership, so women of color are underpaid, undersponsored, and ultimately, often stuck in dead-end jobs. Many white men who enter, on average, with higher starting salaries are promoted up the ladder at significantly higher rates. They're given opportunities to shine and are sponsored by other white men, leading to lucrative executive jobs. In totality, when women of color are underpaid because they're not expected to lead, it's no wonder more than half of the women of color surveyed plan to leave their jobs in the next two years—not for lack of ambition, but for lack of support and opportunity.[11]

Don't Expect Women of Color to Negotiate Away Pay Inequality

In 2003, economist Linda Babcock's book *Women Don't Ask* focused on how women's reticence to negotiate their salaries caused a persistent gender gap—to the tune of half a million dollars in lost earnings over a lifetime when women failed to negotiate their first salary. Babcock addressed how the gender schema (the way that we are socialized to think about gender roles and behaviors in society) impacted women's negotiation. Essentially, many experts say women don't ask for more because many are socialized to believe that advocating for themselves would run contrary to societal expectations of being agreeable.

Then there's the flipside of negotiating as a woman. Gender norms are so entrenched that a study confirmed what I have seen in real life: women do ask for raises as often as men; they just don't get them.[12] When we urge women to negotiate their salaries, we are setting them up for failure if we do not simultaneously address the prevailing biases in society. Too many of us, myself firmly included, were socialized to believe that women should conform to being agreeable rather than display ambition.

Babcock's book and the study cited above did not examine how the racial bias faced by a woman of color can be an additional barrier to a successful negotiation. Newer research finds that women of color are 19 percent less likely to receive a raise when they asked for one when compared to white men, according to a 2018 PayScale report that concluded, "Simply expecting people from underestimated backgrounds to ask for a raise will not close the wage gap." The study also found that while white women were slightly less likely to receive raises compared with white men, this number was statistically insignificant.[13] This is why intersectionality matters. Women of color face significant backlash for negotiating pay that is compounded by the expectations people have of their behavior, according to gender *and* racial norms.

One study found that Black candidates were expected to negotiate less than their white counterparts and penalized by receiving lower pay when they didn't conform to this expectation.[14] A number of Black women in the United States whom I've interviewed have spoken to me about how fraught any negotiations around pay can be. "You're constantly worried that you'll be relegated to the 'Angry Black Woman' trope, so I practice salary conversations for months, literally at all hours of the day, to strike the right balance between firm, but not too firm, while trying to appear grateful," Anna, a Black woman based in New York City, told me in an interview.

For Asian women, negotiations are a tricky business because they have to navigate the prevailing stereotype in Western workplaces that they are submissive. I've personally faced pushback and thinly veiled surprise when I negotiate my rates.

Aurora Lewis, who identifies as mixed Black and Filipina, tells me that most people immediately think she's Asian and white. When I met Lewis at a conference, I immediately assumed she was too because of her light skin and curly hair.

Her biracial background gives her a unique vantage point on how women of color experience bias, based on others' perception of their racial background. She has seen covert and overt bias directed at other Black women when she's in the room because people don't know that she also has Black heritage. She is sensitive to the privileges and shortcomings of presenting as an Asian woman as well; she's frequently thought of as competent, but expected to conform to the stereotype of Asian women who don't assert themselves.

Lewis experienced this during her first major salary negotiation. When she was negotiating her salary for a new job that would require a relocation with her spouse and young child, Lewis was offered $10,000 less than what her market research had shown.

"I was asking for $90,000 and the [white male] supervisor offered me $80,000. I didn't really push back after stating my expectation, but he could see on my face that I was disappointed. And he said to me, 'I can tell you're disappointed and I'm offended that you don't seem grateful,'" she recalls.

"It was so clear to me that I had insulted him by not seeming grateful enough, which I now know a man would never say to another man. I think it was a mix of sexism and racism, with the message that I should just be happy with what I was offered—literally, he used those words," she says.

As long as negotiations are an acceptable way to conduct pay discussions, they will always perpetuate pay inequities. This is why it's so incumbent on those with power at the negotiating table to take responsibility for creating equitable outcomes. Do away with salary negotiations altogether. Take a transparent approach to all salary conversations.

The conversation can look like this: "We are offering $100,000 for this role, after conducting a pay audit of comparable roles in the field. We don't negotiate job offers, and any successful candidate—regardless of gender, race, or any other identity—will be offered this amount."

Many of us are socialized to believe that lowballing people, especially those we consider as having less social status, is an acceptable way to gain advantage in negotiations. Back in 1995, economist Ian Ayres found that car dealers routinely quoted Black people and women higher prices than white men for identical cars. When there wasn't transparency about cost, dealers exploited the existing social hierarchy to make better offers to white men.[15] While the internet may have brought in more transparency about cost—whether the price of a car or starting salary of a software engineer—a culture that rewards negotiators has inequality built into it.

To be inclusive on purpose, you have to lead pay conversations *without* negotiations.

In situations where I am asked to recommend a candidate, speaker, or consultant from my network, I ask the requester for their budget up front to pass on that number to the person I'm recommending. You already know that I'll always recommend a woman of color where possible. But I also typically ask the requester their budget or highest salary offer. I only pass on opportunities to women of color where I can also provide a ballpark compensation number. As a third-party reference, I know that I can take the risk of asking this up front.

I wish for it, but I don't know when organizations will do away with negotiations altogether—even though research largely proves that negotiations create inequality.[16] But you can be intentionally inclusive by being direct in the conversations you're responsible for having related to compensation and pay.

Disaggregate the Data

Start by running a pay audit to understand the existing pay disparities. Managers often have some data at their disposal about how much employees on their team are making. Each company's way of accessing these data will differ. Some may have a fancy online system that allows managers to easily compare the salaries of different people on the team, spliced narrowly by the click of a button. Or a manager may have to build a homemade option like plugging in the numbers manually into an Excel sheet.

Regardless of the approach, ensure that you disaggregate the data by race *and* gender. I once worked with a client who had run a pay equity audit at their technology company by gender. They were delighted to learn that not only were they paying men and women equally for equal work but also that some women in leadership (including their white woman CEO) skewed the data such that it seemed all women were in high-paying positions.

When I urged the company's chief people officer to run the numbers to include pay by racial demographics, however, the numbers were less encouraging. Not only were no women of color represented in the high-paying roles at the organization, the intersection of race and gender actually created a wage gap in which women of color were earning less money than their white counterparts in all similar roles. The company instituted a policy to level up the salaries of these women. Without looking into the data by race *and* gender, the company would have lauded itself for being equitable while unintentionally allowing discriminatory practices to continue.

I cite this example because while the results of the audit positively impacted the organization as a whole, and the policies were
changed to benefit every employee, it took the inclusion mindset of
one person—the chief people officer—to understand why disaggregating the data was so important.

This can begin with you; when you compare the data available to
you, they can be powerful in remedying the systemic barriers that
cause pay inequality—such as the racial wealth gap, gap in access
to education, and compounding negative biases against people of
color in the workplace.

There is absolutely no excuse to pay people doing the same work
differently. And the only way to find out if there are disparities is by
making time to look into these data, and disaggregate them by race
and gender. Begin with whatever you have, and where possible, add
in more lenses of intersectionality such as ability and education.
Without this intentionality, we're likely to let biases go unchecked.
We could believe that we're being fair, but good intentions do not
always lead to good impact.

Managers have the power to disrupt this vicious cycle. When we
disaggregate the data within a team, or really, keep an eye out for
biases with anyone we work with, we can be inclusive on purpose.

And if you have influence within your organization, urge other
leaders to do the same.

Sponsor Women of Color for High-Paying Jobs

But that's only part of the puzzle. In the years that I've been speaking on the gender wage gap, I've come to realize that only looking at
apples-to-apples comparisons of whether women of color are making the same as men in the same job is a distraction from a larger
issue: Who gets access to the highest-paying jobs? Of course, it's
deplorable when people are paid differently for doing the same job
because of their race, gender, disability status, sexual orientation,

or any other marginalized identity. It's also fixable; if, say, Rachel's making eighty-nine cents and Robert's making a dollar for the same job, the fix is a no-brainer: up Rachel's salary to a dollar.

The staggering gap in *opportunities* between women of color and their white counterparts in reaching the highest levels of pay is what's more insidious and underdiscussed. Women are underpromoted to reach the highest-paying jobs. McKinsey data finds that "if women are promoted and hired to first-level manager at the same rates as men, we will add one million more women to management in corporate America over the next five years."[17]

This lack of opportunity to advance impacts pay too. While all women face barriers to promotion to these lucrative jobs, women of color are the most impacted. White women make up 30 percent of entry-level jobs in US corporations and 27 percent of the next level up to manager. In contrast, women of color only make up 18 percent of entry-level jobs, and that drops to 12 percent represented at the next level as managers. Men are 70 percent more likely to be executives than women by mid-career.

To fix this, managers must be intentionally inclusive, taking a laser focus on advancing women of color to these high-paying jobs.

Managers must audit who gets the highest-paying roles at the organization too. When you have the data in front of you, it's hard to argue against the fact that women of color are systematically left out of these lucrative jobs. Understanding and accepting this opportunity gap is the first step in fixing it.

Taking an Institutional Approach to Pay Parity at Adobe

What does an organization-wide commitment to pay equity look like?

In 2015, Adobe started facing increased shareholder pressure for transparency on whether employees at the company were being paid equitably. As vice president of global rewards at the software company, Rosemary Arriada-Keiper had already been collecting pay data by race and gender at the twenty-two-thousand-employee company. But like at most companies, those data remained confidential.

In 2016, Adobe decided it would closely review its data by disaggregating them by race, gender, *and* underrepresented racial minorities (in the United States, white and Asian employees are overrepresented in technology companies, while Black, Latinx, and Indigenous employees are underrepresented, compared with their demographic numbers). This approach is commendable, and more organizations would benefit from taking it. After a two-year study into the data, which also resulted in fixing disparities and leveling up underpaid employees, Adobe announced in October 2018 that it had achieved global gender parity.

"That analysis, essentially, is what drives any decisions we make to adjust people's pay, and we've been so fortunate because of the executive sponsorship that we have to do this," Arriada-Keiper says. "We've generally had pretty decent practices, and we've been in a position where as we do this analysis annually and we identify gaps, we've been able to fix it."

To begin the global pay analysis, Adobe first defined what it wanted to measure: pay parity, which it defined as "ensuring that employees in the same job and location are paid fairly relative to one another, regardless of their gender or ethnicity." Then it took the time to clearly define jobs before beginning the comparisons—not an easy task given that employees with different skills and functions were often classified the same by HR.

Adobe then started reviewing its job classifications to assess whether they accurately reflected the roles performed by employees, establishing new job families and levels where needed, and aligning and realigning employees to these new categories. Once this was done, Adobe began its audit first on 80 percent of its employees—those based in the United States and India—before rolling it out across the organization.

Since it began publishing its audit in 2018, Adobe now conducts an annual audit of pay parity and has institutionalized the practice of not asking new candidates for their salary histories, thereby helping to break the cycle of historical inequities for women, especially women of color.

In 2020, when I interviewed Arriada-Keiper, the organization's annual pay audit revealed that 112 employees globally were facing a pay gap. "So, not huge, but still worth noting," she says. "Once the analysis is complete, we go to the line managers and we let them know that our analysis shows there's a variance in compensation." Where a salary difference can't be explained by factors such as time in a role or location, the manager has to adjust the compensation, no questions asked.

"And we've created a centralized budget for this, so it doesn't come out of a manager's budget. So there's no question whether that employee's compensation will be adjusted or not. It just will," she explains.

In 2019, Adobe embarked an even more ambitious endeavor, which it called Opportunity Parity: assessing who had the most opportunities to ascend to the highest-paying roles. As Adobe started assessing fairness in promotion across its employees, it found that in 2019, promotion rates were 0.3 percent higher for men, and 0.3 percent higher for white employees. Women of color were disadvantaged by being in both categories.

Adobe is working to create a standard to measure the average promotion gaps in large companies and ways to fix them. There is no industry standard on how to objectively measure promotions by race and gender, and no easy fix, as there is with leveling up pay to reach pay equity. The organization is still figuring out how to address these gaps.

"It's a fairly new area for us, and we're trying to understand it a little bit better. But it's highlighting challenges in our processes—from promotions to hiring processes," notes Arriada-Keiper.

Adobe's exploration of this level of inequity and inclusion can provide useful lessons to other companies. The leadership of every well-known technology company headquartered in the United States—from Apple to Amazon to Google and Facebook—skews white and male. High-paying technical jobs also disproportionately go to men, and companies have blamed that on the lack of qualified female technical talent. This argument, called the "pipeline issue," is one issue; indeed, we need more women, especially women of color, to get technical degrees. In 1984, 37 percent of US computer science graduates were female; it's now at 18 percent, which is an alarming backward trend. But even among women in technical jobs, the rate of retention is dismal; 41 percent of women leave technology compared with 17 percent of men.[18]

As Arriada-Keiper tells me, there are no easy fixes to that larger problem of the opportunity-pay disparity.

"When you dig, you actually get more questions. And I think that's the mindset that you have to go in with: 'We're probably going to end up with more questions than we can answer, but it's the right thing to do.' Sometimes that does mean it takes longer," she says.

That's where leadership commitment to unearth disparities, assess which policies are perpetuating biases, and work to fix them make all the difference.

"The level of commitment, willingness, and executive sponsorship makes the most difference because these things are hard," she admits. Her approach reminds me of the BRIDGE framework I introduced in chapter 2.

Why Fixing This Gap Is Mission Critical

Fixing pay and opportunity gaps is absolutely critical to creating more equitable workplaces. The ensuing impact on society would be profound. I see women of color around me struggle in every way;

many do not come from generational wealth, and frequently even have to support previous generations that have been impacted by systemic racism and poverty. As they battle a compounding number of barriers, such as, though not limited to, gender, race, and caregiver biases—I find a remarkable resilience and tenacity among women of color.

It is why more of us spur each other forward to not settle for less. I routinely coach younger women of color to up their fees, negotiate their salaries (using available market data), and refuse to work for free. Most of all, I remind them of Arlan Hamilton's quote: "I came for the cake, not the crumbs."[19] For far too long, women of color have been forced to settle for crumbs, but this is not our problem to fix. While we're doing our parts to negotiate using data—asking for more and refusing the crumbs—we need managers to meet us halfway by being inclusive on purpose.

"If people are not familiar with the many barriers that women of color face day to day, it's nearly impossible to make sure that they're doing their actual part to counter them. Probably, at least once a day, every *single day* of their workplace, they're missing opportunities to advance, include, lift up, and amplify women of color around them," Raena Saddler, a leader in the equity and inclusion space, tells me. "And it has a deeper impact on us, our families, our generational capacity to build wealth and advance that for our kids."

Inclusion on purpose refers to the big and small opportunities to make change. Pay women of color equitably, but also assess the barriers holding them back from receiving what they deserve, such as lack of access to transparent salary information, bias when they negotiate, and biased and racist systems. Until we find a new way to wield power, money is still the greatest currency to building influence within an organization. You have a big role to play in ensuring that money and, yes, power is distributed equitably. We're counting on you to pay it forward.

■   ■   ■

KEY REFLECTIONS

1. What pay insights do you currently have access to—for example, the direct reports on your team, how much vendors are paid, what speakers usually get paid to keynote at an event, or organization-wide pay data? What is the easiest way to audit these data by race and gender?

2. What are some opportunities for you to practice pay transparency in your own life?

3. If you were to be entirely honest, how do you feel when you encounter women of color negotiating for raises? Do the same feelings come up when you have encountered men who negotiate?

4. Who are the most well-paid or wealthy people you personally know? What is their race and gender? Has a woman of color you know ever held a comparable position?

5. What is one thing that you could do to take action today? Write it down here:

7

How Effective Feedback Drives Inclusion

The way to right wrongs is to turn the light of truth upon them.

Ida B. Wells

Katherine Kim was courted to become a senior executive at a Fortune 50 company. She relocated at short notice, optimistic that this new job would someday propel her to the C-suite. At a leadership retreat in her first few months on the job, she was asked to share her observations about the company's culture. She was told to be as candid as she could be in a closed-door setting with other leaders. Kim (whose name has been anonymized) was honest about what she liked about the culture, but as asked, also shared her critical observations and experiences. She believed that the other leaders would welcome her candor in wanting to prioritize an inclusive environment.

Soon after this meeting, Kim, who requested to be identified as an Asian woman to ensure utmost anonymity, received feedback that "she was a team player who lacked executive presence." When she asked for examples from her manager, a white British woman, she wasn't given any. When she requested feedback to improve, the organization agreed to assign her a coach to improve her "executive presence."

Every technique that she learned from her executive coach was, in practice, met with resistance. When she spoke up more often in meetings, she was told that she was "too aggressive." When she used data to emphasize her point of view, she received feedback that she was being disagreeable. When Kim was quieter and listened more in meetings, she was told, yet again, that she lacked executive presence. When she changed her dressing style to be more formal, she was told to be more mindful of the technology company's casual dress culture. But when she dressed in jeans and T-shirt, she was sometimes mistaken for employees with less seniority, which when she brought up with her manager, was advised that this issue would be fixed when she cultivated more executive presence.

"It became clear to me that *executive presence* was a coded phrase to mean I didn't fit in there," says Kim. "It was interspersed in all feedback I received, likely because the company knew other words could be interpreted as biased. But how can you argue against not promoting an employee who lacks executive presence? You can't."

The experience took an emotional and psychological toll on Kim, who found herself at a breaking point. After years of trying to stick it out, she felt burned out. She did what so many women of color do: she chose her health over what had the potential to turn into hundreds of thousands of dollars in stock options had she stayed. She resigned right before the 2020 pandemic, and as a result, was out of work even a year later, despite having a top MBA and decades of work experience.

Feedback Matters

Retaining women of color will continue to pose a challenge for organizations today until leaders prioritize inclusion on purpose. That's a shame because as established in this book, women of color are highly ambitious—even more so than their white women counterparts.

LeanIn.org and McKinsey research found 83 percent of Asian women, 80 percent of Black women, and 76 percent of Latinas say that they want to be promoted, compared to 75 percent of men and 68 percent of white women.[1] As experts Zuhaira Washington and Laura Morgan Roberts posit in a *Harvard Business Review* article, women of color are more likely to face barriers to advance due to a variety of factors, including bias, double standards, and microaggressions. But women of color are also blocked from receiving a key ingredient that would fuel their success: access to time-sensitive, critical, and actionable feedback from their managers.[2]

Women often receive two types of harmful feedback. The first is vague feedback that doesn't help them advance at work. The second is biased or racist feedback that is underpinned by stereotypes or tropes, like when Black women are called "aggressive," Latinx women are told they're "feisty," or Asian women are called "docile" or "submissive." Both types of feedback, vague or biased, are harmful, and every woman of color whom I interviewed for the book had been on the receiving end of both.

First, let's address why vague feedback is an issue. Stanford University scholars Shelley Correll and Caroline Simard studied performance evaluations at three high-tech companies and a professional services firm, finding that men—compared with women—consistently received feedback related to business outcomes. Across their research, they found that women received vague feedback that they were doing good work generally, but the feedback didn't specify which actions were valuable or how their accomplishments were positive. "We also learned that vague feedback is correlated with lower performance review ratings for women—but not for men. In other words, vague feedback can specifically hold *women* back," they wrote of their findings. They posit that this could be attributed to stereotypes about women's capabilities such that reviewers are less likely to connect women's contributions to business outcomes or technical expertise. Stereotypes about women's caregiving responsibilities may "cause reviewers to more frequently attribute women's accomplishments to teamwork rather than team leadership," they observe.[3]

Their research wasn't broken down by race, but ineffective feedback often compounds for women of color. Ironically, because of the heightened awareness of workplace racism and bias, sometimes managers don't want to say the wrong thing. So they engage in what the Stanford scholars call "protective hesitation" when delivering effective feedback.[4] In essence, reviewers don't deliver the critical feedback needed to advance a woman's career—ironically—for fear of hurting their feelings, or that they will be perceived as sexist or racist (or both).

This is a pity because *all* employees greatly benefit from receiving specific, actionable, candid feedback, especially when delivered by a manager who cares personally. The last part is a component of "radical candor," a feedback framework created by author Kim Scott.

Women of color usually receive the opposite of effective feedback in informal exchanges and formal performance reviews alike. It's often unhelpful, such as "you're doing fine" or "I can't put my finger on what you're doing well, but you're good," without offering specifics on actions or behaviors taken, and thus they don't know exactly what to repeat. Effective feedback would instead be, "Here's exactly what you did and here's exactly the impact it had." In this way, they would know exactly which actions to repeat or avoid.

Style Not Substance

Then there's biased feedback, where women of color receive comments on the style in which their work was delivered rather than the substance of the work completed. As opposed to focusing on the content—the substance—of what was communicated, the manager delivers feedback on her style, including the tone of voice, what the woman was wearing, or how others perceived the way that she said something. One way is through tone policing, or the "conversational tactic that dismisses the ideas being communicated when they are perceived to be delivered in an angry, frustrated, sad, fearful, or otherwise emotionally charged manner."[5] It impacts many women, especially Black women, in the workplace and is an ad hominem attack that silences women from speaking up further. I've even seen non-Black women give biased feedback to Black women.

Urban planner Nadia Owusu was surprised to be tone policed by a non-Black woman of color. It felt, to her, among the more negative experiences in her professional career.

In a recent meeting, she brought up how one of the programs that her nonprofit organization was working on would need to address racism, particularly as it was serving the Black community. "I was disagreeing with the CEO in a heated discussion, but we were wrestling with it in a way that was necessary. I don't think our tones were any different from each other."

A non-Black woman of color disparaged Owusu for her tone and said, "Oh, I would not want to get on your bad side," indicating that she was being angry and unprofessional.

The woman's racist feedback shut down Owusu's ability to further her point—a necessary one that was informed by her experiences as a member of the Black community. "I felt dismissed and as if being treated like what I was saying was a fully emotional reaction," she says, when in fact her passion and expertise were perfectly appropriate for the situation.

Owusu's example illustrates that biased feedback can come from anyone, and also that anti-Blackness is unfortunately common in the workplace. Weaponizing Black women's anger has specifically harmful consequences on Black women in and out of the workplace. The expectation that women in general should not display anger harms all women.

We have all been socialized to accept dominance, passion, and especially anger in men but not women. These expectations of accepted behavior can be more pronounced, depending on where in the world you live and work.

"The disparagement of anger more generally is problematic because in fact, anger when used by men is a tool of leadership. When people see an angry man, especially an angry white man, that confirms their notions of dominance and control and leadership, and they don't question that association," says Soraya Chemaly, author of *Rage Becomes Her: The Power of Women's Anger.*

Men's anger is rewarded, whereas for women, any demonstration of legitimate, necessary anger is still seen as transgressive and unfeminine. "And in women," remarks Chemaly, "it actually undermines our leadership."

As in Owusu's case, though, what about attributing anger to a woman of color where there is none?

"That has everything to do with asserting dominance, silencing people, putting them in their place," says Chemaly. When white women display anger, which eschews traditional norms of femininity and nurture, they're often called crazy, but that's treated as an individual character flaw. For women of color, the feedback becomes racialized, "such as being called a 'hysterical Latina woman,' or 'angry, Black woman,' or 'sad Asian woman,'" Chemaly notes. A white woman's race isn't weaponized on top of the gender bias that they face. When white women are perceived as angry, it's considered a one-off character trait, but for women of color, it builds on a negative stereotype that already impacts their career growth and can impact even other women of color in the organization.

Becoming aware of these nuances and empathizing with the difference in how the same words may impact a person because of their gender as well as racial identities is key to delivering feedback that is appropriate and antiracist. A white woman's anger may be penalized at work, but she will likely be perceived as an individual with an anger problem—a negative perception that will impact just her career, not every white woman in the office, says Chemaly.

A Black or Latinx woman's perceived anger, conversely, will have wider consequences; other Black or Latinx women in the office (or those who are being interviewed) are likely to be painted with the same brush. This is why applying the lens of gender *and* race becomes so necessary to providing feedback that doesn't inadvertently curtail the careers of many women of color. In short, if you notice heightened emotions in a woman of color, take a pause and ask yourself some questions. Is anger really the right word? Is it a justifiable emotion for the situation that she is dealing with? Could my feedback fuel the trope of an "angry woman of color," thereby impacting her career and even others' more negatively?

Setting and Stating an Intention

In fact, it's always a good idea to pause and consider your intention in delivering feedback in the first place, says Amy Gallo, workplace conflict expert and author of the *HBR Guide to Dealing with Conflict*. "To give helpful and fair feedback, get real clear on the 'why.' Oftentimes we give feedback because we believe it's our job as managers and we think it's the right thing to do," she says. But before you even utter the feedback, take a moment to ask yourself, What is my intention here? "And if your intention is not focused on that person's development and growth, then reconsider giving the feedback."

Gallo recalls an incident when as a young manager, her boss told her to speak to the person who directly reported to Gallo about taking too many days off. "I hadn't even noticed how many sick days she was taking off. And it didn't appear to me that it was affecting her ability to get her work done. But I thought, 'I should deliver this because my boss asked me to,' she recalls. "My intention was completely wrong. Sharing that feedback didn't really serve my employee at all. I was just trying to do what my boss told me to." In hindsight,

Gallo says that she wished she had interrogated her own intention and possible bias before giving the feedback.

Many of us feel an obligation to pass on all feedback, but without focusing on the intention (*Will this really help the recipient?*), we are likely to pass on unconstructive feedback.

"Critical feedback conversations are often tense for everyone involved. Articulating your intention from the beginning ensures that it's not open for interpretation," Gallo says. Of course, the intent must be genuine, but initiating a conversation with, "My intention by sharing this feedback is . . ." can make all the difference. When we tell anyone, but especially women of color, that we're invested in their success (and mean it), we're more likely to deliver constructive feedback that also prompts the recipient to listen without defensiveness.

Safeguarding against Vague or Biased Feedback

Once you've gotten clear on the intention behind delivering your feedback, concentrate on substance not style. Do this by using specific examples of what an employee *did* that had positive outcomes and specific *actions* that she could take to improve.

The Situation-Behavior-Impact (SBI) feedback framework is well known and effective.[6] It was developed to deliver on-the-spot feedback. SBI safeguards against vague feedback by establishing the *situation* that you're referring to clearly and specifically, the precise *behavior* that you're addressing, and the *impact* of the person's behavior on you, the team, or the organization. First, be specific about the situation that you're referring to. Say, for instance, "in the customer meeting yesterday" rather than "that time last week." Next, be precise about the *behaviors* that you're seeking to address, and avoid subjective feedback or hearsay. Say, for example, "you didn't mention the customer's feedback in your presentation" not "you probably got lazy and didn't collect customer feedback, that's why you didn't mention it" or "Tom told me you didn't ask the customer for feedback and rushed preparing for the presentation last night." Only the impact part of the feedback should be subjective—how the behavior landed for you or others in the organization. Use "I" statements where possible.

I've added one more layer to it. Include one positive reinforcement when delivering critical feedback. In interviewing women of color, it became clear that I'm not alone in spending too much time ruminating over critical feedback, even when it's delivered effectively. The overthinking is likely a side effect of the bias experienced by women of color at work for far too long. Therefore I recommend adding one positive reinforcement to the SBI framework when delivering critical feedback.

Here's an illustration. The typical SBI framework would dictate this as adequate feedback: "Your presentation on the importance of social media marketing this morning could have been more effective [situation] because there were no customer testimonials [behavior]. When executive team members don't see customer data, they may not see the value of using it [impact]. Include this next time to bring more visibility to your work."

My edit to this SBI would be: "Your presentation on social media marketing this morning had robust research, which was really effective [situation and positive reinforcement]. It could have included customer testimonials [behavior]. When executive team members don't see customer data, they may not see the value of using it. Include this next time to bring more visibility to your work [impact]."

Aim to gather objective feedback even when other colleagues are talking to you about your direct report. If a colleague tells you that Anna is "aggressive," ask for specific examples where she demonstrated the behavior that was perceived as aggressive. Remind your colleague that even if Anna's actions were perceived as aggressive, it's important to distinguish the behavior from characterizing her as an aggressive person. Precise feedback can help contextualize that a person's behavior in a specific situation doesn't necessarily mean that's their character. This benefit of doubt is typically given to men, but not women, and more frequently to white women rather than women of color.

The beautiful thing about institutionalizing the SBI feedback framework is that it benefits all employees, even if they're not women of color. When any human being receives affirmation and understands exactly what they're doing well, they are likely to do more of it. When they receive critical feedback that's specific, actionable, and judgment free, women of color win, but so does everybody else. Better feedback mechanisms will also advance women of color leaders. When you create a culture that values objective feedback, women leaders are likely to be appreciated—not penalized—for providing direct feedback.

Round out the SBI framework by asking the recipient to repeat back the feedback that you just delivered, especially how *they* heard it. Gallo reminds us that because feedback can often be uncomfortable, we either become too verbose (SBI can help safeguard against that) or exit the conversation too quickly so as to avoid discomfort.

"Sometimes, even though we think we're clear in what we're saying, it's not clearly heard by the other person. And so, I will often ask at the end, 'Was that clear? Can you repeat back to me what you heard?' I don't want them to repeat my words verbatim, but to articulate what they heard and possibly learned. Did it resonate? This helps turn the conversation into a coaching opportunity," Gallo explains.

Examine How the Biased Code of Professionalism Feeds into Biased Feedback

One hindrance to giving bias-free feedback is that the concept of "workplace professionalism" in and of itself is biased. Women of color often receive biased feedback when they don't or can't conform to these invisible codes of professionalism—codes that were created and reinforced so that mainly white people, especially white men, are best positioned to succeed.

When US scholars Tema Okun and Keith Jones examined corporate workplace professionalism, they found that it largely centers around white supremacy, or the "systemic, institutionalized centering of whiteness," writes thinker-organizer Aysa Gray in the *Stanford Social Innovation Review*. "In the workplace, white supremacy culture explicitly and implicitly privileges whiteness and discriminates against non-Western and non-white professionalism standards related to dress code, speech, work style, and timeliness, Gray adds."[7]

Accepted workplace norms privilege those who already have an advantage, such as because of a white-sounding name, familiarity with Western culture and norms, and a Eurocentric appearance. One example is the so-called professionalism of straight hair for women, which disproportionately disadvantages women of color, particularly Black women with natural hairstyles or women who cover their hair for religious reasons. A Western hegemony has specifically privileged those who have the most proximity to Western and white culture, while disadvantaging those who are further from it.

Many women of color receive feedback that is biased against their authentic selves and favorable to their white counterparts. This could be related to their hair, speaking style, or behavior. Those who can do so cope by code-switching, a technique of adjusting their appearance, speech, or behavior in ways that help white people feel more comfortable, according to Cornell University assistant professor Dr. Courtney L. McCluney.

Code-switching most often happens in workplaces where people of color benefit from downplaying their identity in a stigmatized racial group. It also occurs in workplaces where it's advantageous for these employees to distance themselves from negative stereotypes of their racial identity or help them build affinity with white people so that they may advance if they're considered more similar, says McCluney. An illustration of this could be a Muslim woman choosing not to wear her hijab in the workplace for fear of being rejected, but covering her hair when she leaves the office.

My ability to code-switch has been a powerful advancement tool personally as well as for the women of color whom I spoke with for this book. I frequently get clues on how much I benefit when managers have lauded me for "being so normal" or "not like other Indians," or rewarded me with positive feedback for being different from their preconceived notions of what women of color are like in the workplace. But code-switching is exhausting, psychologically and emotionally. Constantly trying to fit into a container that wasn't made with you in mind can take a deep toll in many visible and invisible ways, McCluney says.

Further, code-switching isn't an available option for everyone. If your name automatically reveals that you're nonwhite, or you can't change your non-Western accent, code-switching isn't a solution.

As we know, women of color aren't the problem. Workplaces that expect them to hide parts of themselves to fit in are. This is why we need more managers to be aware and thoughtful before giving women of color feedback related to their professionalism. In many cases, this type of feedback is steeped in bias. The code of workplace professionalism, as it stands, only rewards women of color when they are able to code-switch to fit in. Biased feedback about professionalism is usually the first marker of rejection when they don't. Once again, focus on substance of their work, not style, when delivering feedback to safeguard against this.

Reset Vague Definitions of Leadership/Executive Presence

Related to so-called professionalism, until we remove bias from what we believe is "leadership" or "skills to advance," we will continue perpetuating a system that disadvantages women of color. It's neither quick nor easy, but examining and reframing what—and whom—we consider to be leaders could truly create more effective feedback systems. If we do this right, we're likely to accept a more expansive variety of leadership and communication styles. We can widen the aperture of what is considered leadership to move away from a one-size-fits-all vision. Imagine a world where we didn't ask women of color to change to fit a model that was never designed with them in mind but rather rewarded them for being authentic, as they are?

Many workplaces are complicit in holding up biased, narrow models of leadership, or basically, "think leader, think male." A number of women of color whom I've spoken with were given feedback that they lacked leadership or executive presence—concepts that many have tied to men's demonstration of leadership and executive presence. There's no existing playbook for how women, especially women of color, should exhibit these traits, so they're penalized for being too dominant or overconfident.

These vague concepts can have far-reaching consequences on a woman of color's career prospects.

Safeguard against this by having clear definitions of what leadership and executive presence mean. Taking time to define the traits that the organization values and rewards (through advancement) can help prevent biased criteria that often leave out women of color. Go one step further and audit who *does* embody executive presence in your organization. What skills and behaviors do they explicitly demonstrate? If only white men and women are promoted for evidencing "executive" or "leadership" presence in your organization, create explicit criteria that ensure that skills and behaviors, not biased "gut-feel" traits, are rewarded.

Flip It to Test It

One of my favorite tools to reduce bias generally, but especially in feedback delivery, is "flip it to test it." Kristen Pressner, a white

Switzerland-based HR executive for Roche Diagnostics, found that even she, a woman, was prone to bias against other women.

When both a male and female member of her team asked for a salary raise, Pressner realized that she was ready only to evaluate the compensation of her male employee, but not her female one. As she began researching how many words are naturally associated with a certain gender ("think leader, think male"), it suddenly dawned on her that she was perpetuating bias. When two team members had asked her for a raise—one man and one woman—she realized that she had subconsciously associated the man with the word "provider" and took his salary request more seriously, while dismissing the woman's. Pressner not only became aware of her own conditioned bias but also developed the flip it to test it framework.

Think of words that we frequently use to provide critical feedback to women: emotional, angry, and submissive. Would we use the same words to describe men? Mentally flip whomever or whatever you're talking about to test it. You're likely to have uncovered a bias if the flipped characterization feels odd—like describing a man as "fragile" or a woman as "the provider."

Gallo agrees, and challenges us to use flip it to test it on ourselves. "Managers must investigate, 'Would I give this feedback if I saw the same behavior in someone who looked like me?' If you're about to give feedback to a Black woman that she's aggressive, you have to ask yourself whether you'd say the same thing to a white man? Would you still use that word?" Taking a moment to flip it can help think through and hopefully catch your own biases.

Flip it to test it takes a little more nuance in the context of feedback provided to women of color, but it's worth applying in most cases. However, the same feedback that is positive for white women, especially as corporations have rewarded more leadership models of white women, can be fraught for women of color. Awareness about racial bias is necessary because flip it to test it isn't foolproof. For example, a white Western woman could be described as "articulate" and that's not an exclusionary comment because white people are *expected* to be articulate. When people of color are called articulate, however, this perpetuates the biased narrative that people of color generally aren't articulate—and therefore this one individual is the exception versus the norm.

When Senator Kamala Harris was appointed to be the Democratic US vice presidential nominee in August 2020, a slew of media pundits and other politicians called her articulate. Scholars H. Samy Alim and Geneva Smitherman urged caution when giving a person of color, particularly a Black person, the feedback that they are articulate:

> Intentionally or not, when Black people are given the "compliment" of being "articulate," it's often combined with other adjectives like "good," "clean," "bright," "nice-looking," "handsome," "calm" and "crisp." When someone feels the need to point out that an individual Black person has these qualities, it's understandable that Black people who hear this will infer that the speaker thinks this is unusual and that Black people are usually the opposite—bad, dirty, dumb, mean-looking, ugly, angry, rough and inarticulate."[8]

I'm not only taking issue with this feedback simply because it causes hurt feelings but rather because it can impact a woman of color's career advancement since it's also discriminatory. A woman of color is seen as an exceptional individual at that moment, but she's also fighting an uphill battle against the perception that people of her group are not expected to be exceptional. She constantly has to prove her merit to be thought deserving of the accolade and often ultimately isn't awarded it.

Below I've created a list of common biased feedback and suggested alternatives. It's not exhaustive by any means but instead a starting point. Create your own by researching the words that are most commonly used to describe behaviors or personalities of your direct reports. Spend time researching and reflecting on how you most often characterize similar behaviors of people you work with by gender and race. Are there words you use that would be a positive or neutral descriptor for a man (like "bossy") that would negatively impact a woman of color?

Instead of . . .	Use . . .
Angry	Passionate
Aggressive	Leader-like
Hostile	Confident
Bossy	Leader-like
Submissive/meek	Deliberate
Disorganized	State exact examples using the SBI framework along with objective examples on how to improve
Selfish	Judicious with her time
Lacks leadership skills	State exact examples using the SBI framework
Lacks executive presence	State exact examples using the SBI framework
Articulate	Powerful, leader-like, and inspires action

To be clear, biased feedback most harms a woman of color's career when it comes from her manager or another leader. But anyone delivering it in a group setting—such as the way that Owusu was tone policed by a peer—can feed into negative stereotypes about women of color, especially Black women. While all professionals must watch out for giving biased feedback, *anyone* in that meeting could have shown up as an ally and shut down the feedback that she was given in the meeting—most of all, the white male leader present. Inclusion on purpose means using your privilege, whether from race, gender, and/or status, to disrupt bias as you see it in action. The onus shouldn't be on women of color to fix this.

Reducing Bias in Performance Evaluations

Unchecked bias in formal performance evaluations can have long-standing consequences on the advancement of women of color.

The vast majority of performance evaluations are biased, even when they strive for fairness, write Stanford University researchers in *Harvard Business Review*. Managers often believe "that by reflecting on people's performance and codifying it in an evaluation form, we will be able to assess their merits objectively, give out rewards fairly, and offer useful feedback to help them develop in the next year. But while we may strive to be as meritocratic as possible, our assessments are imperfect and all too often biased."[9]

All managers must familiarize themselves with what these biases could be. Then work to identify and disrupt them. Bias Interrupters lays out the four most common types of biases that show up in performance review feedback.[10]

Prove-it-again bias: Women of color are expected to constantly prove their competence and ability to perform their jobs, but the same is not expected from employees from dominant groups. For example, men are promoted on their potential while women are promoted on their track record. Or the mistakes that women of color make are judged more harshly or remembered for longer than their white male counterparts. In feedback, this shows up as "isn't ready for the next step" or "hasn't demonstrated the ability to . . ."

Tightrope bias: A far narrower range of acceptable workplace behavior is allowed for women, especially women of color, compared with men and white people. As the previous section described, flip it to test it often exposes tightrope bias in feedback: the same behavior that's acceptable for men and white people frequently isn't fine for women of color. While women in the workplace have to walk a narrower tightrope of being considered effective but not too aggressive and adhering to tricky standards of being respected yet likable, these expectations compound for women of color. Men do not have to do so, research shows.

Maternal wall: Mothers or caregivers are penalized for their role outside work, particularly in terms of experiencing pay, promotion, and opportunity gaps. I haven't spent much time on the role of women of color as caregivers, but even women of color who are not parents usually take an outsize responsibility in caregiving for their community. Beware the maternal/parental wall that often appears in feedback with phrases like "distracted," "priorities lay elsewhere," "is not ready for a promotion," or "never stays late."

Tug-of-war bias: When there's limited opportunity for women of color to progress, they may feel like they have to be pitted against each other to succeed. Feedback from a woman of color manager to a woman of color employee may be biased because there's a perceived threat due to this scarcity of opportunities.

Reducing Bias in Performance Reviews at Culture Amp

Culture Amp prioritizes reducing bias in employee performance review systems. Afterall, it is a software company that helps other organizations manage employee feedback. Culture Amp managers are trained to spot common biases in employee feedback and encouraged to intentionally audit whether these concepts have shown up in the feedback that they give their direct reports.

"Auditing performance evaluations and feedback will allow you, over time, to look for your patterns," says Aubrey Blanche, director of equitable design and impact. "I often look at what I'm commenting on between genders, or if there's a difference in the feedback I'm providing my colleagues of different races. I can audit myself to see if I'm falling into those socialized stereotypes." Culture Amp's software allows managers to do this.

Even if you don't have software to evaluate bias in feedback, Gallo recommends a more homemade though still effective option like keeping a handwritten file or a spreadsheet on the computer to consistently document the feedback that managers provide. "It's helpful to go back and check whether you're only being really frank with employees who look like you. So as a white woman, I ask myself, Am I comfortable giving direct, honest feedback to other white women, or conversely, am I going easy on people who look like me?" she says.

Blanche recommends providing specific goals and expectations for employees so that performance evaluations are analyzing objective criteria, rather than biased or "style versus substance" feedback. Unfortunately, only 50 percent of employees say they know what's expected of them at work.[11] Instead, create objective, measurable goals and communicate them to your direct reports. When you start a performance evaluation process with clearly stated goals, there's less room to insert your opinions or biases, which even the Stanford researchers cited above recommend. When you align expectations, you're also more likely to support, sponsor, and mentor your direct reports to meet their targets.

Write performance review assessment questions in the positive as opposed to the negative, Blanche says. "Research shows that under-represented people tend to get questioned in the negative, which essentially questions, 'Why won't you fail?' while well-represented people get questions on how they'll succeed. So we try to be really careful about being aspirational at our organization."

Culture Amp performance reviews frame critical feedback in the positive by asking managers to answer:

1. What would you have liked to see this employee do?
2. What are key areas or deliverables you recommend that the employee focus on?
3. What actions or behaviors have you seen this employee take to improve their skills?

"We don't talk about failure; it's not about what they failed to do but rather what would you like to see them do because it creates more space to have a dialogue about why something didn't happen, and what could be done the next time to deliver it," explains

Blanche. "Fundamentally, this is just good management, but because certain people tend to lack this, institutionalizing it tends to have a disproportionately positive impact."

Most of all, normalize continuous feedback instead of having all promotion decisions rest on a once-a-year performance review— something that Gallo also recommends with her file approach. "At Culture Amp, we use continuous feedback tools. That's really powerful because it actually creates documents of accomplishments," Blanche says. This becomes particularly important for women of color because a long-standing record of excellence can be used to combat biases in the moment. "Every time someone gives you a compliment at work, you would put that in the platform. We must create records of our own brilliance because society assumes they do not exist."

I interviewed Blanche in August 2020 against the backdrop of the COVID-19 pandemic and a large, global movement for racial justice that was especially challenging for Black employees. Culture Amp had updated its performance evaluation criteria to account for both external circumstances and the upheaval that they caused for its workers. It was an innovative move at a time when many organizations were penalizing women and people of color for not performing at regular levels.

"We evaluated skills and growth in a different way from before, accounting for behaviors such as remote work effectiveness, [employees] building their own resilience, supporting others, adapting their way of working. We explicitly gave managers this guidance ahead of their reviews to count these behaviors from employees as growth."

Culture Amp also proactively changed its criteria to positively recognize employees who had taken time off during this difficult time rather than penalize them. Employees impacted by challenges like caregiving, mental health, and community trauma such as ongoing police brutality were rewarded for taking time off. "We recognized taking extended flexible leave when it was needed as good performance," Blanche notes.

Much literature on better management and leadership intersect beautifully with more inclusive leadership. In short, be empathetic and human.

Get Comfortable with Feeling Uncomfortable Delivering Feedback

Effective feedback, especially effective critical feedback, can be deeply uncomfortable. That's OK and is actually a good sign. Work through the discomfort, Gallo urges us. "People might get defensive or even upset when you deliver feedback. But their emotional reaction can't be an excuse to stop giving feedback," she says. Managers may feel like they must back off to protect a woman of color's feelings, particularly if she reacts negatively.

Gallo reminds managers that defensiveness to critical feedback may not be just about the conversation you're having. Defensiveness often comes from years of being told that you're not good enough, or getting vague feedback about how you're doing great and yet never getting the promotion. We know this happens frequently to women of color.

"So when you get a defensive or upset reaction, just accept that that's part of the process and keep going—with the right framework [like SBI]," advises Gallo. "But the worst thing a manager can do is just say, 'Well, they got defensive, so I'm not going to give feedback anymore.'"

I've worked in three different countries over the course of my career so far. I've certainly observed how cultural norms dictate the way feedback is delivered. I've found remarkable differences even within the United States. Without a doubt, direct feedback delivered with the right intention, with evidence and concrete advice on how to improve, wins every time. If you have always believed that to create an inclusive workplace it's better to refrain from delivering critical feedback to a woman of color, I'm here to tell you that exactly the opposite is true.

Giving effective, fair feedback is not something most of us are socialized to do. Factors that impact whether we engage in candid feedback giving or not include our upbringing, our racial and gender identities, the expectations around those, and even the industry that we work within. But with practice and the tools I've detailed in this chapter, we can all improve our feedback-giving prowess. With an inclusion mindset, we can all grow and learn to become better feedback providers. Next, I'll evaluate how to take action when we receive difficult feedback in order to create psychologically safe workplaces for women of color.

■   ■   ■

KEY REFLECTIONS

1. Can you think of a time when you witnessed a woman of color being called biased words (such as angry, hostile, bossy, or submissive)? How could you have intervened or behaved differently in that situation?

2. How do you approach feedback conversations? Do you lean into or avoid them? How can you practice having them more often?

3. How can you apply the SBI framework to feedback conversations? (If you want practice, try also using it outside work-related situations.)

4. Which of the four common biases (prove-it-again, tightrope, maternal wall, or tug-of-war) identified by Bias Interrupters have

you experienced or witnessed? How have these biases impacted how the women of color around you have been categorized?

5. What is one thing that you could do to take action today? Write it down here:

8

How Psychological Safety Powers Innovation and Growth

I pattern match for grit.

Arlan Hamilton

Shefali Kulkarni had never seen as much security as she did at the 2016 Republican National Convention. As an experienced journalist, she had reported on a variety of political events and rallies, but this one felt different. The day before, she had witnessed a single protester surrounded by armed military guards. The energy was hostile and even militaristic. At the front and center of the convention was Donald Trump, a presidential nominee who had built a campaign on fear and xenophobia, with a history of violence at his campaign rallies.

It was a hot, sticky day in Cleveland, Ohio, and Kulkarni was waiting in the press security line to begin her work reporting on the second day of the convention.

As an Indian American woman who had spent many hours in security lines in US airports, Kulkarni knew that she had a high chance of being randomly selected by security officers due to her skin color. She was prepared to be stopped or asked questions. Kulkarni had already taken extra care to ensure that all her digital equipment was contained in clear, plastic bags, ready to pass through the X-ray machine.

As all her colleagues went by before her without trouble, Kulkarni still remained on guard.

Suddenly her monopod, the stand used to hoist up her camera, was targeted by the security officer.

"What is this? This can't go in," he said, lifting up the monopod, after flagging it as a weapon and attempting to throw the expensive media equipment away, into a box with other banned items like water bottles and selfie sticks.

"Sir, I work at this media organization. Please look at my badges. It is not a weapon," she replied, trying to de-escalate the situation, recalling all the tactics that she knew to decrease tension when around authorities—something that most people of color develop early. She held up multiple pieces of identification, including various press passes.

The white male officer menacingly took a step toward her, saying, "Do you not understand English? This can't be taken inside."

Kulkarni was quickly encircled by armed officers, shouting at her to toss away the monopod or be thrown out of the convention. In turn, she tried to plead her case to let through security a standard piece of media equipment—one that she had been let through with the day prior—so that she could do her job effectively.

"We'll need to escort you out. You're acting hostile," the security officer said to her.

Kulkarni started shouting, getting angry and refusing to let the officers touch her, as she was led to a bench several yards from the security tent. She looked at her cell phone, filled with frantic texts and missed calls from her boss wondering where she was.

"Once I sat down, I kept wondering, 'Should I have called him?' I don't know what would have happened if I called him. My boss is a British white guy, so I started thinking to myself, 'Everybody's a white person. I don't know who to trust,'" she says.

"I just kept hearing the security guy saying, 'Do you not understand English?' in my head. I know what he was really saying with that. That I'm nobody, that I don't belong here."

Kulkarni debated whether to leave the event and go back to her hotel, but did not want to feel like the officers had won. "I felt very lost and alone," she says.

Eventually, after drying her tears and feeling calmer, Kulkarni called a fellow colleague, a white British woman, to come get her outside.

Her colleague finally arrived, nonchalantly eating a bag of chips, and offered one to Kulkarni, remarking, "I've never seen US racism before. This is really messed up."

Kulkarni was tired and didn't want to discuss the humiliating incident.

She asked her colleague to open her bag to put in one part of the dismantled monopod, and Kulkarni planned to carry the other in her second attempt through security. When her colleague opened up her own bag, it was filled with a number of items that had been prohibited by the convention's authorities—a water bottle, aerosol sprays, and even a pocketknife. The woman had passed through security a number of times with these items and even remarked to Kulkarni how nice all the security staff were to her.

When Kulkarni went back into the line with her colleague in an attempt to reenter the event, the security office smirked at her, "Make sure you play nice this time." After an extended security check that included a full pat down, dogs sniffing her, and having to remove her shoes—which no one else was asked to do—the officers finally waved her through. Her white colleague, who had gone before her, wasn't stopped by security, once again passing through with a bag full of items explicitly prohibited by the authorities.

Reunited with her team, Kulkarni told them that she was fine, she just needed to wash her face in the restroom. Her white male manager joked, "Do you need a white person to come with you?" She realized, true to her original assessment, that no one else on her team understood the gravity of what she had just experienced.

After that, Kulkarni and her manager never talked about the incident. Even on returning to the office in Washington, DC, after the convention, Kulkarni did not tell her white bureau chief about the incident. Some colleagues knew about it and urged her to file a report so that the organization could write a letter of complaint to the Republican National Convention.

But she didn't trust any of her colleagues or managers enough, she says. "I didn't think anybody had my back, which is a terrible thing to think about, but it's true. And it was obviously a very traumatic experience, but I never felt I was psychologically supported at work," she recalls. Even today, when there is rising awareness of the racism that employees of color face, Kulkarni says that she believes her white colleagues would not understand the humiliation she experienced that day at the hands of the white male security officer and passive bystanders. "I would have just gotten gaslit in some way or another that to some extent would almost be like I imagined all this."

Kulkarni didn't feel psychologically safe in her organization—not to bring up the incident or to fully contribute her ideas in future discussions at the organization on how to reduce bias in journalism. Eventually she moved to a different media organization. She has yet to work in a company that prioritizes her mental health, or makes it safe for her to speak up against incidents of bias and racism. "White comfort is often prioritized over people of color's emotions. It's taken me years to realize that I shouldn't have to shoulder the burden of racism alone."

Why Teams Must Prioritize Creating Psychological Safety

The lack of psychological safety that Kulkarni experienced is all too familiar for most women of color in the workplace. Psychological safety describes a work environment in which employees believe that they can speak up candidly with ideas, questions, and concerns without fear of retribution, according to Harvard Business School professor Dr. Amy Edmondson. Employees in psychologically safe environments can dissent, disagree, and even fail, but ultimately they believe that they will still be respected and able to advance precisely because of their contributions by speaking up.

Psychologically safe environments benefit both employees and the organization's success as a whole.

For a company to be truly innovative, hiring smart and motivated people isn't enough, says Edmondson. Without psychological safety, even knowledgeable and well-meaning people cannot contribute at the critical moments that they are needed, because they're reluctant to be wrong, stand out, or upset their manager. "For knowledge work to flourish, the workplace must be one where people feel able to *share their knowledge*! This means sharing concerns, questions, mistakes and half-formed ideas," Edmondson writes in her book *The Fearless Organization*.[1]

Most important, they must feel like they can speak up without fear of retaliation—such as being demoted, fired, or labeled a troublemaker. Edmondson's research has shown that hospital teams with psychological safety can alter the course of life and death, like when a nurse is able to speak up at the critical time to correct her superior, the doctor, about administering a lifesaving intervention in a neonatal intensive care unit.

This seems like a no-brainer, and yet creating psychological safety for most employees, let alone women of color, continues to be a challenge. Research shows that we're constantly trying to influence how others perceive us by managing the flow of information to them in social settings.[2] At work, we're often managing the risk that we will come off as less knowledgeable or problematic, versus speaking up at the right time and possibly being rewarded for it. Apply an intersectional lens and it becomes immediately apparent how much

more risky it is for women of color, who have to navigate preconceived stereotypes while calculating the interpersonal risks when
they speak up.

Women of color are especially prone to receiving pushback when
they speak up about experiencing bias or racism. In 2020, Harvard-
trained emergency medicine doctor and professor Dr. Uché Blackstock left teaching at one of the United States' top medical schools
after facing close to a decade of racism. "I made the difficult decision to leave my faculty position at an academic medical center after
more than nine years there because of a toxic and oppressive work
environment that instilled in me fear of retaliation for being vocal
about racism and sexism within the institution," Blackstock wrote
in an op-ed, lamenting that without institutional support, more
Black doctors will leave academic medical centers.[3] This is an alarming trend considering that only 6 percent of US doctors are Black.
Currently, the Black American community faces some of the worst
health outcomes in the country due to systemic racism, particularly
in health care. Research shows that many people of color feel unsafe
going to white doctors and instead prefer receiving treatment from
health care providers of the same ethnicity.

When women of color experience psychological safety, they experience greater inclusion in their workplace. When their perspectives
and feedback are welcome, everyone benefits. The last chapter was
about giving better feedback to women of color. Now I will explore
how to create a culture where women of color can deliver critical
feedback without facing retaliation.

Four Warning Signs of a Psychologically Unsafe
Culture for Women of Color

There are four problem areas that I see to improving psychological
safety in healthy organizations that generally have a good work culture. I make this distinction because there are organizations that

are run by bullies, and the only way to create psychological safety in them is to completely overhaul a toxic culture. But in other cases where managers are generally supportive and learning is welcomed, psychological safety is still far from a given. That's why it's so necessary to be inclusive on purpose.

The four warning signs of a lack of a psychologically safe culture for women of color are:

1. There is a lack of safe mechanisms to report bias
2. Women of color are penalized for speaking up
3. White comfort is prioritized and employees of color are penalized for speaking up about issues that disproportionately impact their communities
4. There is a lack of advocacy for women of color

I will break each one down before offering solutions in my ADAPT framework.

The Lack of Safe Mechanisms to Report Bias

My assessment for a technology client found that their organization generally had a healthy work culture. But I also found that several women on a team were feeling harassed by a male team member. This male teammate would often enter a shared office room occupied by three women and spend hours trying to make conversation with them, sometimes making inappropriate or sexual comments. He also would stand too close to the women, making them feel uncomfortable. While one of the women had subtly commented on his behavior, there was no change. The women who responded to my survey said that his behavior likely stemmed from a lack of self-awareness rather than malicious intent. Yet it's always necessary for employers to take action when a manager is making other employees uncomfortable. The behavior had gotten so pervasively uncomfortable that some of the women preferred working from home, even if that meant negatively impacting their careers. Others were considering leaving the organization.

These cases are far too common. Acts of bias and harassment can have major consequences on the safety of as well as sense of belonging for women, particularly women of color, who may have the most to lose by reporting this behavior. Also, these situations, while uncomfortable for the person facing it, can be difficult to report face-to-face.

Our conclusions led the organization to immediately institute a confidential employee hotline to report harassment or bias. Having safe, confidential ways to report issues in the workplace is key to creating psychological safety.

In 2016, Intel realized that it had a problem retaining women and people of color. One effort to address this was the creation of Warm-Line, a confidential online hotline for employees to be paired with a DEI case manager to listen and provide feedback. The company wanted to "ensure we are creating a safe space where employees feel heard and valued," Barbara Whye, then Intel's global chief diversity and inclusion officer as well as corporate vice president of social impact and HR, tells me.

Intel's employees are encouraged to use the WarmLine to discuss a variety of concerns, from problems with their manager to feeling stuck in their current position to feeling overlooked or excluded, she says. So far, this confidential hotline seems to be working. Intel has an 82 percent "save rate"; over eight in ten employees who once wanted to leave decided to stay on at the organization. "WarmLine advisers listen, provide resources such as communication strategies, and assist employees on their path to desired opportunities within the company," she notes. In turn, the WarmLine provides Intel with a robust data set to identify patterns and locate problem areas, so that the company can "address issues proactively and systemically"—an approach that is unusual and highly effective. More companies could benefit by following suit.

Understanding that not all employees feel safe approaching a manager with concerns, employing alternative complaint systems such as "Employee Assistance Plans, ombuds offices and transformative dispute resolution systems can play a critical role in not only reducing retaliation but also provide fuel for organizational change," Harvard sociologist David Pedulla writes.[4] In smaller organizations, having an external vendor run a tip line and coaching assistance like this is more useful than having it in-house, where complainants could be easily identified. Of course, once the anonymous tip line is created, leaders must communicate its existence to employees, including how tips and complaints will be handled.

The organization must follow up by reviewing anonymized complaints, identifying problem areas, and taking action.

Women of Color Are Penalized for Speaking Up

A lack of psychological safety for women of color runs deep in the implicit and explicit messages they receive that it isn't safe for them to speak up. Ironically, speaking up at critical moments can most positively impact the organization, but this is when employees often face the most barriers to be able to do so. About half of all discrimination cases in the United States result in retaliation, according to the Equal Employment Opportunity Commission. Employees who complain suffer from career obstacles as well as physical and mental health challenges, compared with their peers who experienced discrimination but didn't complain, so I can see why so many women of color hesitate to report facing bias.

In September 2020, Dawn Wooten, a Black female nurse who worked at an Immigration and Customs Enforcement detention center, emerged as a whistleblower. She alleged that the detention center allowed mass nonconsensual hysterectomies to be performed on female immigrant detainees and there was "gross mishandling" of COVID-19 cases. Wooten took her case public after being demoted when she raised her concerns of the human rights violations with her bosses and stayed home when she showed symptoms of the highly contagious COVID-19 disease. Due to the highly politicized nature of immigration detention centers in the United States, Wooten took extraordinary risk to come forward publicly about the gross mistreatment of Spanish-speaking immigrant women of color and has since faced death threats.

Naturally, not all concerns in the workplace will be as serious as Wooten's, but women of color far too often find themselves labeled as troublemakers, demoted, or even fired for speaking up.

Instead, organization leaders must intentionally create an environment that doesn't penalize women of color for coming forward with concerns. Intel's Whye says that it requires managers to acknowledge that each of us require different things to feel a sense of belonging and psychological safety at work. Friction should be expected as people work with others who are different from themselves.

Most important, this friction can benefit the organization; it can be turned into "productive thinking when establishing a foundation of open communication," Whye says. "We think of this as a muscle and have used it as a developmental opportunity, instead of avoiding the issue. This has helped us develop a culture around candid and constructive conversations."

Stating a commitment to psychological safety up front is half the battle. Putting it into practice to ensure that truth tellers are not penalized is the other half.

White Comfort Is Prioritized while Employees of Color Are Penalized for Speaking Up

In a previous job, Sacha Thompson was the global diversity and inclusion marketing lead for a technology company. Her role required her to engage the organization's community through social media by sharing resources and articles. Soon she started noticing a discrepancy. Whenever she would share a news article on racism on her own personal social media, it would send up red flags immediately with some of her leaders. "But when my white male colleague would say the exact same thing or post the exact same article, nothing would be said," she notes.

It became clear that the messages, which never violated the company's social media policy (she was well versed in it), wasn't the issue. It was the fact that she, a Black woman, was talking about racism in the workplace, and that her advocacy was making white leaders uncomfortable. She didn't feel psychologically safe in an environment that prioritized white comfort over her sharing her own pain about encountering racism.

"I realized that I didn't have the freedom to express myself, even when I was completely in line with company policy. Particularly if I was expressing the feelings or sentiments of other Black women, not even just within the company, but within technology or within the corporate space, I didn't have the freedom to express that because I was told that it made the company look bad," she says. "And that's a very toxic environment to be in."

Tone policing, which I've explored in the previous chapter, can even occur on social media. As we see more backlash against women and people of color for expressing solidarity with racial justice movements, both in the office and over social media, those environments will continue to struggle with creating a psychologically safe workplace for women of color. In 2017, after the inauguration of US president Trump, the annual Women's March took place in Washington, DC, all over the United States, and in several cities around the world to protest his election as well as his antiwoman stance.

That year, while I was speaking on a panel, an Asian American woman in the audience raised her hand to ask me, "My company gave us the day off to march for women and even sponsored matching T-shirts for employees who would march together. But a few weeks later, I was asked to remove a 'Black Lives Matter' sign from my desk. My manager told me it made some of my white colleagues uncomfortable. The message I got was that the company was in support of white women and their issues, but not Black women or allies of Black people. Should I stay or go?"

I remember hesitating in my response; the reality is that my own experience in the technology industry in Seattle (where she worked) corroborated that there was infinitely more tolerance for movements for gender equality than racial equality—so I was worried that if she left, she'd find that other workplaces were similar. At the same time, I knew that if she stayed at this workplace too long, she would become resentful and frustrated. I advised her to begin looking for other workplaces, but to check about how psychologically safe the environment was before she took a new job there.

This is an imperfect solution to a grave problem. When leaders prioritize white comfort over confronting the reality of racism and bias that too many communities of color face, women of color will never feel safe and supported.

The landscape shifted some after the worldwide reckoning for racial justice unleashed in 2020. A number of corporate organizations made statements in solidarity with Black lives and promised to create more antiracist work environments. Unfortunately, much of it was fanfare, and many Black and other employees of color felt there was little progress, as more leaders were focused on supporting external causes related to the Black community rather than addressing racism and bias internally.

I urge leaders reading this to ask themselves, What mechanisms do we have to ensure that women of color are not penalized for highlighting issues of racism or injustice that impact their communities, even outside work? How do we handle complaints when white employees express discomfort with how women of color show up?

The lack of psychological safety to call out bias when women of color experience it can also impact their willingness to contribute to key initiatives related directly to their jobs. At the same company that Thompson was chastised over her social media posts, she felt unsafe when she shared her ideas on topics directly job-related with her managers.

In one meeting, she brought up the point of centering "accessibility" in the company's inclusion efforts. But after being met with derision initially, she didn't feel safe to keep pressing the issue. Without psychological safety, productive debates can't take place. Too often, great ideas fall by the wayside. The company could have strengthened its inclusion efforts if it had created an environment where Thompson felt like she could contribute her knowledge, but instead it lost out on an innovative idea.

Eventually, Thompson left the organization to pursue entrepreneurship.

Managers Must Become Active Bystanders or Success Partners to Women of Color

Women of color consistently lack the advocacy and allyship (solidarity of people from other groups that don't face the same obstacles) that they require from their white peers. And without organization-wide common language around what constitutes bias and racism, many will continue to create workplace cultures that exclude women of color.

"Many managers don't have the necessary tools or the skills to manage from a diversity, equity, inclusion, and belonging lens. Oftentimes, people are promoted because they're seen as good people, but that doesn't necessarily mean they're good managers," Minda Harts, author of *The Memo: What Women of Color Need to Know to Secure a Seat at the Table*, tells me. While women of color certainly end up leaving organizations because of toxic bias and exclusion, it's also common for them to leave because of well-meaning managers who are unable to recognize, stop perpetuating, or call out everyday bias (not just overt racism) in themselves and others. A generally healthy work culture can still end up missing the mark on creating psychological safety for women of color without the language and tools to root out bias.

Some organizations that I've worked with now have workshops to coach managers to recognize what sexism and racism looks like at their organization, with proactive coaching on how to eliminate bias, be antiracist, and stand up to others who perpetuate it. As Lean In's *State of Black Women in Corporate America* report argues, training should "emphasize tangible ways that employees can practice allyship, such as speaking out against discrimination and advocating for opportunities for Black women colleagues."[5]

Unfortunately, the bystander effect is disturbingly common when people witness incidents of bias or bullying. The bystander effect refers to when people in a group setting don't disrupt or shut down toxic behaviors, frequently because they expect someone else will jump in or they don't feel confident in their ability to effectively intervene. More managers must become *active bystanders* and use their in-group privilege to directly stop exclusionary behavior.

When managers operate as active bystanders or success partners (Harts's framing) to women of color, using their privilege to advocate for others, women of color are more likely to feel psychologically safe and included. Conversely, when women of color don't feel like there's anyone who "has their back or is batting for them," they're more likely to become withdrawn or leave an organization, Harts stresses.

Women of color specifically need white women to step up as success partners.

"It's not enough for white women leaders to send the elevator back down for women of color. Sometimes it will even require you to get back in the elevator and ride with them. That's active commitment," observes Harts. She says that more work cultures must explicitly state that allyship and advocacy for women of color is valued, and reward those who practice it. Until then, many will feel psychologically unsupported, operating in an atmosphere where they can't bring their authentic selves to work.

I think back to Kulkarni's story—one that is particularly close to me as a former journalist and now journalism professor. I know that the lack of diversity in the media deeply impacts the diversity of stories told and plurality of viewpoints represented. Experts say this erasure can even impact the future of democracy. Much of this lack of representation is blamed on people of color, particularly women of color, not being able to "make it" in the cutthroat journalism industry. But as Kulkarni's experience illustrates (among countless others), without psychological safety in their workplaces, we risk losing bright and determined women of color. It is to the detriment of society.

The ADAPT Framework

Above I addressed large, long-term goals for managers to work toward. The ADAPT framework below focuses on immediate actions that organizations can take to create an environment of psychological safety, centering women of color.

A: analyze employee engagement data

D: develop a code of conduct

A: accept failure

P: propel and fund ERGs

T: team tenets on DEI

Analyze Employee Engagement Data

More organizations now collect employee engagement data. But many don't expressly measure psychological safety or belonging—an important measure of how included marginalized employees, especially women of color, feel at the organization. All too often, leaders only analyze the data by gender or race, without taking an intersectional approach.

To be inclusive on purpose, regularly survey your employees and specifically ask questions around experiences of bias as well as how included and psychologically safe your employees feel. Culture Amp, the software platform for employee engagement, shared the five questions that elicited the most insight into inclusion. I identify the specific area of culture that each question addresses:

1. I feel like I belong at this company (inclusion)
2. I can voice a contrary opinion without fear of negative consequences (psychological safety)
3. Perspectives like mine are included in decision-making (psychological safety)
4. My company believes that people can greatly improve their talents and abilities (growth mindset)
5. Administrative tasks that don't have a specific owner are fairly divided (fair distribution of office housework)

As always, ensure that you disaggregate the data by gender and race.

"If you don't dig into a cut of the key questions along race and gender lines, you're going to miss a story," says Nicole Sanchez, founder and CEO of Vaya Consulting. Specifically focus on Black women's experiences, she recommends, if you are able to splice the data while maintaining anonymity and confidentiality.

"Black women will tell you what hurts most in your organization because they're the ones living with it disproportionately," she says. If your organization calculates an engagement score, it's crucial to compare the overall score of engagement with what women of color, especially Black women, are scoring. "That is the bellwether data about 'where do I start.' Many leaders talk about centering people on the margins, what that really means is centering women of color's opinions.

What isn't going well," she explains. "Take an extra look at that data, because when you center Black women, you build an employee experience where not only they're safe, the rest of us are also safe."

Develop a Code of Conduct

Most organizations have a weighty employee conduct handbook that no one reads. A handbook that's full of legal jargon will do little to safeguard against exclusion. Instead, organizations must create transparent and specific guidelines for employee conduct, focused on reducing bias as well as creating psychological safety and inclusion.

Ideally this code of conduct will be short and tangible, detailing what an inclusive culture looks like and what constitutes unacceptable behavior, according to Lean In's *State of Black Women in Corporate America* report. "To be treated seriously, these guidelines must be supported by a clear reporting process and swift consequences. Companies should also hold periodic refreshers to drive the guidelines home and make sure all employees understand them."[6]

Without explicitly creating a tangible employee code of conduct (ideally no more than a page), and one that involves women of color in its creation, we may unintentionally be carrying forward systems of bias.

I've seen this in my own classroom. I assume that all new students will understand that racism will not be tolerated in my class, especially given my public writing along with the texts and concepts covered in my course. So I have never explicitly stated that our classes will operate under the guidelines of an antiracist classroom. Unfortunately not everyone is on the same page, and every year I'll find myself or my students of color facing incidents of racism or gender bias.

In 2020, I reversed roles and became a student in a yearlong writing class. Theo Nestor, the white female writing instructor, began the first class putting in place guidelines for an antiracist classroom, including that "we agree that our classroom will be a safe place for writers to speak up about racism, whether the racism be inside or out-side the classroom," and "we understand that white fragility will often be present when instances of racism are presented in text or discussions, and white students will strive to deal with their fragility outside class discussions." She also shared resources that students could use to identify, call out, and root out racist behavior.

As one of two people of color in a class of seventeen white people, I felt reassured that I could bring my true self to this course and would have the instructor's support if I encountered racism. As a woman of color, I felt much more at ease, and that there might be more place for my stories and contributions than when I, at first glance, saw myself racially outnumbered.

Women of color report facing more *everyday discrimination* than white women and men in several areas including the exclusionary behaviors that I've outlined earlier, like hearing surprise at their lan-guage or other skills, and needing to provide more evidence of their competence, according to the same Lean In report. A code of conduct must spell out that not only egregious forms of discrimination (such as racial slurs or sexual harassment) won't be tolerated but what exclu-sionary behaviors look like instead. This is necessary in creating psy-chological safety for women of color, especially, so they can surface these behaviors without fear of retaliation.

Accept Failure

Women of color typically feel a significant pressure to prove them-selves and outperform, especially if they are tokens ("the only") or one of the very few at the workplace. Several women of color whom I interviewed told me they felt like they could never fail because their failures would impact not just them as individuals but the future of all women of color like them too. That's a heavy burden to carry, yet one that is all too familiar.

Too many teams focus only on celebrating successes, but don't take time to understand, examine, and learn from failures. One of the organizations that I worked with had a "no bad news" culture, so not only did the few women of color there feel psychologically unsafe to speak up about errors but many white men whom I interviewed there also said the same. Yet we know that innovation is born out of failure.

The team that I advised started having an annual "fail fest" during which it would gather at the end of the year to discuss and even celebrate mistakes. This exercise allowed the team to bond over errors—large or small—and started normalizing failure, given that failure is normal! Later, when I informally checked in with members of the team, a number of employees from a variety of backgrounds reported feeling relief that mistakes could be aired more freely and a greater sense of belonging on the team.

In Edmondson's research in hospitals, the explicit use of a "failure event analysis" was key in creating psychological safety within teams. "It doesn't have to be something really bad that happened, it could be a near miss," she says. She recommends a rigorous (not necessarily lengthy) process, where everyone who was involved in the incident "goes around and talks about what they saw, what happened from their point of view and their little part in it, with the aim of getting to what really happened. And what we can change to make sure that it doesn't happen again."

Edmondson says that normalizing failure and having a process to discuss it are central to creating psychological safety on a team. "A team may be busy, people may feel like they don't have an hour to discuss a failed incident, and yet the recognition is by doing this particular learning process," she explains. By taking this action, her research has shown that teams can potentially avoid countless, undesired, and preventable failures.

To really drive team psychological safety, Edmondson says any culture that accepts and learns from failure involves people committing to being honest, and being aware that they only see part of the reality of the entire situation. "They have to be humble about that, but also curious about what really happened. This probably isn't their favorite way to spend an hour, but while they're there, the process forces them to be pretty interested in what their colleague's perspective was too."

For underestimated employees, creating a culture that accepts, normalizes, and learns from failure can drive greater belonging and psychological safety.

Propel and Fund ERGs

ERGs are known by a variety of different names including business resource groups and affinity groups, but I will keep to ERG for consistency. At their core, ERGs are made up of voluntary groups of employees who have shared life experiences or identities, and gather on a regular basis in their workplace.

The first known corporate ERG was formed in 1964, when Xerox corporation's CEO Joseph C. Wilson organized a caucus for Black employees to address racial discrimination and inclusion, against the backdrop of racial violence and riots at that time. The ERG had a significant and meaningful genesis, but unfortunately, nearly fifty years later, many ERGs operate as a symbolic gesture, with little opportunity to drive change. By some estimates, 90 percent of Fortune 500 companies have ERGs, but less than 8 percent of employees participate in them.[7]

"When set up well, ERGs should create psychological safety for people, period," Sanchez emphasizes. Frequently, however, what had originated as a meaningful endeavor to address racism has in many companies become a networking opportunity for white women. Most organizations concentrate on propelling and funding the women-focused ERG, which often doesn't create psychological safety for women of color.

Instead, Sanchez recommends that any organization dedicated to inclusion should first create ERGs focused on racial affinity, particularly an ERG for Black employees and their allies. "Centering the experiences of Black women, especially, can create some of the best outcomes for your organization," she says.

Then ensure that those ERG leaders are leveraged in business decisions and regular conversations with leadership, not "as the head of a party planning committee or when it's Black History Month, not like that," asserts Sanchez. As strategic decisions are being made and initiatives are being rolled out, organizations can benefit from being in open conversation with a diverse group of employees within an ERG.

Sanchez's retail client leveraged a committee of ERG leaders (of different racial affinity groups) for early retail product reviews. "Having ERG leaders involved with reviewing a product in early stages actually helped the company avert a disaster, from going in a direction that would be considered cultural appropriation," she says.

Cultural appropriation refers to "the unacknowledged or inappropriate adoption of the customs, practices, ideas, etc. of one people or society by members of another and typically more dominant people or society," according to *Oxford English Dictionary*, which only entered the phrase in 2018, despite the term's origins over seventy years ago.[8] Cultural appropriation not only exacerbates inequities in the workplace (I've observed white women in prior workplaces complimented for wearing Indian clothing to events, whereas I know that I would be seen as "less assimilated" into the Western workplace culture for doing the same) but also can create a chasm between a company and customers from that community.

"In this case, Latina women ERG leaders flagged the issue and really saved the company from embarrassment. When you center the experience of women of color and really listen, it can be a win all around," says Sanchez. Leverage the expertise inherent in ERGs to make strategic decisions for the organization; done right, leaders should be deeply involved with ERGs.

Next, ensure that ERGs have adequate funding. Instead of having ERGs "beg" for small budgets, the organization should take a proactive approach in determining the charter of the ERG. "Figure out what you want the ERG to accomplish, then resource that accordingly," advises Sanchez. Goals that are actionable tend to fare well, such as tracking whether there was a rise in employees of color that cited belonging to an ERG as a benefit of working at the organization, or leveraging ERG leaders in hiring plans, strategy conversations, or community outreach.

"Until we're clear about what the charter and the responsibility of the ERG is, we won't know how to attach money to it." Well-funded ERGs with leadership buy-in can be a truly powerful environment for women of color to feel safe and advance. To be clear, the ERG should never be the *only* place in the organization that women of color feel safe, but when an organization explicitly shows (through action) that women of color are not expected to hide their identities, psychological safety can be created. When ERGs have high visibility and impact throughout the organization, they can also signal that it's safe for women of color to surface issues of bias without worrying about being penalized for offending white people and men.

Wilson may not have known it at the time of founding Xerox, but centering Black employees' voices back in 1964 created a pathway for a truly groundbreaking outcome for the company's future. In 2009, Xerox's Ursula Burns became the first Black female CEO on the Fortune 500 list.

Team Tenets on DEI

Women of color often read employer commitments to inclusion in marketing materials, but in practice find that inclusion is not prioritized. That's because inclusion takes commitment—and sometimes that commitment can be in conflict with business as usual. How does a team prioritize two conflicting interests? If you need to make a decision that pushes up your organization's cost yet makes life easier for your customers, would you make that decision?

Recognizing that teams constantly make decisions that pit seemingly opposite priorities against each other, online retailer Amazon came up with the concept of creating tenets to solve these challenges. "Tenets get everyone in agreement about critical questions that can't be verified factually," a blog post on Amazon's website states.[9] Simply put, a tenet allows a team to decide which of the two competing priorities it would prioritize in a recurring situation so that the conversation doesn't get derailed every time the situation arises.

I first heard about the concept of tenets in 2019, when I was pondering an issue that too many of my clients have: a team needs to hire new people urgently, but it wants to prioritize drawing from a diverse slate of candidates too, and that takes time. It seemed like the two goals were constantly bumping up against each other and being revisited regularly, with no definitive answers.

A friend who worked at Amazon introduced the concept of tenets, an evolving set of "how-tos" used to solve recurring issues at the company. To my knowledge, the concept of tenets has not been used in the context of DEI, and I want to state that I have not worked with Amazon on tenets, so I do not have knowledge on how tenets are applied to its business.

I see value, though, in developing team tenets around DEI to codify a team's intentions related to creating an inclusive, psychologically safe environment. As always, it is necessary to have women of color involved in creating these tenets.

Some problems that could be decided through tenets could include:

1. Between speed and diversity of candidates in hiring, we will prioritize . . .

2. When an incident of racism or exclusion comes to light, but the perpetrator is a well-liked employee otherwise, we will prioritize . . .

3. In making a key team deadline without a diversity of members present or delaying a deadline to ensure that there are people of color involved in the decision, we will prioritize . . .

Once the team has developed DEI tenets, put them into action. So if your recruiter brings a homogeneous slate of candidates to the table for expediency, but your tenet was to prioritize diversity, there's no gray area about what to do next; your recruiter must go back to the drawing board until you have more candidate diversity, even though it will take longer to fill the role.

When leaders come to me and say, "We care about creating a diverse and inclusive environment, but hiring immediately matters most," then they have decided to prioritize speed over representation.

If these considerations come up often, take the time to discuss and evaluate these with your team to create a pathway forward.

Harts says that nothing jeopardizes psychological safety for women of color more than when leaders prioritize the success of otherwise star employees who are biased or discriminatory over the concerns of women of color. This conundrum can be addressed through the creation of tenets.

"A lot of the language used to justify bad behavior in an organization is very harmful to women of color," she says. Using a hypothetical example of "Tom," a white male employee who is being reported by a woman of color for being racist, she remarks, "We'll hear, 'Oh well, that's just Tom being Tom! Tom didn't mean any harm.' And it totally dismisses the experience of the woman of color. What people don't understand is that two things can be true at the same time. Tom can be a good man to you, but he also could be doing these other things that you're not on the receiving end of." Instead, seek a shift in accountability and language that does not defend oppressors.

Creating tenets around how exclusive or discriminatory behavior will be handled may seem uncomfortable at first, but it can be incredibly beneficial in the long run. In this case, the tenet could be: *We prioritize the psychological safety of team members, so even if a stellar employee behaves in a manner inconsistent with our code of conduct, we will investigate and take action.*

"If we keep giving passes to bad behavior then that creates more of a toxic work environment and women of color will never have equity because we keep still putting these offenders on pedestals," Harts says. By contrast, if a team explicitly prioritizes the safety of women of color—even if that means addressing the bad behavior of a well-liked employee—women of color are likely to feel safe speaking up and airing concerns. They will know that their issues will be taken seriously, without fear of retribution.

Everyone benefits when a team prioritizes the psychological safety of women of color.

Edmondson reminds us that the world has never been more unpredictable or interdependent. Innovation will help us overcome a variety of challenges—from a global pandemic to the movement for racial justice to huge political movements. "That means, truly anyone's voice might be mission critical, and organizations must be in a place where different perspectives are allowed to be heard," she says. "Our future depends on psychological safety."

■   ■   ■

KEY REFLECTIONS

1. What does psychological safety mean to you?

2. When have you felt psychologically safe at work? When have you felt psychologically unsafe?

3. Have you observed some or all of the four warning signs of a psychologically unsafe culture for women of color in your workplace?

4. How are women of color generally treated when they speak up at your organization?

5. Looking at the ADAPT framework, what are tools that you already use? Which can you prioritize in the short, medium, and long term to create greater psychological safety for your team?

6. What is one thing that you could do to take action today? Write it down here:

III

Looking to the Future of Inclusion on Purpose

We are facing global challenges that will continue on into our future if we don't take an intersectional, interconnected approach. These chapters focus on the ways that inequity and exclusionary behaviors in society are similar in workplaces around the world, and left unchecked, could create harm on a massive scale, especially within the technology industry and the technologies that are created. Women of color must be centered in designing the future.

9

A Future Powered by Inclusive Technology

> Those of us who have been privileged to receive education, skills, and experiences and even power must be role models for the next generation of leadership.
>
> —Wangari Maathai

Ifeoma Ozoma, Pinterest's former public policy and social impact manager, was shocked to learn from the advocacy group Color of Change that her company was advertising wedding venues that were former slave plantations to its users. She immediately began to push for change with leadership, intuitively understanding the reputational risk if Pinterest didn't take quick action to remove them.

"As a company, we were promoting slave plantations as wedding and event venues, which is just absolutely offensive, because we would not do the same for concentration camps," she recalls telling her former manager, when she flagged the issue in multiple emails and meetings.

But her manager, a white man, chastised her in her performance review. Ozoma was also told that the way she presented the issue was biased. Instead, she was told that she should have provided the *pros and cons* of ceasing the promotion of former plantations on the company's platform. She was rebuked for promoting her own "agenda" rather than taking an unbiased view, her manager wrote in her review.

"My performance was dinged, which affected my pay," Ozoma says. "All because I advocated for a policy that when we eventually made the change, the company was celebrated for doing so externally. But internally I was punished for pushing for it."

The pushback that Ozoma faced in this instance underpinned a history of discrimination that she and other Black women had already been dealing with at the organization. Previously, she raised repeatedly that she was paid less than her white male peer in a similar role. Ozoma also observed that Black women were routinely hired at more junior roles than their experience warranted, especially compared with white employees.

In 2019, a white male engineer became so enraged by Ozoma's commitment to safeguarding against health misinformation and white supremacist content on the platform, he "doxed" her and two other female colleagues. Doxing is an extreme form of online harassment in which a person's sensitive information, like their home address and cell phone number, is published—often on nonmoderated platforms—with the malicious intent of having that person attacked online and in real life. Doxing particularly impacts women of color who are more likely to have this information posted online without their consent and receive "greater amounts of unwanted, vitriolic messages," according to experts.[1]

It took a week for Pinterest to fire the engineer, but Ozoma had already experienced unspeakable online harassment by then.

Fed up after facing compounding indignities, Ozoma and another Black woman, Aerica Shimizu Banks, left the company in May 2020. For context, Pinterest has garnered a positive public reputation for being the kindest and most inclusive technology company in Silicon Valley, especially compared to its peers like Facebook and Uber. Ozoma had seen firsthand how untrue that was, but she knew it would be close to impossible to get another job in the industry if she publicly disparaged the company. She was ready to put this painful chapter behind her.

But in June 2020, when she saw Pinterest make public statements in solidarity with Black Lives Matter—as many companies were doing during the national racial justice movement that year—she couldn't take the hypocrisy any longer.

Ozoma and Shimizu Banks bravely spoke out about how, despite the organization's public commitment to racial equality, internally, racism and sexism was rampant. Ozoma says that the company's leadership has yet to publicly acknowledge or address her public grievances, but privately, the company's CEO and his largely white male leadership team have disparaged her and other women of color who have spoken out. She persists and is determined to change the workplace for others like her.

In February 2021, Ozoma was a leader in pushing legislation in California to protect employees who have experienced workplace discrimination or harassment against nondisclosure agreements enforced by employers to silence them.[2] The new bill, called Silenced No More, seeks to expand previous state legislation that only protects women who publicly disclose workplace gender discrimination, not racial discrimination. As Ozoma reminds us, intersectionality matters.

We know that no one industry is unique in propagating racism and other biases. But what is condoned at large technology companies (as of this writing, Pinterest is valued at close to $40 billion and used by more than 320 million monthly global users) has a significant impact on their employees *and* customers worldwide. The technology industry deeply influences which company cultures are rewarded, which products get created, and how we live our lives.

Only recently are we beginning to understand the power that a handful of technology companies, such as Google, Facebook, Twitter, and Amazon, wield the world over. Technology companies are rarely created by a diverse group of founders (the large technology companies are almost entirely run by white and a few Asian men), don't have women in decision-making roles (30 percent of technology employees are female), and don't hire people of color, especially Black people (the average Black employee base of large technology employers in the United States hovers at lower-end single digits). It's not a stretch to imagine the role of technology and technology companies to spread inequality at scale.

When Silicon Valley sneezes, the whole world has the potential to catch a cold.

Grappling with the Outsize Impact of Technology in Our Lives

If you're reading this book, you probably can't imagine a world without technology now. I certainly can't. Billions of people around the world use it to make life easier. But there is a flip side to many of its conveniences—some that we are only starting to learn, such as how much personal data about us are collected and owned by technology companies. We have yet to fully uncover the extent to which these data will be used, whether to benefit or one day harm us. We all need to pay attention to inclusion in the technology industry. We all have a part to play in advocating for greater diversity among technology creators and leaders, and ensure that technology does not further harm underestimated communities. This chapter has some specific messages for leaders within the technology industry, but it's essential for every reader, no matter how distant you may consider yourself from it, to advocate for greater equity and inclusion in technology. If you have a smartphone with even a single application downloaded, this impacts you.

First, let's step back a little to learn the early origins of the industry. Computer science descended from the field of mathematics.

Mathematics is often paraded as an unbiased industry; numbers can't have a social agenda—they either add up or they don't. But more experts have been pushing back against this narrative, seeking to highlight how the field of mathematics has long institutionalized sexism and racism. Many of these norms have been carried on by the modern technology industry—one that's wrongfully garnered a reputation for being unbiased.

New York University data journalism professor Meredith Broussard frequently points to the fact that the prestigious American Mathematical Society membership has never consisted of more than 20 percent female members since 1985, and that number has begun declining precipitously since 2012. While women PhDs in STEM fields are on the rise, and in some cases reaching parity with men, they are still absent from leadership in the vast majority of technology organizations, academia, or shaping the policy of how technology is governed.

For many years, the belief was that women and non-Asian people of color were unable to excel in these fields. And largely, Asian technology employees are seen as able to do the grunt work, yet lacking the leadership skills to influence modern technology. As a result, almost all modern technology that we use was created by white men in the West.

Are white men genetically predisposed to be better at creating technology? Only recently have we started peeling back the curtain to investigate the flawed narrative that girls and women inherently can't grasp these concepts. I've had to correct a white male computer science lecturer at the University of Washington in the media who posited that women were biologically hardwired to be less competent at coding.[3] The bias against people of color in the industry has been investigated even less, but persistent racism pervades STEM education. This excludes students of color and graduates from entering or staying in these professions.

Women of color face outsized barriers to entry even when they have tech qualifications. Tracy Chou, a Taiwanese American software engineer who has two technology degrees from Stanford University (including a master's in computer science), noticed a surprising pattern when she started mentoring other Asian women computer engineering college students. Many like her were steered by mentors to pursue nontechnical jobs in technology companies rather than lucrative engineering jobs. It wasn't enough to be technically qualified to fit the industry; she encountered bias because she was expected to fit the personality type of a socially awkward software engineer, usually a white or Asian man.

"There's some supposition that if you are going to be an engineer and you're a woman, that you need to fit some super nerdy stereotype. I'm not even that social, but I'm just not painfully shy or awkward," she says.

While women struggle to gain a foothold in this hostile industry, women of color face more barriers. White men and women are twice as likely as Asians to become executives, and hold almost three times the number of executive jobs in the technology industry, according to an Ascend Foundation study on Silicon Valley leadership. Although white women are substantially more successful in reaching the executive level than all men or women of color, white men are still 47 percent more likely than white women to be executives.[4]

White men (51 percent) and women (20 percent) dominated the STEM professions in 2015 in the United States, according to the National Science Foundation.[5] Women of color make up less than 12 percent of STEM professionals. This is truly tragic because the growth of STEM occupations has consistently outpaced non-STEM jobs in the United States over the last decade, according to a 2017 report from the US Bureau of Labor Statistics.[6]

These jobs are highly lucrative, at nearly double the average wage for non-STEM occupations, according to the same report. When women of color are blocked from entering and advancing in the industry, wealth creation is concentrated among those who already have privilege—white men. To be clear, this impacts all of us, even those who are not employed in the industry. When the products that we cannot imagine our lives without are designed, funded, and regulated by a small, privileged subset of society, we are already experiencing some of the downsides. Those downsides include apps that prioritize convenience over privacy, the addictive nature of social media, and billions of dollars being thrown to solve issues like ordering food and taxis faster, as opposed to solving societal problems like poverty, hunger, and climate change.

Why Bias in the Industry Is Bad for Society

The potential harm of this lack of diversity and inclusion among technology creators is even more alarming for society at large. Coupled with the fallacy of an unbiased, meritocratic industry, the homogeneity among technology creators and leaders has allowed biased technology to proliferate unchecked.

MIT technologist Joy Buolamwini was working on an exciting new program to project digital masks onto faces. But when she used generic facial analysis software to build it, Buolamwini, a Black woman, found that the software would not detect her face unless she wore a white mask. How did that happen? In a TEDx Talk, she describes how computers "learn" facial recognition from machine learning techniques: computers are fed hundreds or thousands of data sets to recognize patterns over time.[7] In this case, it was faces. If the training sets don't include a diversity of faces, though, the machine itself learns that faces only look a certain way. It doesn't detect others that aren't consistent with what it has been trained to recognize. Buolamwini didn't only encounter this problem in the United States across multiple labs that she had been working in, but even when she was at an entrepreneurship competition in Hong

Kong, one of the robots couldn't detect her face. It's frightening how even one biased algorithm can travel to be used in technology in a different part of the world.

"Algorithmic bias, like human bias, results in unfairness. However, algorithms, like viruses, can spread bias on a massive scale at a rapid pace. Algorithmic bias can also lead to exclusionary experiences and discriminatory practices," she says in her talk.[8]

A variety of issues feed into this problem, such as lack of diverse data training sets, but also the fact that the creators of the generic software had fairly homogeneous skin tone and facial features, so they didn't even detect the problem when they tested it on themselves. This is among one of many examples of how technology has replicated existing biases in society, especially anti-Black racism. Photo-labeling software has tagged photos of Black people as gorillas. If you query "unprofessional hairstyles" on Google, you're more likely to be returned photos of Black women with natural hair. Health care algorithms favor providing extra care to white patients, but not equally sick Black patients.

Women of color technologists are leading the charge on how biased technology is enabling and perpetuating discrimination.

In 2016, over 117 million US adults—half the country's population—were in police face recognition networks. These unregulated networks are in frequent use, but far from fail-safe, and experts say that they disproportionately make errors in detecting Black faces, again related to a lack of diversity in the training data sets. The American Civil Liberties Union has called for greater examination of how bias shows up in and is perpetuated by these systems: "A growing body of evidence suggests that law enforcement use of face recognition technology is having a disparate impact on communities of color, potentially exacerbating and entrenching existing policing disparities."[9]

Other instances of how biased technology could impact our lives are plentiful and need urgent rectification. Artificial intelligence already in use by US courts to predict the likelihood of a criminal reoffending was more likely to predict Black people as reoffenders, all other information being equal. Facebook targets job advertisements for nurses to women, and janitor and taxi driver ads to men. Biased algorithms are often used in job-screening functions, which frequently screen out women and applicants with non-Anglo Saxon names. In the future, as self-driving cars may become ubiquitous, one study finds that the technology is less likely to detect (and stop for) darker-skinned pedestrians, thereby endangering their lives.[10] Everyone in society should be alarmed by this.

Technology Companies Must Immediately Regulate Harassment and Misinformation

Women of color face severe and sustained online harassment. It's unacceptable morally, but has far-reaching consequences too, like the risk to free speech and a country's democracy. We risk losing women journalists, particularly women of color, due to this issue, a study by my Seattle University colleague Caitlin Carlson and her collaborator Haley Witt found. "Some respondents avoided certain stories for fear of online abuse they would receive. An overwhelming majority of U.S. women journalists (79%) agreed that online harassment affected press freedom," Carlson and Witt's study concludes.[11] Yet technology platforms (which are largely run by men) have refused to seriously crack down on harassment. Over time, I've seen incredible women of color leave social media platforms after they experienced shameful harassment and abuse online. What a loss at a time when their voices are needed the most!

Another area of concern is how many technology organizations have not cracked down on misinformation (false information) and disinformation (deliberately deceptive information with harmful intent). Leaders at these multibillion companies choose profit over principle, knowing that misinformation and incendiary speech garner more interest as well as users on their platforms. And that translates into more money for these companies. I blame the large gap between the average person and the white male technology leadership that makes these decisions on how to manage misinformation and hate speech online. This is why empathy and inclusion on purpose matters.

In 2017, prominent technologist Ellen Pao (also known for suing her venture capital employer for gender discrimination) wrote an op-ed with Laura Gómez (whom you met in chapter 4) calling on Twitter CEO Jack Dorsey to suspend then president Trump from Twitter for violating the platform's policies and terms of service. Both authors are women of color who have experienced abuse online.

"People's lives are actually at stake here, and each day our goodwill for Twitter erodes as Trump and his followers overshadow the good of the platform. For a long time, internet pundits blamed anonymity for online bullying. But we saw at Trump's rallies that harassment moves easily from behind the screen to in-person behavior, as his supporters shouted at and physically attacked protesters and reporters. As this behavior escalates from the web and lands in real life, Twitter needs to set an example for other social media platforms by holding its users, and itself, accountable," they urged.[12]

The warnings went unheeded. In 2020, two days before the US presidential elections, Pao once again urged Dorsey to suspend Trump's account, citing the rise of violence against Asian Americans because of the former president's racist use of "China virus" to refer to the coronavirus, and his use of the platform to spread misinformation about voter fraud as well as incite violence online and in real life.[13] Still nothing. Twitter did not permanently suspend his account until January 8, 2021, two days after white nationalists stormed the US Capitol, inciting violence that was spurred on by Trump on social media.[14] Lives were lost because of Twitter's decision to take no action earlier.

So many women of color who call for the creation of ethical technology and careful regulation of it to ensure the safety of society often face the most severe online harassment, particularly as they become more vocal in their advocacy of creating a diverse, equitable, and inclusive technology industry.

The combination of how technology can reach people at rapid speed and the spread of misinformation can have truly monumental consequences. The same possibilities that have allowed millions to connect and unite for important causes (it's arguable that movements like #MeToo would never have gained worldwide momentum without social media platforms) can also be used to spread hate speech and lies at scale. The same platforms that allow women of color to band together in solidarity are used by white supremacists to radicalize impressionable members to cause harm to them too.

An Exclusionary Ecosystem for Women of Color Entrepreneurs

One way that we can create more inclusion in the industry and in turn society at large is by supporting more women of color to start successful, well-funded technology companies. Unfortunately, women of color technology entrepreneurs, like their counterparts working in existing technology companies, also face barriers to advancement. After seeing the rise of and personally facing vicious online harassment, Tracy Chou left a lucrative technology job to launch Block Party, a consumer app to help prevent online harassment and abuse. The problem disproportionately harms women of color. It's one that established technology companies simply were not doing enough (and still don't) to protect users from on their platforms, she says. But being a female technology entrepreneur of color proved even harder for her than her experience as a software engineer in top Silicon Valley companies.

"Compared to getting into software engineering versus getting to be a founder, I have felt much more pushed out by the entrepreneurial ecosystem," she observes, although she has faced exclusionary behaviors and even overt sexual harassment in previous technology jobs.

"Maybe it's because Asian women are considered the worker bees but not leaders," she muses. Chou faced a number of challenges getting her start-up off the ground, like being told by white male investors that online harassment is a niche problem and being "mansplained" that her approach to solving the problem isn't the correct way, despite her personal experience with online harassment, combined with her technical acumen. She has also been sexually harassed by well-known white male technology entrepreneurs and investors when asking for advice or raising funding. Unfortunately, her experience is consistent with the data: 46 percent of women of color founders report being harassed by a potential investor, compared with 36 percent of white men.[15] In early 2021, Chou was dismayed to learn that a knockoff of her company had been launched by a white man and funded by several prominent investors. Even when brilliant women of color technologists create useful technology, the industry still excludes them.

The lack of support for underestimated technology entrepreneurs should concern us all. Almost 80 percent of new small businesses in the United States are founded by women of color, but only 4 percent are in the technology sector.[16] What begins as a small technology start-up has the potential to one day employ thousands, if not hundreds, of thousands, of people. Some of the world's most valuable public and private companies are technology companies founded by white men. A strong myth of the "lone wolf" founder—always male—has fed the pervasive narrative about what it means to be a successful entrepreneur. As a former business journalist, I would see media stories about white male founders who were characterized as brilliant and visionary. I've met many technology entrepreneurs who cite Microsoft cofounder Bill Gates and Amazon founder Jeff Bezos as their inspiration. Both men are admired for starting their now giant companies in a garage with no funding. The only thing is that this story is incomplete. Both men were indeed visionaries, yet they not only received significant early funding from their parents but also were enabled to succeed in an industry that mostly propels white male founders.

The chips are stacked against women of color entrepreneurs, who face a number of barriers to getting a shot at powering the next billion-dollar ("unicorn") company. What a shame, because a number of brilliant women of color are working to create more ethical technology as well as build inclusive work cultures and products that could benefit society at large. While the lion's share of attention (and investment) goes to white or Asian male Silicon Valley entrepreneurs, many women of color entrepreneurs are tackling large societal issues like creating greater access to jobs, capital, opportunities, and safety especially for women of color.

But women entrepreneurs receive an insultingly low amount of investment. In 2017, for instance, out of $85 billion of venture capital funding given to entrepreneurs, only 2.2 percent went to women founders. Every year, women of color get less than 1 percent of venture capital funding; 0.2 percent of it goes to Black women technology founders.[17]

On the other side of the table, the investors writing the checks are disproportionately white and male too. Investors tend to be people who have either gotten wealthy from their own employment or entrepreneurship in the technology ecosystem, or come from generational wealth, or both. So an inclusive and ethical future truly depends on creating opportunities for women of color to surface innovative ideas. It is also a matter of priority for women of color to have their ideas funded and gain access to investors who are women of color too. This is why gender and racial pay equity (and opportunities to ascend into highly paid roles) is so important as well. It's all related.

A Call to Action to Inclusive Tech Leaders

So how can we be inclusive on purpose to ensure a technology industry that includes and is created by women of color? First, more women of color must be recruited in and advanced across the industry, whether as technology company employees or entrepreneurs. That's according to the chief operating officer at the Wikimedia Foundation, Janeen Uzzell, one of the most influential Black women leaders in the industry today. Growing up, Uzzell had to press on despite facing surprise and hesitation from teachers and her school principal when she showed her interest in pursuing an engineering degree. She then went on to be one of the few Black people and women in her college. As famous showrunner Shonda Rhimes writes in her book *Year of Yes*, when you are the first, only, or different in any environment, "you are saddled with that burden of extra responsibility—whether you want it or not" to represent your whole community in every interaction.[18]

Facing inhospitable environments in many STEM workplaces can further deter technically qualified women of color. "Many of these places are incredibly biased, I will say for women, even more so for women of color," Uzzell remarks. "The catcalling is still real in engineering and manufacturing." When women of color are barely represented, they may not be safe reporting incidents of bias. As I repeatedly recommend here, taking personal responsibility to foster an inclusive and safe work environment is central to being inclusive on purpose. Only then can we encourage more women of color to enter and advance in the industry.

Take a holistic approach to nurturing the pipeline by actively engaging with organizations that are building and enriching STEM education for girls of color in local schools. When engaging with these programs early, leaders at technology companies must not only fund these programs but also work closely with this pipeline of girls of color to ensure that the workplaces they graduate into are inclusive. Inclusion on purpose takes the long view.

More technology leaders must understand that the challenges begin early; the sexist tropes that girls aren't good at math and science have filtered out generations of girls from participating in these classes from a young age. Psychologist Claude Steele's research on the stereotype threat—when girls or students of color subconsciously conform to the stereotype that they are not good at academic test taking—highlights how believing that they're inferior has often caused these students to self-select out of academic achievements.[19] This happens despite the data showing repeatedly that there is no gender gap in mathematical aptitude. For many girls of color, the intersection of gender and race can compound this further. A confluence of factors, as I've discussed earlier in the book, contributes to deeper exclusion for girls of color, such as financial and educational barriers, a lack of role models, and facing negative stereotypes that reinforce low self-confidence and interest in these fields. There is much to be done to make STEM education more equitable and accessible, but that topic goes well beyond the scope of this book.

Technology companies can partner with programs led by women of color that are seeking to solve the problem. In the United States, Black Girls Code and Girls Who Code are national programs both run by women of color and focused on building a more robust, diverse pipeline of future women engineers.[20] When technology organizations support and host graduates of these programs, many women of color can often be exposed for the first time to the possibilities of a career in the industry.

Next, more leaders must actively understand and address the unique biases faced by women of color technologists. Chou found that the code she wrote was routinely subject to extra reviews compared with codes written by her male peers. Once when she caught a huge coding error, her manager didn't believe her until a white male engineer verified that it was a red flag. Uzzell was paired with a more junior white male with no technical expertise to run a global technology program at a former employer "because they didn't trust me. He didn't have an engineering degree, but he was the guy that they trusted."

When leaders are inclusive, they openly name biases and listen to women of color with the intention of believing them. If a woman of color engineer is telling you that she is facing bias or discrimination, believe her. In overt instances of bias, including sexual harassment, it is incumbent on you as a leader and the organization as a whole to create the psychological safety for women of color to surface these issues. Take swift action to address concerns. As I previously stated, do not ignore harassment and exclusionary behavior directed at women of color just because the perpetrators are considered to be too brilliant or valuable to lose—a problem that we frequently encounter in the industry. Not addressing bad behavior early allows it to normalize and proliferate.

Leaders must also constantly sponsor women of color to keep advancing in technology. A lack of finding role models like her became the strongest barrier that Uzzell faced to staying the course for the three decades that she has been in technology. "It makes it difficult to stay encouraged, to know that there's even a future for you," she says. "If there are no women at this level in engineering, then I tell myself: surely, I'll never be plant manager or I'll never be the chief technology officer . . . that's impossible! How do I even perceive that that's an option for me?"

We are fortunate that Uzzell persevered, advanced, and now has turned her sights to building a future in which upcoming women in the technology industry can ascend to technical roles with big budgets and decision-making capabilities. She drove large workplace initiatives to accelerate women in technical roles at various organizations that she has worked in, always taking an intersectional approach in her endeavors. "Leadership is critical because that's the only way we can hire and build teams that look like the world. Otherwise, we're kind of just catching the ball and running with it," she says.

A Quick Blueprint for Creating Ethical, Inclusive Technology Products

The recommendations that I made in previous chapters to advance women of color broadly apply across industries, including technology. Apart from hiring and advancing women of color as well as creating psychologically safe work cultures, however, technology managers and leaders have a unique opportunity to build inclusive and ethical technology.

First, prioritize using a diversity of data sets when designing and building technology *with* women of color as part of the designing and creating team. Without ensuring—from day one—that women and people of color are central to the technology, there is a grave risk of creating exclusionary technology that could pose risks to marginalized people in society. As you are building, keep these two questions at the top of your mind: *Who is this technology helping and who may we be harming in the process? How can we optimize for the former and reduce the impact on the latter?*

Second, prioritize collecting feedback from diverse and traditionally underestimated voices on your service or product when determining product/market fit. Many ride-sharing technologies, initially lauded for their innovation, often had glaring safety concerns for women riders, who were usually left out of early customer testing. Center women of color, and most important, make it safe for them to share feedback candidly. Far too many platforms punish women of color users when they report issues, such as banning the accounts of women of color who report abuse on social media platforms rather than the accounts of abusers.

Third, intentionally look for biases that may otherwise go undetected. The "default" is frequently biased, such as using women's voices in voice technology designed to be assistants and lighter-skin people in images. Dive headfirst into this by evaluating where these biases are showing up and then address them. Relentlessly create mechanisms to safeguard against bias, hate speech, harassment, and abuse, no excuses made for "brilliant" harassers.

Lastly, as someone with the privilege to invest in start-up companies, I have specifically committed to advising and funding women of color entrepreneurs. Many people in the existing technology industry become investors, whom we know are overwhelmingly white and male. If you are in this position, invest with intention—not just in entrepreneurs who look like you, but those who don't. Mentor and sponsor aspiring technologists from underestimated backgrounds, and then connect them with people working in technology within your network.

Women in technology—Ozoma, Chou, Uzzell, and the countless others I've spoken with—express a sense of resignation that the industry, as it stands, is so powerful yet so broken. Most tell me that they don't have much hope for the industry if it continues in the way it is structured right now—growing rapidly without DEI, and enabled to reap maximum profits without regulation or repercussions of any kind.

That's why so many of women of color with a background in the industry are working tirelessly and fearlessly to create a more inclusive future, especially for the women of color who are coming up behind them. Many are calling for more robust governmental regulation of the industry. Working with, not against regulators, remains a key opportunity for the inclusive leader to truly create technology for, by, and that benefits all.

Your Role in Creating Inclusive Tech as a User

Even if you're not in technology, you can make a difference in creating a more inclusive and ethical technology future.

Here are some ideas to get you started:

1. Give more gender-inclusive gifts to young girls in your life, such as age-appropriate STEM toys. Encourage girls, especially girls of color, in your life to take an interest in exploring STEM education and sign up for opportunities that can expose them to it.

2. If you use social media, follow, learn from, and amplify women of color leaders. Be intentional about the demographics of who you follow on platforms like Twitter and Instagram. "We spend so very much of our time on these social networks, and there's so much we can do to right the wrongs we've seen in other media, through simple, small actions. This one's been a delightful and fun place to start," male technology leader Anil Dash concluded after an experiment where he intentionally did not retweet men for a year on Twitter.[21]

3. Call out and report harassment that you see online, even when it is not directed at you.

4. Be more thoughtful in the images that you select for use on your own social media or website. Seek alternatives if the professional images available are only of white people, or people of color are shown in stereotypical or negative ways.

5. Stay informed on how technology companies are treating their workers and users. When I learned about one ride-sharing company's refusal to address its sexual harassment issue, I started using alternatives. If you can find alternatives run by women of color, all the better! I have also stopped using and have encouraged my loved ones to rethink using platforms that willfully spread misinformation and disinformation.

6. Communicate with your lawmakers to engage in the greater regu-
    lation of big technology companies. Focus on greater regulation on
    privacy issues as well as against harassment, and misinformation.

7. As remote and hybrid work arrangements have become the norm
    for many of us, we must ensure that the people we work with and
    manage have the technology access they need to be successful.
    Moreover, while remote work has created new opportunities for
    inclusion, like allowing people to participate who may have pre-
    viously been excluded by geography, it has also resulted in some
    biases and allowed exclusionary practices to take new forms. One
    example is when people who have status dominate online meet-
    ings, likely because they can't rely on behavioral cues during
    in-person meetings. The intentionally inclusive leader will priori-
    tize adapting to new technologies to ensure that they're used to
    include, not exclude.

If all of us take personal responsibility by being active and engaged
in creating the technology industry (from within and/or as customers), we can work toward a future that is powerfully innovative and
intentionally inclusive. We can design a future in which women of
color can be technology leaders and creators, and can use technology
to share ideas as well as connect to build community and movements
without the fear of online harassment. Most of all, we can build a
future in which technology is distributed equally so that everyone
has access—one in which factual, fair information is the norm, not
the exception.

I'm betting on a collaborative, cocreated future that is diverse,
equitable, and inclusive. Won't you join me in working toward it?

■   ■   ■

Reflect on my recommendations above on your role in creating
inclusive technology as a user.

What is one thing that you could do to take action today? Write it down here:

10

Inclusion in the Global Market

There's really no such thing as the "voiceless." There are only the deliberately silenced, or the preferably unheard.

—Arundhati Roy

Ruby Manaulo walked into a restaurant in Madrid, Spain, ready to celebrate a big win for the Switzerland-based multinational company where she worked. The restaurant had been reserved just for the leadership team, consisting of twenty men and five women, including herself.

Manaulo, who requested anonymity, is a Black Frenchwoman who was born in Cameroon. She was the only woman of color present, and almost everyone else was white.

The man slated to be the company's next chief information officer arrived at the restaurant just after her. He walked around the table, greeting every person one by one. As is customary in Swiss French culture, he kissed the cheeks of the four white women and shook hands with all the men. Once he shook the hands of the man on Manaulo's right, he looked at her, ignored her, and went to kiss the cheek of the white woman on Manaulo's left.

"I was completely astonished. I thought I must be dreaming," she tells me.

Manaulo's manager, a white Swiss man who was at the bar getting a drink, witnessed the exchange and rushed over to verify what he saw: that Manaulo had been rudely snubbed in front of all her colleagues.

"I told him, 'Now you've seen it with your own eyes. I don't exaggerate or lie about the discrimination I experience,'" she says. She had brought up multiple instances of facing racism at work in the past to him, but was usually brushed off, and told that she was overreacting or imagining things.

Manaulo knew that while the leader's behavior was outright racism, the fact that not one of her peers in that restaurant stood up for her was just as painful. It was yet another illustration that she would never be valued as one of the team.

Racism has shown up in other painful ways in all of Manaulo's work experiences. While her project deliverables always exceeded objective expectations, her promotions were either delayed by years or outright denied after years of being promised them. In her professional experience spanning multiple cities in France and Switzerland, she has yet to find a work culture in which Black women are made to feel welcome.

In 2015, Manaulo became Emilie's manager as a result of her taking on additional responsibilities to lay the groundwork for a promotion that she was vying for. Emilie was a white Frenchwoman with whom she developed a friendship alongside her professional relationship. Initially, all was cordial. But after two months, Emilie started disparaging Manaulo as a "bad manager" behind her back. When Manaulo asked Emilie for direct feedback and examples of her management failures, Emilie had none. Instead, she became defensive and publicly shouted in the office that Manaulo was "aggressive." Manaulo quickly began de-escalating the situation, knowing that as a Black woman, she would be perceived in a negative light if she defended herself.

Determined to have this matter resolved officially, she went to her manager to initiate a mediated discussion with Emilie with HR present. But her manager discouraged Manaulo from this, citing that it would impact the case they were building for her promotion.

"Looking back, that was a huge mistake. I had already been waiting for a promotion for two years, and was told to keep doing my work and that my manager would make sure I would get recognized internally," she says. "I did everything I could to deliver in advance of deadlines, keeping quiet when I saw men who were hired after me getting promoted before me. But the promotion never came."

Months later, Emilie got the first-mover advantage by reporting Manaulo to HR and accusing her of poor management. Manaulo painstakingly collected evidence to prove that she wasn't in the wrong, including multiple examples from other white colleagues that she was a competent manager. Emilie resigned soon after, and Manaulo was relieved that the matter was finally resolved.

Unfortunately, it came back to haunt her with a vengeance. Manaulo was summoned, months after Emilie had already left the organization, to a two-hour meeting with a team called "global investigations." The meeting turned into a six-hour interrogation in a windowless room where she was asked to "confess" to how she treated Emilie, and was repeatedly manipulated into believing that her team had turned against her and that others—not just Emilie—had lodged complaints against her. She had never heard of complaints about her management from other team members. When she responded by asking for evidence, for specific instances and the names of colleagues who had complained about her, nothing was offered. She later learned that one of the investigators was formerly with the KGB and used interrogation tactics on her.

Her interviewers were gaslighting her—emotionally manipulating her to question her own recollection of events and her feelings. So deep was their gaslighting that she began questioning her own sanity after the interrogation. And for years after, Manaulo was so traumatized by the experience that she couldn't enter rooms without windows.

"I left the meeting after 9 p.m. For days after, I couldn't sleep or eat. My sister became so worried about me, she forced me to see a doctor." She was diagnosed with depression and post-traumatic stress disorder.

Manaulo's abuse continued even after she was fired while on leave. The compay refused to release the correct version of her "employment reference letter," a document that future employers would need to employ her in Switzerland, thereby jeopardizing future job opportunities for her.

"To this day, I don't know what I did to deserve this, except that I was a Black, ambitious woman leader," she tells me.

Her heartbreaking story, factored in with so many others, highlights pervasive discrimination that women of color can face, no matter which country they are employed in.

Taking a Global Approach to DEI

The inclusive leader will understand that there are specific issues and challenges to inclusion across geographic and cultural borders. No doubt, any attempt to capture the nuances of DEI that are evenly applicable across the globe will fall short. But there exist some clear overlaps between how women from marginalized and underestimated backgrounds experience the workplace in countries around the world.

The phrase "woman of color" itself doesn't translate globally. Yet both misogyny and racism are global issues, and the entire world has been touched in some way by our intertwined histories of Western colonization, slavery, and more recently, neocolonial capitalism.

Like the socioeconomic dominance of white women in the West, we can identify dominant-group women in other parts by assessing which women generally comprise higher-income and wealth groups, have more access to education, and are better represented in leadership positions as well as favored in that country or region's workplaces. By contrast, nondominant-group women overwhelmingly experience economic insecurity or even poverty, higher rates of gender-based violence, and lack of access to education or representation in corporate workplaces, and in general are disadvantaged in workplaces.

A quick and incomplete list of examples of women from marginalized communities include Dalit and other lower-caste Hindu women in India, Muslim women in non-Islamic countries, Afro-Latinx and Indigenous women in Latin America, Indigenous women in Southeast Asia, Aboriginal women in Australia, immigrants (documented and undocumented), refugee women, and darker-skinned women, who experience colorism. Identifying the underestimated women in any community in a given region or country helps us develop an intersectional and context-specific approach to global inclusion.

This isn't reserved just for those of us who work or manage teams outside the United States or western Europe. "Many people within Western workplaces have roots elsewhere, whether it's where they were born, where they were raised, where their families are from, and the cultures they relate to," says global diversity and inclusion practitioner Diya Khanna, who has worked across North America, Europe, and Asia.

Looking at the Past to Draw Broad Connections Globally

Inclusion on purpose requires leaders to first understand the barriers that hold back the advancement of any society's most marginalized women.

Social hierarchies dictated by gender and ethnic/racial divides have existed for centuries. The caste system in India, where my ancestors are from, was a hierarchy dictated by the interpretation of an ancient Hindu text. It still uniquely influences the career of any person in India even today, centuries after the system was first derived to "regulate society." Work and advancement opportunities are allocated to Hindu Indians based on this system. At the top of this social hierarchy are Brahmins, who can achieve coveted jobs such as teachers and priests. At the bottom of the hierarchy are Dalits, translated into English as "outcastes"—once called "untouchables"—who were assigned to clean latrines and streets.

As in any patriarchal society, cisgender men (Brahmins) are at the top of this artificial pyramid, and Dalit women were—and to date, are—deeply discriminated against. While India has struggled to fully engage women in its workforce, the intersection of caste and gender still casts a long shadow on an Indian woman's work and life experiences. Upper-caste women who seek professional careers are highly preferred over lower-caste Dalit women.

New research has shown that while the caste system was prescriptive for centuries in India, it was not as rigid until the British colonization of India.[1]

The British colonizers began using the hierarchy to assign other rights—not just professions—such as landownership and self-governance, based on caste and religion. It fortified a system of discrimination that would alter the course of India's destiny and has had consequences on people of all castes even in modern India.

Caste discrimination was legally prohibited in India in 1950, fourteen years before the Civil Rights Act was passed in the United States to ban racial discrimination. Seventy years later, its legacy endures. Oxfam finds that inequality in employment opportunities for nondominant-caste women is a significant contributor to poverty and social inequality in India.[2]

This caste hierarchy is also being exported across borders. A growing number of Dalit Indians who work as engineers in Silicon Valley are surfacing the discrimination that they face today from other Indians at top US tech companies. "We have had to weather demeaning insults to our background and that we have achieved our jobs solely due to affirmative action. It is exhausting," wrote thirty Dalit female engineers in a statement published in the *Washington Post* in October 2020. They are seeking to include caste as a protected category against discrimination in the United States.[3]

Does the caste struggle in India sound familiar? Perhaps you can identify an unofficial caste hierarchy in your own country with similar markers.

Pulitzer prizewinning US writer Isabel Wilkerson deftly draws parallels between the caste hierarchy in India and the anti-Black racism prevalent in the United States in her seminal book *Caste*. She even uses "casteism," not racism, to define the expectations, laws, and customs that have held, and continue to hold, Black Americans to a "fixed place" in the United States. An unofficial caste system, she posits, has prevented the social mobility for Black Americans that has been readily available to white Americans and newer immigrants.[4]

"A caste system is an artificial construction, a fixed and embedded ranking of human value that sets the presumed supremacy of one group against the presumed inferiority of other groups on the basis of ancestry and often immutable traits, traits that would be neutral in the abstract but are ascribed life-and-death meaning in a hierarchy favoring the dominant caste whose forebears designed it," Wilkerson notes.[5]

Every society globally has a caste system—a hierarchy that sorts communities of people into artificially engineered categories to enforce power. These hierarchies normalize and justify some people getting access to resources, opportunities, and power, and others being denied them. If you cannot easily identify it in your own country, assume that you're somewhere at the top of this artificial hierarchy. Like with the issue of privilege that I explored in chapter 1, if you haven't had to ever think about it, assume that you're benefiting from the hierarchy.

Wilkerson's interweaving of the racial hierarchy in the United States (where she describes European-ancestry white people as the dominant caste, Asians and Latinos as the middle caste, and Black and Native Americans as the subordinate caste) is applicable throughout the world.

The caste system in your country will usually be signaled by which communities are the most prosperous, contrasted with those who have experienced generational wealth disparities. Also spend time reflecting on which hierarchies have existed for a long time and which are newer (such as discrimination against newer immigrants). Ask yourself, How are these different hierarches reinforced in the workplace?

Without understanding the origins of the hierarchy along with how they influence all people even in modern societies and workplaces, we will not be able to fully include women from underestimated groups.

Examining the Bias That Has Bolstered Sexism and Racism Globally

Globally, women from underestimated communities experience more discrimination because of the intersection between their gender and other marginalized identities. Dominant-group women in non-Western countries, while harmed by patriarchal societies and workplaces, are privileged by their proximity to dominant-group men—like white women in the United States and western Europe.

In Singapore, I've seen presumptive biological differences carelessly bandied about to explain why local Indians and Malays (the latter who are largely Muslim and face religious discrimination too) do not have the innate ability to succeed like the Chinese locals. To be clear, there are no scientific bases for these claims, but Singapore-born Indian and Malay women continue to face the double jeopardy of racial/religious and gender bias in the workplace. Singaporean Chinese and white Western expatriate women as well as even newer, wealthier immigrants from other countries, including India, largely do not. As ever, intersectionality matters.

Are women everywhere at a disadvantage due to their gender? Absolutely. Patriarchal attitudes have been bolstered by long-standing—although now largely disproven—science. Biased science relied on exaggerating slight biological differences between the sexes to justify gender bias in the workplace, according to Angela Saini's book *Inferior*.[6] Sexist attitudes about how capable women inherently are continue to create barriers for women in developed countries. These unscientific claims can be even more harmful for women in poorer countries.

Biased science has been used to justify why men are in higher-paid "analytic" positions and women are in lower-paid caregiving work. Presumed inherent sex differences have also been used to justify why girls should not receive an education, or as comprehensive an education as boys.

Saini's research shows us that the biological differences between the sexes are so minimal, it really makes no sense to assign education or career prospects based on sex. Sex differences are artificially exaggerated to "keep women in their place," Saini tells me. It's a narrative bolstered by biased research, which has often allowed us to let power continue unchecked.

The intersection of gender, which is a social, not biological construct, and other marginalized identities exacerbates oppression for women of color (or nondominant women where this categorization doesn't apply). In fact, many dominant-group women believe that they are inherently superior to nondominant-group, underestimated women. They can frequently even be complicit in allocating dangerous or undesirable lower-paid work to them. That's why the demands for women's equality and progress are usually loudest from dominant-group women—whether white feminists in the West, upper-caste women in India, or the lighter-skinned women of color in other countries who are most often the face of these movements. Many movements do not address the urgent challenges that underestimated women face, such as engaging in high-risk, low-paid work, or the associated risks of physical, mental, and sexual harm.

Sometimes it's even dominant-group feminists that fight to keep these narratives of sex differences alive. "It's easier to assume that there is some biological basis that can be more difficult to challenge, even within feminist circles," says Saini. "There are many feminists who do believe that, for example, women are more empathetic or that we're more nurturing, . . . that we have qualities that men don't have, and also that men are naturally more violent or have negative qualities that women don't have. And that's quite deep rooted."

Biased science has been applied even more dangerously throughout history to justify racial discrimination, violence, and even genocide. After *Inferior*, Saini wrote *Superior*, which details the horrifying race science that perpetrators used to justify slavery and the Holocaust.[7] International communities of mainstream policy makers and scientists collectively decided to remove the concept of race as a biological construct after the Second World War (it has still continued on in fringe communities), but Saini and other scholars have tracked the frightening comeback of scientific racism into the mainstream. It is gaining momentum in politicized white nationalist movements in the United States and across Europe.

I'll restate this: race and gender are social constructs; neither have genetic or scientific basis. Yet in most parts of the world, the belief in the inherent genetic differences in the abilities of men and women, and between the races, has allowed many to discriminate based on race and gender. Humans are 99.9 percent the same, and there are frequently greater genetic variances between people who are categorized as the same race than between the races.

We will never, I hope, return to the race science used to justify slavery, but a part of the belief that people are better suited to certain careers, or less capable to succeed, based on their race and gender still persists. It can be seemingly positive, such as when I'm told "Indians are naturally good at mathematics." This message, however, reinforces a white supremacist hierarchy that pits one underestimated group against another: "If Indians are good at mathematics, we'll hire them, not _____ group, which is bad at mathematics." Such a statement puts undue pressure on people to conform to a stereotype and shuns those who don't conform. In the end, any race- or gender-based presumptive qualities are harmful, and unscientific. Yet the confluence of racism in our history and the biased science to justify differences has a long-standing legacy that impacts our workplaces today.

Most leaders are deeply uncomfortable with confronting histories that paint their communities in a bad light.

This is where the work for leaders who want to be inclusive on purpose begins. You must understand and even confront historical and contemporary systems of oppression, no matter how uncomfortable it may be. You must examine and disrupt how they may show up in your contemporary life and workplace.

Serious harm is perpetuated when we don't. Until today, eminent members of Western society have made claims that Black people are intellectually inferior, from University of Pennsylvania law professor Amy Wax to disgraced University of Cambridge historian David Starkey.[8] We must confront the reality that scientific racism, though thoroughly disproved, has endured through centuries. It is rampant globally too. Leaders must thoroughly investigate and dispute claims of biological inferiority when they encounter them. Casual statements such as "girls are naturally not good at math" and "Asian women are naturally submissive, not leaders" are biased, incorrect statements that any inclusive leader should immediately discount.

Left unchecked, these narratives only reinforce long-held ethnic, racial, gender, and other divisions in society, and exacerbate the divide felt by the most marginalized of women in any given society.

Worldwide, for women from underestimated groups, bias has snowballed over the course of history, Saini tells me. "There are a lot of stereotypes around what women are capable of, and there are lots of stereotypes around what different racial groups are capable of. In women of color, all those things get compounded together."

Considering together Wilkerson's scholarship on caste hierarchies and Saini's on the biased science used to justify sexism and racism, it is no surprise that women of color, particularly Black women, continue to suffer such deep barriers to inclusion and progress. Using biological differences to rank people can be seductive. Every society uses them to justify why some groups are able to progress and others lag so that privileged individuals don't have to investigate their role in perpetuating discrimination. It's just wrong.

How Colorism Impacts Women in the Global Workplace

Colorism, the bias against darker-skin individuals, is another type of bias that the globally inclusive leader must familiarize themselves with so they can identify and root it out. Colorism is an enduring vestige of colonialism and white dominance around the globe. It disproportionately harms women of color and privileges white-skinned women. The term was coined by US novelist Alice Walker, who first used it in 1983 to refer not only to the preference for lighter skin between different communities but even how lighter skin is privileged within the same communities. While the majority of research on colorism (also called skin tone bias) has been conducted among Black people in the United States—where discrimination cases are high—it is a global phenomenon that disadvantages darker-skinned women in accessing job opportunities, career advancement, and societal acceptance.

Colorism impacts the lives of women around the world, but especially in Asian countries. From China to India, South Korea to

Japan, the skin-lightening industry is a multibillion-dollar one, and lighter-skinned women there are considered more desirable. Growing up in Singapore as a lighter-skinned Indian woman certainly granted me more acceptance in society, but I was never considered light enough, finding myself often accosted by beauty counter salespeople attempting to sell me skin-lightening products. While critics have urged cosmetic companies to stop profiting off discrimination and instead widen accepted norms of beauty, we have only scratched the surface of the depth of colorism in the workplace.

The biggest challenge that I see to addressing it is first even spotting this insidious and covert form of bias.

"In a skewed, unequal global economy, it is important to understand how the experiences of white or light-skinned migrants compare to darker-skinned migrants," writes University of the Witwatersrand research associate Melissa Tandiwe Myambo in an article about how the experience of immigrants in new countries can differ by skin color. "In South Africa, as in India, whiteness or lightness often denotes power and prestige. When a migrant enters the new society, the local population tends to 'read' the migrant's skin tone and then assign it positive or negative associations. Thus to understand the migrant experience, we must understand these associations and stereotypes."[9]

Scant research exists on how it impacts the careers of darker-skinned women outside the United States, but American studies have shown that it can create wage and job opportunity penalties. The only academic study that I could find that specifically looked at colorism in India not only found how detrimental this bias is for darker-skinned women's career achievements but that it harmed darker-skinned Indian women's own career aspirations too. Darker-skinned women frequently self-select out of applying for roles or promotions, or find their own self-confidence eroding once in the job. But leaders must not expect women to fix this and instead must proactively address colorism to create more inclusive environments. "They must support recruitment, selection, and promotion policies and practices that ensure equality for women of all skin tone," authors Cynthia Sims and Malar Hirudayaraj write. "Workplace issues that result from unearned privilege and the power it grants certain employees in specific fields must be discussed more deliberately and openly so that it is no longer a taboo subject that is passively accepted and silently perpetuated."[10]

A Nuanced Approach to How Immigration Impacts Women in the Workplace

Immigrant women face outsized challenges to inclusion, and leaders must familiarize themselves with these challenges in order to address them.

One German study finds that "women with a Turkish migration background are less likely to be invited for an interview, and the level of discrimination increases substantially if the applicant wears a headscarf. The results suggest that immigrant women who wear a headscarf suffer discrimination based on multiple stigmas related to ethnicity and religion."[11]

Against rising Islamophobia globally, professional Muslim women confront mounting challenges, whether they're immigrant women or a religious minority in their native countries. Black Muslim women in the United States whom I interviewed for this book also reported having significantly negative workplace experiences, compounded by race, gender, and religion. The migration journeys, policies within a given nation toward immigrants, and exclusionary attitudes of the locals toward immigrants in general all impact how immigrant women of color will be treated by employers. Again, taking an intersectional approach to inclusion is key. Some immigrants will arrive to the shores of another country with a multitude of intersecting identities that privilege them, such as socioeconomic, language, and even skin color privilege. Their experience will be distinctly different from those who immigrate with less-privileged identities.

Immigrants with socioeconomic or white privilege (sometimes called "expatriates") may be able to advance easily in Western workplaces, or push back against bias without worry of losing their immigration status or position in society. Their experience of "success" should not be mistaken for the experience of all immigrants to that country. For example, as a Singaporean immigrant to the United States with economic and education privilege, my right to apply for permanent citizenship was expedited. My experience is not the norm. Many immigrant women of color are stuck in decades-long immigration processes, beholden to a job for fear of being deported. The privileges granted to me—such as the ability to leave exclusionary workplaces or choose to work for an employer not because I rely on them to sponsor my visa—is the exception, not the norm for most immigrant women of color.

So take a nuanced approach to the challenges that immigrant women may face related to inclusion and corporate advancement opportunities. Being an immigrant can be a significant disadvantage for women of color who immigrate from less economically developed countries, and may find impediments to being hired or retained. Other immigrant women (usually white immigrant women) from Western countries that have been glorified for their sophistication, like France, may have a positive experience.

In my interviews, Black women whose ancestors were formerly enslaved would clearly make the distinction that newer African immigrants to the United States still had more opportunities to progress in the workplace compared with them. This is because Black immigrant women outside the United States grow up without the specter of the generational barriers to housing, education, and jobs that haunts the vast majority of Black Americans who have descended from enslaved ancestors.

All the Black immigrant women whom I interviewed reported experiencing racism once they arrived in the US workforce. But the Black women whose ancestral lineage was so inextricably bound up with having enslaved ancestors reported having to navigate centuries of oppression, such as racist policies that denied them secure housing, neighborhoods with good schools, and access to quality health care. All this impacted their ability to amass intergenerational wealth, which in turn blocked their ability to enter and progress within the workforce. This reality also prompts some African immigrants to distinguish themselves from Black Americans—a familiar phenomenon to me when I consider how Indian immigrants to Singapore distance themselves from the marginalized Singaporean Indian community so as to enjoy greater economic and career privileges.

Identifying this distinction—particularly the experience of Black American descendants of formerly enslaved people compared with all other women of color in the United States—is a necessary examination for the inclusive leader. Many newer immigrants come to the United States fully understanding that the rules of progress in society and especially the workforce are inextricably linked to upholding the US racial hierarchy. Indeed, many immigrants' careers and futures depend on upholding white-centric systems of power as well as anti-Blackness.

That's not true just in the United States. Immigrants the world over quickly understand that to progress, they must play nice with the dominant group, while eschewing solidarity with the underestimated and oppressed.

While new immigrants everywhere can struggle with assimilation in a new culture and feeling included in the workplace, the socioeconomic and other privileges that they enter a new country with can uniquely impact the availability of career opportunities in their new countries. The inclusive leader will not simply look to the economic progress of certain communities—particularly those that have chosen to immigrate, and enter with educational and other privileges—and use the same brush to paint the experience of all immigrant women of color in the workplace.

Questions to reflect on include:

- What are the general social, education, and economic privileges or barriers experienced by this group?
- What are the contemporary and historical barriers faced by this community, such as colonialism, slavery, civil war, and religious persecution?
- Where are the gaps in my own understanding about communities different than my own?
- How can I bridge these gaps?
- What is fact and what are my own assumptions about immigrants from a different culture?

As every chapter in this book emphasizes, no community is a monolith and sweeping generalizations do more harm than good. Instead, the inclusive leader will seek out more context, contemporary and historical, center voices from the community, and approach inclusion efforts intentionally and with nuance.

Below are my recommendations to get you started on taking a global approach to inclusion.

Cultivate Cultural Humility, Not Cultural Competency

Simply applying a US- or Western-centric approach to DEI without local customization will not be successful. Instead, leaders must seek out local cultural context in the global marketplace. Cultivate cultural humility, not cultural competence, advises Khanna.

For years, cultural competency has been hailed as the standard to becoming more proficient in the way that other cultures operate, but more racial equity practitioners have begun questioning its efficacy in inclusive engagement, especially as it originates within the dominant culture and Eurocentric thinking. Cultural competency refers to learning about other cultures while retaining the idea that your culture is dominant. Cultural competency allows stereotypes to proliferate like "people from non-Western cultures are always late" or "we don't discuss business over work meetings in China." The belief is that the nondominant culture's way of doing things may be considered exasperating and perhaps even exotic, or a quirk to accommodate, not something that one could respect or learn from.

Cultivating cultural humility means "approaching this work with the premise that we don't know everything—and so the goal is to invest resources in the experts on the ground who have the lived experience," Khanna says. This also means familiarizing yourself with and even deferring to local customs, laws, and practices where relevant. It means acknowledging that while we may have a bias toward thinking our culture's way is best, we can approach a different culture with a mindset of learning and growth—that we are not always the experts.

While doing business in an Islamic country, for example, cultural competency would lead us to sweepingly assume that no women would shake hands with a man. Cultural humility would guide us to wait and observe the specific practices in different countries, work cultures, and local environments, and then adapt to the situation. Cultural competency is broad and fixed; cultural humility allows us to have nuance and flexibility. It prompts us to observe visual and body language cues, not just verbal ones.

Cultural humility is particularly useful for leaders working with nondominant-group women, no matter where in the world they are. Even one team based in the United States could be comprised of a number of immigrant women of color, second- or third-generation Americans, and US-born citizens who represent a plethora of religions, cultures, and languages. Every inclusive leader must make the effort to ask the correct pronunciation of a colleague's name if it's unfamiliar, practice it (in private), and demonstrate an unwavering commitment to get it right. Cultural humility reminds us that all names are meaningful to their owners; stumbling through an unfamiliar name, or worse, asking someone to anglicize their name for your comfort, is unacceptable.

Lastly, don't let assumptions about a country or non-Western culture's work environment cloud your judgment so that you fall prey to biases, particularly about the imagined plight of non-Western women compared with Western women in the workplace. One only needs to look at the fact that countries around the world, from Bangladesh to Liberia, Brazil to Sudan, have had women heads of state. The United States has still not had a female president to date.

Customize and Cocreate DEI and Culture Initiatives Locally

Recognize that "inclusion" can mean different things in different parts of the world. In individualistic societies in the Western world, the concept encourages us to magnify and celebrate the differences that we bring to an organization. In more collectivist societies, like countries in Asia, standing out for being different may not be a positive thing. I have found that the term "belonging" often resonates more deeply in non-Western cultures.

It's therefore necessary to bring context-specific DEI strategies to your global offices rather than what India-based Ruha Shadab calls "a copy-paste from the west strategy." Shadab transitioned from being a physician to starting Led By Foundation to develop Muslim women leaders in India after observing a critical need for role models and support for professional Muslim women in corporate India. While the country's multinational corporations have "started having conversations about women, there's very little of diversity and inclusion frameworks that originate in India," she says. One US organization with a large presence in India simply took its US DEI strategy and broadly began applying it to India, she recalls.

One of this organization's policies focused on including veterans in the workforce, but Indian military veterans do not face the same workplace discrimination that they do in the United States, notes Shadab. Instead, the organization's leaders would make more meaningful progress by assessing local issues and barriers to inclusion and diversity such as faith-based initiatives.

Leaders looking to engage in a global DEI strategy must spend time getting to know the local marketplace and what may constitute challenges to fully engaging the workplace. Finding local studies, media articles, and experts to talk to should guide any strategy for local offices. Specifically evaluate, *Who constitutes the nondominant groups in this country, and what are some barriers holding back their representation and advancement here?*

Do this by conducting focus groups with local teams to find out whether employees feel like they belong to the community and organization. Inquire about any obstacles to their progress there. A more psychologically safe way to do this may also be through conducting country-specific online surveys or bringing in facilitators outside the organization. In addition, you can leverage the expertise of headquarters-based ERGs to recommend local office approach and culture. Larger organizations in the United States tend to have Asian, Afro-Caribbean, and Latinx ERGs, which may be a place to start, particularly so as to inform cultural and professionalism norms. Seek advice specifically on which in-country groups generally constitute the dominant group and which ones are historically marginalized. Seek to learn the barriers faced by women in these groups.

Accordingly, adapt your company norms, which were likely created when the organization was small and localized. As the company grows, so does the responsibility to tailor company principles and values to concepts that are easily recognized and practiced by a global employee base. Some norms simply do not translate and can end up harming nondominant-group women. One US-headquartered company places much emphasis on being able to disagree at work and even openly challenge your superiors. The organization makes hiring and advancement decisions with this company principle as a central guideline. This norm works well ... for white men at the organization, multiple employees tell me. But it is especially harmful to women of color even in the US locations, especially when considering the stereotypes that they have to deal with, as I've covered in previous chapters. When the company was expanding aggressively across Asia, it could have benefited from understanding how from a cultural standpoint, disagreeing with your superiors would not fly. Moreover, leaders at the organization should have spent time familiarizing themselves with the prevailing cultural norms and adapted the principle to be context specific.

Practice Intersectionality on a Global Scale

Global organizations must stop focusing on policies simply geared toward "women," and instead "create policies and strategies based on the intersections that transect gender, like ethnicity, sexuality, caste, and disability," which are relevant not only in Western countries but even more so outside them, says Snehanjali Chrispal, an Australia-based academic who studies casteism and other forms of discrimination in the Indian workplace.

As explored previously, the same measures of what constitutes leadership and confidence in white men do not apply unilaterally to women of color. This is even more relevant in the global context, where people from other cultures are often not socialized to operate with the outward confidence and self-assurance of North Americans.

For nondominant-group women who may have experienced multiple layers of societal oppression, this could be even more pronounced.

As leaders begin to manage more global teams, or indeed even global employees in Western offices, it's incumbent on them to understand the local customs and norms that contribute to an employee's communication style. A quiet woman may not be lacking confidence; she just may be processing during a meeting and follow up with ideas in another way.

When managing a global team or employees in other countries, recognize that professionalism and communication styles are typically Eurocentric, and frequently set nondominant-group women up for failure if they're measured against those standards. As a team of Stanford researchers advise in a *Fast Company* article, "Whenever you feel the urge to correct a behavior or appearance as 'nonprofessional,' pause. Ask yourself, 'Is this ineffective *or* different?' and 'Can I expand my expectations to include this?' Instead of dismissing what you see, try to understand why you are having the reaction and learn to make room for it."[12]

Without intentionality and intersectionality, even existing policies can propagate bias across boards. Facebook Inc. sought my counsel on inclusive hiring practices when recruiting for a global advisory "Oversight Board" to inform controversial decisions about content on its platform. I made two main recommendations to ensure that the board could include more nondominant-group women outside Western countries. First, I suggested that the firm ensure that interview questions were locally and culturally appropriate by engaging local experts to review the questions; this differed from the company's standard process. Second, I advised that the firm ensure that all board members would get paid equally, no matter where they were in the world, as they were expected to complete the same duties. This also was new to Facebook, which like most companies, adjusted employee salaries by location—a discriminatory practice. The organization had not considered these ideas before our conversation. By including my input, the final board consisted of a number of prominent nondominant-group women around the globe.

Center the Voices and Expertise
of Nondominant-Group Women

Gender mainstreaming, the concept of centering women's experiences and concerns in decisions, is not new; it was formally introduced in 1995 at the United Nations' fourth conference on women. Gender mainstreaming is "the process of assessing the implications for women and men of any planned action, including legislation, policies or programs, in all areas and at all levels. It is a strategy for making women's as well as men's concerns and experiences an integral dimension of the design, implementation, monitoring and evaluation of policies and programs in all political, economic and societal spheres so that women and men benefit equally and inequality is not perpetuated. The ultimate goal is to achieve gender equality."[13]

What is less common, and has been my emphasis throughout this book, is to center the experiences, voices, and expertise of *nondominant-group* women. Women of color have too often been excluded from making decisions that impact their own lives and communities, and that's why the ultimate goal to achieve gender equality globally still lags, close to three decades later.

Centering the experience of nondominant-group women will ensure inclusive and equitable outcomes in a variety of sectors. Technology and health care are top of mind.

We can see why applying gender mainstreaming is necessary in solving worldwide poverty and health disparities. Large global health initiatives have stumbled when they haven't taken women's voices into consideration. Vaccine distribution is one example where even while the science and technology to deliver vaccines in formerly colonized countries advances, vaccines don't always get distributed effectively. Gender mainstreaming is key; without addressing the sociocultural factors that hamper women who make a household's health decisions, the science alone cannot ensure that the vaccines reach those who need them the most.

Gavi, a global vaccine alliance, realized that without training and deploying female health workers in its distribution strategy, vaccines would not reach enough families. Due to prevailing cultural norms, women were refusing to let male health workers enter their homes to vaccinate them. Households covered by a female health worker were 15 percent more likely to have vaccinated children than other households.[14] When you center the voices of those most impacted by a decision, you are most likely to create outcomes that benefit even those in the majority. Even the Western world grappled with the immense inequality in how richer, white people disproportionately received the COVID-19 vaccine, compared with poorer people of color, who were at much higher risk of being exposed to the disease.

My recommendation is not just to apply a gender lens to strategy and policy design but ensure that this lens is intersectional too, and includes the impact on and voices from communities of marginalized women.

Taking this one step further, more Western leaders would benefit from adopting the attitude that there is much to learn from the wisdom of women outside Western countries. During the coronavirus pandemic, a striking picture of global female leadership began to emerge. As Western countries struggled to contain the pandemic, a number of women-led countries, particularly in Southeast Asia ones such as South Korea and Taiwan, emerged as especially well equipped to deal with it.

A study into 194 countries in the first three months of the pandemic found that female-led countries saw lower infection and fatality rates when compared with male-led countries.[15]

A number of non-Western women leaders were praised for acting decisively, such as Bangladeshi prime minister Sheikh Hasina and Taiwanese president Tsai Ing-Wen, and urging that there be more testing early on, such as H. E. Amira Elfadil Mohammed Elfadil, the social affairs commissioner of the African Union, and Aminata Touré, president of Senegal's Economic, Social, and Environmental

Council. While there was much more global media praise for Jacinda Ardern, the white female prime minister of New Zealand, there is no doubt that nonwhite women also displayed remarkable leadership in the time of crisis. More Western male leaders would have benefited from learning from these women.

Recently I learned of a start-up geared around providing financial services to underbanked women around the world. The start-up's website boasted that its service was built "for women by women," but when I clicked through to the leadership team, the cofounders of the company were a white European man and woman, who had gathered a largely white, European female leadership team. Their target audience at launch was lower-income female entrepreneurs in Asian countries. While I could see the business and social potential behind the idea, I couldn't help but wonder, Why had the cofounders not brought on women from the countries that they were hoping to serve? Surely there were a number of qualified women who were already trying to solve the barriers to financial services access within their own communities! Why not partner with them? Wouldn't their cultural acumen and proximity to the communities that they were trying to serve be an asset? These are questions that more leaders with privilege should be asking in every situation:

- Whose perspectives should be here but aren't?
- Am I always the right person to lead an initiative, or are there women who are often overlooked yet eminently qualified to lead?
- Could I better support this not from the front but instead by taking a learning and support role?

Taking a globally inclusive approach means making room for the expertise, wisdom, and leadership of nondominant-group women. It means making room for them to lead and then stepping out of the way.

We cannot solve the complex, worldwide problems that we're currently facing without cultivating cultural humility and dismantling long-existing oppressive social hierarchies, many of which stifle the innovation and growth of too many women around the world. With purpose and intention, I believe that we can write a different story, with global women of color as the protagonists.

■   ■   ■

KEY REFLECTIONS

1. Which cultures do you most interact with, outside your own? Can you determine who are the dominant- and nondominant-group women within them?

2. How do race and/or caste hierarchies play out in your society? How are they reinforced in your workplace?

3. Does the concept of cultural humility resonate in your life? What are ways that you can cultivate it?

4. What do global DEI efforts look like at your organization? If they aren't customized to be location specific, what can you do to change this?

5. What is one thing that you could do to take action today? Write it down here:

Conclusion:
The Future Is Ours to Create

In January 2021, Kamala Devi Harris was sworn in as the vice president of the United States. Harris, a Black and Indian woman with immigrant parents, became the first woman and person of color elected to hold the office in the 208 years since it was created.

Her ascent is a testament to the ideals of opportunity and justice that many globally have looked to the United States to model. It restored some hope to what drew me, like millions of immigrants, to the United States after we had painfully endured a hostile and xenophobic administration.

Harris's first and middle names are *different, unusual, and unfamiliar*, and her skin color is like mine. I can never accurately capture the full meaning of her success for *all* women of color who have aspired to the highest levels of leadership, but were never shown a possible pathway to get there.

But the journey is far from complete.

It was a bold choice to have a woman of color on the ticket in the first place, and even more so given that the opposition party ran on status quo messaging—preserving the homogeneity of white male leadership, threatened by "others." Harris commended President Joseph Biden for having "the audacity to break one of the most substantial barriers . . . and select a woman as his vice president." In any society that prides itself on fairness and equality, a woman of color leader is a strength, not a risk.

As I continue advocating for inclusive, equitable workplaces, I am heartened to see growing acceptance from male and white leaders that sexism and racism does in fact exist. Without naming it, we cannot conquer it. I see more commitment from these leaders to push for progress. When I first started speaking up about strategies to advance gender equality at work, I was expected to present mountains of data to make my case. People would publicly dispute my claims of an existing gender and racial gap after keynote presentations. White organizers asked me explicitly to refrain from mentioning "race" or "racism" in my work.

Fortunately our world is changing. The movement for racial justice in 2020 did not just spark a reckoning in the United States but also quickly exported it the world over. For the first time in recent memory, I witnessed a global movement that challenged how the most marginalized, especially women with intersectional identities, are left behind by those in power.

Centuries of oppression persist throughout our societies, and that has reinforced the exclusion faced by women of color in the modern workforce. To move toward action, I turn to Archbishop Desmond Tutu's saying, "If you are neutral in situations of injustice, you have chosen the side of the oppressor." All the stories of the courageous women of color detailed in these pages capture acute racial trauma—not only because of the bias of their perpetrators, but because of the complicity and silence of their peers.

This book is my dedication to women of color. My hope is that it provides them the validation that I once desperately needed. It's not *us* who need to change to fit in. Experiencing everyday bias, the overt and covert racism compounds until even the most driven, qualified woman of color has thwarted ambitions, unable to compete in a rigged system. Women of color already have the grit, ambition, leadership, and coalition-building capabilities that are easily celebrated in their white counterparts. What they need is to have that power and ambition recognized, fueled, and rewarded.

This is precisely why we need all hands on deck. Inclusion on purpose demands that leaders not stand by passively when they see yet another woman of color overlooked and underestimated. It is not nearly enough to condemn bias, but then shrug our shoulders, thinking, *Well that's just how it is*. It requires daily practices to recognize, name, and undo discrimination, knowing that the small actions you take to be inclusive and equitable have the potential to add up to transform the workplace to foster cultures of belonging for all employees. Inclusion is leadership because until we are not becoming a force multiplier for *all* around us, we are not operating at our full capacity as leaders.

Inclusion on purpose is simultaneously internally motivated and action oriented. It requires us to examine in ourselves, *Where could bias be appearing in the way that I show up as a friend, colleague, manager, and leader? What could I do differently?* Only then can we get to work.

It is inherently uncomfortable. It is easier to protest that you are not biased, that you would help advance qualified women of color, if only *they* would reach out for help. But when we don't take personal responsibility to understand and undo barriers that women of color face, we can never actively propel them forward. We become even more the perpetrators of injustice when we choose ignorance over action. The challenge is seeking out that discomfort and perhaps even shame, emboldened by the belief that this is the only way to progress toward a society without exclusion.

Inclusion on purpose is a lifelong practice. It's one worth engaging in. It is the key way to differentiate between average managers and great leaders, between struggling organizations and the ones that are paving the way for our future leaders. The definition of inclusion will continue to evolve as new generations enter the workforce and bring measures of diversity that we may not yet even consider. Adaptability and readiness for these changes is the hallmark of an inclusive leader—to live up to the ideal, daily, that until *everyone* is intentionally included, someone will always be excluded from bringing their whole, authentic selves to work.

Indeed, it is not a "one and done" activity. It does not come from hiring *one* woman of color, or offering the lone or few women of color on your team effective feedback or career sponsorship. It is an ongoing, never-ending practice—akin to practicing antiracism. Being exclusionary *or* inclusive are not onetime activities or even fixed states of being but rather a set of practices that deepen and develop with consistent use.

To begin you must first begin internally. As my BRIDGE framework recommends, **B**e all right with being uncomfortable as this work is not easy. **R**eflect on what you don't know and **I**nvite feedback. Know that **D**efensiveness doesn't help. Normalize **G**rowing from mistakes, and know that you, like everyone, will likely make errors when working toward greater inclusion and equity. That's when the most meaningful change can happen. Most of all, **E**xpect that change takes time.

We must seek out a diversity of people in our social and professional networks. We must make room for women of color to shine and then get out of their way to let them lead. We must normalize asking, *Who is missing from this decision table, and how can we ensure that they are represented?* More leaders benefit from cultivating a reflexive awareness that decisions made without the representation of women of color are not only a missed opportunity for greater success but also perpetuate harm.

As this book has demonstrated, inclusion on purpose requires us to take responsibility for recruiting and advancing women of color. To disrupt affinity bias and work doggedly to fix pay and advancement gaps across the workforce. To ensure psychological safety for women of color by engaging the ADAPT framework: **A**nalyze employee engagement data (disaggregated by race and gender) so that you know how employees are experiencing the workplace. Develop a code of conduct that is widely understood by everyone, specifically laying out what an unbiased and antiracist workplace is. Accepting and celebrating failure is the hallmark of a psychologically safe workplace, and ensures that women of color can take risks and "fail up" like dominant-group team members. Propel and fund ERGs, and leverage the expertise of ERGs for business strategy. Lastly, create Team tenets on DEI; plan in advance how you will address competing priorities. In a globally interconnected world, the inclusive leader will prioritize cultivating cultural humility as well as work toward a future fueled by innovation and technology that is free from bias.

I urge more leaders to internalize how the intersection of gender and race impacts *every* other marginalized experience in the workplace. It is not adequate to only seek out the leadership of white male employees with disabilities. You must, for example, ensure that women of color with disabilities are centered in any accessibility strategy.

The philosophy of *Ubuntu*, the Bantu term that is translated into English as "I am because we are," guides much of my work. I advocate for inclusive and equitable workplaces not *only* because I stand to benefit as a woman of color but because as a human being, I am harmed by injustice that others face too. As many of us are realizing, even discrimination that doesn't directly impact us, still hurts *all* of us. In fact, workplaces that operate with a narrow, outdated definition of leadership exclude not only women of color but even cisgender, straight white men who may not be able to conform to these rigid standards. We all stand to benefit when we all prioritize inclusion on purpose.

Moreover, without each one of us rising up to meet the opportunity of truly creating workplaces that work for all, we are not harnessing the full power of our humanity. Many systems of oppression will perpetuate if we continue to prioritize the wants of the privileged over the needs of the many less privileged.

When we solve for the most marginalized in the workplace, everyone rises and benefits. That's why inclusion on purpose is so powerful—for employees, leaders, and organizations.

Inclusion on Purpose at Scale

So what's next? Redefining power. People with power get to influence which ideas shape the world. Most often they power the ideas of others who look like them, and the cycle continues. As long as women of color are not given the agency to shine, they face an uphill struggle to succeed.

Can power ever be fully shared—not competed for—so that each person in the workplace regardless of their race, ethnicity, gender identity, sexual orientation, religion, disability, and immigration status has the opportunity to be deemed powerful? I turned to Nilofer Merchant, author of *The Power of Onlyness*, for an answer.

Merchant urges each of us to connect with the place of power that is *only* within ourselves; each of us stands in our own spot in the world, and from that vantage point, we each have the agency to create the world we want to live in. This unique power is what she calls "onlyness."

Too many existing systems reward an exceptional, lone wolf visionary—almost always a white man—while requiring all others to fit into an existing mold. *Onlyness* posits that power is not a zero-sum game, and that we all win when we create new systems of power that recognize our unique abilities to lead and include others.

Inclusion on purpose will require more leaders with privilege to stop hoarding power and share it with others who don't look like them. It requires a focus on justice—undoing historic harms and rebuilding entirely new workplaces. What I outline in this book is just a starting point toward building workplaces where power is shared and the concept of justice is central to our future.

To move forward, we must build a coalition and community of like-minded people. People with societal power and privilege will need to step up and vocally identify themselves as advocates and allies, as champions of a future that is intentionally inclusive and propels women of color. It's already happening—and the inclusive leader understands that inclusion isn't a nice to have, it's the most important leadership trait for the future.

Women of color (whom we know are not a monolith) are already the largest demographic worldwide. A future with women of color at its center is being created *right this moment*. A growing number of women of color are eschewing existing systems to create their own. Examples include singer and songwriter Beyoncé walking out of a multimillion-dollar partnership after refusing to work with a homogeneous creative team at Reebok, and Arlan Hamilton, who is building a venture capital fund to power underestimated entrepreneurs by including many first-time investors. There are other everyday examples, like my mother, an Indian woman, who first entered the workforce in her fifties, and is now running her own business and turning away from societal expectations of what women like her can achieve. I see it in the women of color who bravely call out bias at tremendous risk, and all the ones who plant seeds so that future generations of women of color can enjoy the fruits of their labor, long after they're gone. I felt it in every conversation that I had while gathering stories for this book.

Expanding the influence of women of color is the only hope that we have to navigate our complex and polarized world—one that is facing massive disruption from climate change, recovery from a frightening global pandemic, civil and political unrest, and rising inequality. We risk standing to lose so much by putting up barriers to prevent women of color leaders from collaborating and innovating. Inclusion on purpose requires every single one of us.

We can all win when we focus on turning away from perpetually seeking the spotlight, which only has space for one person to be illuminated, and toward the sun, where there is more than enough light for all of us to shine.

Acknowledgments

My mother knew that I would write this book starting from when I was a little girl. I was always the go-to storyteller, and would often advocate fearlessly for other girls—and later, women—when I was young. It took much longer to do that for myself, but I learned from my role model. I love you, mum.

I am humbled by the incredible trust that so many women of color placed in me to tell their stories. Many of you spoke despite great risk to your employment status and even your mental health as you recounted stories of workplace abuse and trauma. There aren't enough words of gratitude for your bravery. Thank you to all the experts who remind us this is not a one-off but rather structural problem.

I could not have written this book without my agent, Maile Beal. You saw in me what I could not envision and advocated for me to bring it to life. Thank you.

Thank you to my editor, Emily Taber. Your tireless guidance and also commiseration/compassion on being a working mum during a once-in-a-lifetime pandemic helped see this book to the end. Thank you to the entire MIT Press team for believing in me.

Thanks to the peer reviewers, especially the most critical one. You made me so much better, and I hope this final version makes you proud.

Thank you, Ijeoma Oluo. You lead by being your authentic self and spreading light wherever you go. The world is so lucky to learn from your brilliance, and I am humbled to have your bold voice to open this book.

Thank you to all the people who amplify me in quiet and mysterious ways. It means the world to me.

Thank you to all the champions who cheered me on during the writing process: Sonora Jha, Amy Gallo, Theo Nestor, Diya Khanna, Minda Harts, Deepa Purushothaman, Sarah Stuteville, Shruti Subramanian, and Shareen Pathak. Many, many bubbles/cake when we get to the other side.

Thank you to Mom and Papa; without your support, I could not have achieved this goal.

Ra and Sameer, we overcame so much with strength and hope! Survivors keep on surviving. Hugs to Rahul and Ahi.

Paras, the universe conspired! Just like you said it would. Love you more. I remain inspired by the way you lead your global team as a purposefully inclusive leader, every single day.

Most of all, this book is a written expression of my commitment to create a future where no matter who you are, you can thrive. Thank you, Veer, for fueling that passion and igniting the fire in me to work toward a better world for you and for all children who will go on to become the leaders of tomorrow.

Notes

Introduction

1. Jonathan Woetzel, Anu Madgavkar, Kweilin Ellingrud, Eric Labaye, Sandrine Devillard, Eric Kutcher, James Manyika, et al., "How Advancing Women's Equality Can Add $12 Trillion to Global Growth," McKinsey Global Institute, September 1, 2015, https://www.mckinsey.com/featured-insights/employment-and-growth/how-advancing-womens-equality-can-add-12-trillion-to-global-growth; Kweilin Ellingrud, Anu Madgavkar, James Manyika, Jonathan Woetzel, Vivian Riefberg, Mekala Krishnan, and Mili Seoni, "The Power of Parity: Advancing Women's Equality in the United States," McKinsey Global Institute, April 7, 2016, https://www.mckinsey.com/featured-insights/employment-and-growth/the-power-of-parity-advancing-womens-equality-in-the-united-states.

2. Katherine W. Phillips, "How Diversity Makes Us Smarter," *Greater Good Magazine*, September 18, 2017, https://greatergood.berkeley.edu/article/item/how_diversity_makes_us_smarter.

3. "Closing the Gender Gap Accelerators," World Economic Forum, https://www.weforum.org/projects/closing-the-gender-gap-accelerators.

4. Ruchika Tulshyan, *The Diversity Advantage: Fixing Gender Inequality in the Workplace* (New York: Forbes, 2015).

5. Howard Schneider, "U.S. Labor Shock from Pandemic Hit Women of Color Hardest; Will It Persist?," Reboot-Live, Reuters, October 5, 2020, https://www.reuters.com/article/us-great-reboot-data-idUSKBN26Q1LR.

6. Meredith Covington and Ana H. Kent, "The 'She-Cession' Persists, Especially for Women of Color," *St. Louis Fed on the Economy* (blog), Federal Reserve Bank of St. Louis, December 24, 2020, https://www.stlouisfed.org/on-the-economy/2020/december/she-cession-persists-women-of-color.

7. "The World Bank in South Africa," World Bank, last updated October 10, 2019, https://www.worldbank.org/en/country/southafrica/overview.

8. Pippa Stevens, "Racial Inequality Cost the Economy $16 Trillion over the Last Two Decades, Citi Finds," Economy, CNBC, last updated September 24, 2020, https://www.cnbc.com/2020/09/24/racial-inequality-cost-the-economy-16-trillion-over-the-last-two-decades-citi-finds.html.

9. "Women of Color in the United States: Quick Take," Catalyst, February 1, 2021, https://www.catalyst.org/research/women-of-color-in-the-united-states.

10. Heather Long and Andrew Van Dam, "For the First Time, Most New Working-Age Hires in the U.S. Are People of Color," Business, *Washington Post*, September 9, 2019, https://www.washingtonpost.com/business/economy/for-the-first-time-ever-most-new-working-age-hires-in-the-us-are-people-of-color/2019/09/09/8edc48a2-bd10-11e9-b873-63ace636af08_story.html.

11. "Kimberlé Crenshaw on Intersectionality, More Than Two Decades Later," Stories and News, Columbia Law School, June 8, 2017, https://www.law.columbia.edu/pt-br/news/2017/06/kimberle-crenshaw-intersectionality.

12. Quoted in Katy Steinmetz, "She Coined the Term 'Intersectionality' over 30 Years Ago. Here's What It Means to Her Today," *Time*, February 20, 2020, https://time.com/5786710/kimberle-crenshaw-intersectionality.

13. Ashleigh Shelby Rosette, Rebecca Ponce de Leon, Christy Zhou Koval, and David A. Harrison, "Intersectionality: Connecting Experiences of Gender with Race at Work," *Research in Organizational Behavior* 38 (2018): 1–22, https://doi.org/10.1016/j.riob.2018.12.002.

14. Barbara Frankel, "Half of Multicultural Women Are Thinking of Quitting. Here's Why," Career, *Working Mother*, May 27, 2020, https://www.workingmother.com/why-women-of-color-want-to-quit.

15. Kathleen Fuegen, Monica Biernat, Elizabeth Haines, and Kay Deaux, "Mothers and Fathers in the Workplace: How Gender and Parental Status Influence Judgments of Job-Related Competence," *Journal of Social Issues* 60, no. 4 (December 2004): 737–754, https://doi.org/10.1111/j.0022-4537.2004.00383.x.

16. "How the Pandemic Is Affecting Working Mothers," Public Policy, Knowledge@Wharton, University of Pennsylvania, September 29, 2020, https://knowledge.wharton.upenn.edu/article/how-the-pandemic-is-affecting-working-mothers.

17. Kimberly Seals Allers, "Rethinking Work-Life Balance for Women of Color," Work, *Slate*, March 5, 2018, https://slate.com/human-interest/2018/03/for-women-of -color-work-life-balance-is-a-different-kind-of-problem.html.

Chapter 1

1. Ruchika Tulshyan and Jodi-Ann Burey, "Stop Telling Women They Have Imposter Syndrome," *Harvard Business Review*, February 11, 2021, https://hbr.org /2021/02/stop-telling-women-they-have-imposter-syndrome.

2. John Amaechi, "Privilege Blinds Us to Plight of Others Who Lack It," Opinion, Workplace Diversity and Equality, *Financial Times*, November 17, 2020, https://www.ft .com/content/e394fd7b-5bdb-4d96-8375-a10a24e960c2.

3. Jessica Hamzelou, "Be a Player, Hate the Game: Beating Sex Discrimination," *New Scientist*, May 13, 2014, https://www.newscientist.com/article/dn25555-be-a-player -hate-the-game-beating-sex-discrimination.

4. Joan C. Williams, Su Li, Roberta Rincon, and Peter Finn, *Climate Control: Gender and Racial Bias in Engineering?* (San Francisco: Society of Women Engineers, University of California Hastings College of the Law, 2016), https://research.swe.org /climate-control.

5. Sarah-Soonling Blackburn, "What Is the Model Minority Myth?," Learning for Justice (formerly Teaching Tolerance), March 21, 2019, https://www.tolerance.org /magazine/what-is-the-model-minority-myth.

6. Darrick Hamilton and Trevon Logan, "This Is Why the Wealth Gap between Black and White Americans Persists," How to Be a Success at Everything, *Fast Company*, February 8, 2020, https://www.fastcompany.com/90461708/why-wealth-equality -remains-out-of-reach-for-black-americans.

7. Ibram X. Kendi, interview by Jenn White, "Historian Ibram X. Kendi on 'How to Be an Antiracist,'" *Reset*, WBEZ, NPR, October 30, 2019, https://www.npr.org /local/309/2019/10/30/774704183/historian-ibram-x-kendi-on-how-to-be-an-anti racist.

8. Maxine Najle and Robert P. Jones, "American Democracy in Crisis: The Fate of Pluralism in a Divided Nation," PRRI, February 19, 2019, https://www.prri.org /research/american-democracy-in-crisis-the-fate-of-pluralism-in-a-divided-nation.

9. Emma Green, "These Are the Americans Who Live in a Bubble," Politics, *Atlantic*, February 21, 2019, https://www.theatlantic.com/politics/archive/2019/02/americans -remain-deeply-ambivalent-about-diversity/583123.

10. Rachel Thomas, Marianne Cooper, Ellen Konar, Megan Rooney, Mary Noble-Tolla, Ali Bohrer, Lareina Yee, et al., *Women in the Workplace 2018*, LeanIn.org and

McKinsey & Company, 2018, https://wiw-report.s3.amazonaws.com/Women_in _the_Workplace_2018.pdf.

11. Oswald Yeo, quoted in Christopher Quek, "Company Culture Is What You Reward, Punish, and Tolerate, Says This Founder," Tech in Asia, May 19, 2017, http:// https://www.techinasia.com/talk/company-culture-reward-punish-tolerate.

12. Tiffany Hsu, "NBC News Hits Back against Ronan Farrow's 'Catch and Kill' Book," Media, New York Times, October 14, 2019, https://www.nytimes.com/2019 /10/14/business/media/nbc-news-ronan-farrow-matt-lauer-catch-and-kill.html; Shannon Liao, "Google Confirms It Agreed to Pay $135 Million to Two Execs Accused of Sexual Harassment," Verge, March 11, 2019, https://www.theverge.com/2019 /3/11/18260712/google-amit-singhal-andy-rubin-payout-lawsuit-accused-sexual -harassment.

13. Shirin Ghaffary, "Dozens of Google Employees Say They Were Retaliated against for Reporting Harassment," Recode, Vox, September 9, 2019, https://www.vox .com/recode/2019/9/9/20853647/google-employee-retaliation-harassment-me-too -exclusive.

14. Rachel Thomas, Marianne Cooper, Ellen Konar, Ali Bohrer, Ava Mohsenin, Lar-eina Yee, Alexis Krivkovich, et al., Women in the Workplace 2019, LeanIn.org and McKinsey & Company, 2019, https://wiw-report.s3.amazonaws.com/Women_in _the_Workplace_2019.pdf.

15. Catalyst, Women of Color Executives: Their Voices, Their Journeys, June 19, 2001, https://www.catalyst.org/research/women-of-color-executives-their-voices-their -journeys.

16. Christi Carrasstaff, "Here's What's Happening with Gabrielle Union and 'America's Got Talent,'" Television, Los Angeles Times, December 4, 2019, https:// www.latimes.com/entertainment-arts/tv/story/2019-12-02/gabrielle-union-fired -americas-got-talent-nbc.

17. Quoted in Emily Longeretta, "Heidi Klum Defends 'America's Got Talent' amid Gabrielle Union Drama: I Was Treated with the 'Utmost Respect,'" Us Magazine, January 15, 2020, https://www.usmagazine.com/celebrity-news/news/heidi-klum -defends-americas-got-talent-amid-gabrielle-union-drama.

18. Ross Kerber and Simon Jessop, "The Heat's on Corporate America to Reveal Racial Diversity Data," Reboot-Live, Reuters, July 2, 2020, https://www.reuters.com /article/us-minneapolis-police-corporatediversity-idUSKBN2431JY.

19. Ijeoma Oluo, "Welcome to the Anti-Racism Movement—Here's What You've Missed," Establishment, April 15, 2019, https://theestablishment.co/welcome-to-the -anti-racism-movement-heres-what-you-ve-missed-711089cb7d34/#.ct1d3li7r.

Chapter 2

1. Erika Stallings, "Racism at My Job Literally Gave Me PTSD," Overloaded, Cut, *New York*, August 12, 2020, https://www.thecut.com/article/racism-at-my-job-literally-gave-me-ptsd.html.

2. Judith Warner, *"The Unequal Toll of Toxic Stress: How the Mental Burdens of Bias, Trauma, and Family Hardship Impact Girls and Women,"* Center for American Progress, November 17, 2017, https://www.americanprogress.org/issues/women/reports/2017/11/17/443028/unequal-toll-toxic-stress.

3. Carol Dweck, "What Having a 'Growth Mindset' Actually Means," Managing Yourself, *Harvard Business Review*, January 13, 2016, https://hbr.org/2016/01/what-having-a-growth-mindset-actually-means.

4. Carol Dweck, Mary Murphy, Jennifer Chatman, and Laura Kay, *Why Fostering a Growth Mindset in Organizations Matters*, Senn-Delaney Leadership Consulting Group, LLC, 2014, http://knowledge.senndelaney.com/docs/thought_papers/pdf/stanford_agilitystudy_hart.pdf.

5. Frank Tuitt, Michele Hanna, Lisa M. Martinez, Maria del Carmen Salazar, and Rachel Griffin, "Teaching in the Line of Fire: Faculty of Color in the Academy," *Thought and Action* (Fall 2009): 65–74, https://www.researchgate.net/publication/238743498_Teaching_in_the_Line_of_Fire_Faculty_of_Color_in_the_Academy.

6. Jason S. Moser, Hans S. Schroeder, Carrie Heeter, Tim P. Moran, and Yu-Hao Lee, "Mind Your Errors: Evidence for a Neural Mechanism Linking Growth Mind-Set to Adaptive Posterror Adjustments," *Psychological Science* 22, no. 12 (December 2011): 1484–1489, https://doi.org/10.1177/0956797611419520.

7. "A Follow-up Message from Starbucks CEO in Philadelphia," Starbucks Stories and News, April 15, 2018, 2:22, https://stories.starbucks.com/press/2018/a-follow-up-message-from-starbucks-ceo-in-philadelphia.

8. Andrew M. Ibrahim, "Becoming Anti-Racist," Redesigning Delivery of Surgical Care, https://www.surgeryredesign.com.

Chapter 3

1. Daniel Cox, Juhem Navarro-Rivera, and Robert P. Jones, "Race, Religion, and Political Affiliation of Americans' Core Social Networks," PRRI, August 3, 2016, https://www.prri.org/research/poll-race-religion-politics-americans-social-networks.

2. Ruchika Tulshyan, "Singapore's Social Experiment Key to Economic Success," *Forbes*, June 1, 2015, https://www.forbes.com/sites/ruchikatulshyan/2015/06/01/singapores-social-experiment-key-to-economic-success/#546961596fd0.

3. Rosabeth Moss Kanter, "Some Effects of Proportions on Group Life: Skewed Sex Ratios and Responses to Token Women," *American Journal of Sociology* 82, no. 5 (1977): 965–990, http://www.jstor.org/stable/2777808.

4. "Being a Token Is More Difficult for Some Employees," Academy of Management Insights, January 14, 2019, https://journals.aom.org/doi/full/10.5465/amp.2015.0154 .summary.

5. Quoted in "Research Shows Us Workplaces Need This Level of Diversity to Prevent Tokenism," Future of Work, *Fast Company*, June 13, 2020, https://www.fastcompany .com/90516384/research-shows-us-workplaces-need-this-level-of-diversity-to-prevent -tokenism.

6. Derald Wing Sue, *Microaggressions in Everyday Life*, 2nd ed. (Hoboken, NJ: Wiley, 2020).

7. Ibram X. Kendi, *How to Be an Antiracist* (New York: One World, 2019), https:// www.ibramxkendi.com/how-to-be-an-antiracist.

8. Jonathan Kanter, "Microaggressions Aren't Just Innocent Blunders—New Research Links Them with Racial Bias," *Conversation*, September 24, 2020, https:// theconversation.com/microaggressions-arent-just-innocent-blunders-new-research -links-them-with-racial-bias-145894.

9. Emma Gannon, "Kiley Reid: When Fiction Does What a Thinkpiece Cannot," *Ctrl Alt Delete*, January 30, 2020, 29:00, https://play.acast.com/s/ctrlaltdelete/-242kileyreid -whenfictiondoeswhatathinkpiececannot.

10. "Empathy Quiz," Quizzes, *Greater Good Magazine*, https://greatergood.berkeley .edu/quizzes/take_quiz/empathy.

11. Quoted in Ruth Umoh, "60% of Employees Surveyed Would Take a Pay Cut to Work for This Type of Company," CNBC Make It, June 19, 2018, https://www.cnbc .com/2018/06/12/60-percent-of-workers-would-take-a-pay-cut-to-work-for-an -empathetic-company.html.

12. Umoh, "60% of Employees Surveyed Would Take a Pay Cut to Work for This Type of Company."

13. Jamil Zaki, *The War for Kindness: Building Empathy in a Fractured World* (New York: Crown, 2019), https://www.warforkindness.com.

14. Robin Young, "How Power Erodes Empathy, and the Steps We Can Take to Rebuild It," *Here and Now*, July 9, 2020, 10:47, https://www.wbur.org/hereandnow /2020/07/09/jamil-zaki-empathy-power.

Chapter 4

1. Joan C. Williams and Marina Multhaup, "For Women and Minorities to Get Ahead, Managers Must Assign Work Fairly," Diversity, *Harvard Business Review*, March 5, 2018, https://hbr.org/2018/03/for-women-and-minorities-to-get-ahead-managers-must-assign-work-fairly.

2. Grainne Fitzsimons, Aaron Kay, and Jae Yun Kim, "'Lean In' Messages and the Illusion of Control," Gender, *Harvard Business Review*, July 30, 2018, https://hbr.org/2018/07/lean-in-messages-and-the-illusion-of-control.

3. Ruchika Tulshyan and Jodi-Ann Burey, "Stop Telling Women They Have Imposter Syndrome," *Harvard Business Review*, February 11, 2021, https://hbr.org/2021/02/stop-telling-women-they-have-imposter-syndrome.

4. Danielle Kost, "You're Right! You Are Working Longer and Attending More Meetings," Harvard Business School Working Knowledge, September 14, 2020, https://hbswk.hbs.edu/item/you-re-right-you-are-working-longer-and-attending-more-meetings.

5. Christopher F. Karpowitz, Tali Mendelberg, and Lee Shaker, "Gender Inequality in Deliberative Participation," *American Political Science Review* 106, no. 3 (August 2012): 533–547, https://doi.org/10.1017/S0003055412000329; Deborah Tannen, "Gender in the Workplace," in *Gender and Discourse* (London: Sage Publications, 1997), chapter 4, https://time.com/wp-content/uploads/2017/06/d3375-genderandlanguageintheworkplace.pdf.

6. Alisha Haridasani Gupta, "It's Not Just You: In Online Meetings, Many Women Can't Get a Word In," In Her Words, *New York Times*, April 14, 2020, https://www.nytimes.com/2020/04/14/us/zoom-meetings-gender.html.

7. Tonja Jacobi and Dylan Schweers, "Justice, Interrupted: The Effect of Gender, Ideology, and Seniority at Supreme Court Oral Arguments," *Virginia Law Review* 103, no. 7 (December 2017): 1379–1496, https://www.virginialawreview.org/wp-content/uploads/2020/12/JacobiSchweers_Online.pdf.

8. Zameena Mejia, "How to Combat 'Hepeating' at Work, According to a Harvard Professor," CNBC Make It, October 11, 2017, https://www.cnbc.com/2017/10/11/how-to-combat-hepeating-at-work-according-to-a-harvard-professor.html.

9. Quoted in Juliet Eilperin, "How a White House Women's Office Strategy Went Viral," PowerPost, *Washington Post*, October 25, 2016, https://www.washingtonpost.com/news/powerpost/wp/2016/10/25/how-a-white-house-womens-office-strategy-went-viral.

10. Christine Silva, Nancy M. Carter, and Anna Beninger, *Good Intentions, Imperfect Execution? Women Get Fewer of the "Hot Jobs" Needed to Advance*, Catalyst, 2012,

https://www.catalyst.org/research/good-intentions-imperfect-execution-women
-get-fewer-of-the-hot-jobs-needed-to-advance.

11. Coqual, *The Sponsor Dividend*, 2019, CoqualTheSponsorDividend_KeyFindings
Combined090720.pdf.

12. Shivina Kumar, "New Study: Almost 70% of Professional Event Speakers Are
Male," *Bizzabo Blog*, November 1, 2018, https://blog.bizzabo.com/event-gender-diver
sity-study.

Chapter 5

1. Katherine W. Phillips, "How Diversity Makes Us Smarter," Policy and Ethics, *Scientific American*, October 1, 2014, https://www.scientificamerican.com/article/how
-diversity-makes-us-smarter.

2. Samuel R. Sommers, "On Racial Diversity and Group Decision Making: Identifying Multiple Effects of Racial Composition on Jury Deliberations," *Journal of
Personality and Social Psychology* 90, no. 4 (2006): 597–612, https://doi.org/10.1037
/0022-3514.90.4.597.

3. "'Hire for Culture, Train for Skill': Recruiters Reject Candidates Based on Their Lack
of Cultural Fit," Insights, Cubiks, April 4, 2016, https://www.cubiks.com/insights/hire
-culture-train-skill-recruiters-reject-candidates-based-their-lack-cultural-fit.

4. Jocelyn Frye, "Racism and Sexism Combine to Shortchange Working Black
Women," Center for American Progress, August 22, 2019, https://www.americanprog-
ress.org/issues/women/news/2019/08/22/473775/racism-sexism-combine-shortchange
-working-black-women.

5. Brian W. Collins, "Tackling Unconscious Bias in Hiring Practices: The Plight of
the Rooney Rule," *New York University Law Review* 82, no. 3 (June 2007): 870–912,
https://www.nyulawreview.org/wp-content/uploads/2018/08/NYULawReview-82-3
-Collins.pdf.

6. Helen Turnbull, "The Affinity Bias Conundrum: The Illusion of Inclusion—Part III,"
Inclusive Workplace, *Profiles in Diversity Journal*, May 20, 2014, https://diversityjournal
.com/13763-affinity-bias-conundrum-illusion-inclusion-part-iii.

7. Harvard Business School, "New Report: Degree Inflation Hurting Bottom Line of
U.S. Firms, Closing Off Economic Opportunity for Millions of Americans," October 25,
2017, https://www.hbs.edu/news/releases/Pages/degree-inflation-us-competetiveness
.aspx.

8. Andrew Howard Nichols and Marshall Anthony Jr., "Graduation Rates Don't
Tell the Full Story: Racial Gaps in College Success Are Larger Than We Think," Education Trust, March 5, 2020, https://edtrust.org/resource/graduation-rates-dont-tell
-the-full-story-racial-gaps-in-college-success-are-larger-than-we-think.

9. Peter Arcidiacono, Josh Kinsler, and Tyler Ransom, "Legacy and Athlete Preferences at Harvard" (working paper, National Bureau of Economic Research, September 2019), https://www.nber.org/system/files/working_papers/w26316/w26316.pdf.

10. Lydia Frank, "How to Use Employee Referrals without Giving up Workplace Diversity," Hiring, *Harvard Business Review*, March 15, 2018, https://hbr.org/2018/03/how-to-use-employee-referrals-without-giving-up-workplace-diversity.

11. Katherine Reynolds Lewis, "Diverse Interview Panels May Be a Key to Workplace Diversity," Career, *Working Mother*, June–July 2017, https://www.workingmother.com/diverse-interview-panels-may-be-key-to-workplace-diversity.

12. Lincoln Quillian, Anthony Heath, Devah Pager, Arnfinn H. Modtbøen, Fenella Fleischmann, and Ole Hegel, "Do Some Countries Discriminate More Than Others? Evidence from 97 Field Experiments of Racial Discrimination in Hiring," *Sociological Science* 6 (June 17, 2019): 467–496, https://doi.org/10.15195/V6.A18.

13. Lewis, "Diverse Interview Panels May Be a Key to Workplace Diversity."

14. Amy Dorsey, "Seriously, Why Are Women Expected to Smile All the Time?," *Women's Health*, November 11, 2015, https://www.womenshealthmag.com/life/a19934710/women-expected-to-smile.

15. Melissa De Witte, "Stanford Study Shows How Job Candidates Show Their Emotions May Result in Hiring Disparities, Workplace Bias," Stanford University, July 6, 2018, https://news.stanford.edu/2018/07/06/emotions-may-result-hiring-workplace-bias.

16. Deborah L. DeHaas, Brent Bachus, and Eliza Horn, *Unleashing the Power of Inclusion: Attracting and Engaging the Evolving Workforce*, Billie Jean King Leadership Initiative, 2017, https://www2.deloitte.com/content/dam/Deloitte/us/Documents/about-deloitte/us-about-deloitte-unleashing-power-of-inclusion.pdf.

17. A special thanks to Martha Burwell for her assistance with this list.

Chapter 6

1. "Equal Pay for Work of Equal Value," International Equal Pay Day 18 September, United Nations, accessed February 18, 2021, https://www.un.org/en/observances/equal-pay-day.

2. "Equal Pay for Work of Equal Value."

3. Lilian Wu and Wei Jing, "Asian Women in STEM Careers: An Invisible Minority in a Double Bind," Real Numbers, *Issues in Science and Technology* 28, no. 1 (Fall 2011), https://issues.org/realnumbers-29/.

4. Wu and Jing, "Asian Women in STEM Careers."

5. Damir Cosic, "College Premium and Its Impact on Racial and Gender Differentials in Earnings and Future Old-Age Income" (working paper, Urban Institute, March 2019), https://www.pgpf.org/sites/default/files/US-2050-The-College-Premium-and-Its-Impact-on-Racial-and-Gender-Differentials-in-Earnings-and-Future-Retirement-Income.pdf.

6. Erica Pandey, "The Failed Promise of Education," Politics and Policy, *Axios*, November 14, 2020, https://www.axios.com/hard-truths-deep-dive-education-failed-promise-f89cb2af-79c3-4993-bb7e-65c306cc5a2f.html.

7. "Degrees Conferred by Race and Sex," Fast Facts, National Center for Education Statistics, https://nces.ed.gov/fastfacts/display.asp?id=72.

8. Arya Hodjat, "'White Fragility' Author Paid More for University Speaking Gig Than Black Counterpart, Receipts Show," Unequal, *Daily Beast*, November 24, 2020, https://www.thedailybeast.com/white-fragility-author-robin-diangelo-paid-more-for-university-speaking-gig-than-black-counterpart.

9. Alisa Wolfson, "Why 68% of People Would Rather Talk about Their Weight Than Money," Moneyish, *MarketWatch*, January 25, 2018, https://www.marketwatch.com/story/why-68-of-people-would-rather-talk-about-their-weight-than-money-2018-01-25.

10. Constance Grady, "Black Authors Are on All the Bestseller Lists Right Now. But Publishing Doesn't Pay Them Enough," *Vox*, June 17, 2020, https://www.vox.com/culture/2020/6/17/21285316/publishing-paid-me-diversity-black-authors-systemic-bias.

11. Barbara Frankel, *On the Verge: How to Stop the Tidal Wave of Multicultural Women Fleeing Corporate America*, Working Mother Research Institute, 2020, https://www.workingmother.com/sites/workingmother.com/files/attachments/2020/07/multicultural-women-gender-gap-report.pdf.

12. Benjamin Artz, Amanda Goodall, and Andrew J. Oswald, "Research: Women Ask for Raises as Often as Men, but Are Less Likely to Get Them," Gender, *Harvard Business Review*, June 25, 2018, https://hbr.org/2018/06/research-women-ask-for-raises-as-often-as-men-but-are-less-likely-to-get-them.

13. "How to Ask for a Raise and Get It," PayScale, https://www.payscale.com/data/how-to-ask-for-a-raise.

14. Morela Hernandez, Derek R. Avery, Sabrina D. Volpone, and Cheryl R. Kaiser, "Bargaining While Black: The Role of Race in Salary Negotiations," *Journal of Applied Psychology* 104, no. 4 (2019): 581–592, https://doi.org/10.1037/apl0000363.

15. Ian Ayres and Peter Siegelman, "Race and Gender Discrimination in Bargaining for a New Car," *American Economic Review* 85, no. 3 (1995): 304–321, http://www.jstor.org/stable/2118176.

16. Trish Larson, *Workplace Negotiations, Gender, and Intersectionality*, Gloria Cordes Larson Center for Women and Business, Bentley University, Winter 2020, https://www.bentley.edu/centers/center-for-women-and-business/negotiations-research-report-request.

17. Rachel Thomas, Marianne Cooper, Ellen Konar, Ali Bohrer, Ava Mohsenin, Lareina Yee, Alexis Krivkovich, et al., *Women in the Workplace 2019*, LeanIn.org and McKinsey & Company, 2019, https://wiw-report.s3.amazonaws.com/Women_in_the_Workplace_2019.pdf.

18. Shane Ryoo, "Why Women Leave the Tech Industry at a 45% Higher Rate Than Men," Quora, *Forbes*, February 28, 2017, https://www.forbes.com/sites/quora/2017/02/28/why-women-leave-the-tech-industry-at-a-45-higher-rate-than-men/#5711c91b4216.

19. Arlan Hamilton and Rachel L. Nelson, *It's about Damn Time: How to Turn Being Underestimated into Your Greatest Advantage* (New York: Currency, 2020).

Chapter 7

1. Rachel Thomas, Marianne Cooper, Ellen Konar, Ali Bohrer, Ava Mohsenin, Lareina Yee, Alexis Krivkovich, et al., *Women in the Workplace 2019*, LeanIn.org and McKinsey & Company, 2019, https://wiw-report.s3.amazonaws.com/Women_in_the_Workplace_2019.pdf.

2. Zuhairah Washington and Laura Morgan Roberts, "Women of Color Get Less Support at Work. Here's How Managers Can Change That," Race, *Harvard Business Review*, March 4, 2019, https://hbr.org/2019/03/women-of-color-get-less-support-at-work-heres-how-managers-can-change-that.

3. Shelley J. Correll and Caroline Simard, "Research: Vague Feedback Is Holding Women Back," Giving Feedback, *Harvard Business Review*, April 29, 2016, https://hbr.org/2016/04/research-vague-feedback-is-holding-women-back.

4. Correll and Simard, "Research."

5. "Tone Policing," Dictionary.com, https://www.dictionary.com/browse/tone-policing.

6. Leading Effectively staff, "Use Situation-Behavior-Impact (SBI) to Understand Intent," Feedback, Center for Creative Leadership, November 18, 2020, https://www.ccl.org/articles/leading-effectively-articles/closing-the-gap-between-intent-vs-impact-sbii.

7. Aysa Gray, "The Bias of 'Professionalism' Standards," Human Rights, *Stanford Social Innovation Review*, June 4, 2019, https://ssir.org/articles/entry/the_bias_of_professionalism_standards.

8. H. Samy Alim and Geneva Smitherman, "Of Course Kamala Harris Is Articulate," Opinion, *New York Times*, September 8, 2020, https://www.nytimes.com/2020/09 /08/opinion/kamala-harris-articulate.html.

9. Lori Nishiura Mackenzie, JoAnne Wehner, and Shelley J. Correll, "Why Most Performance Evaluations Are Biased, and How to Fix Them," Assessing Performance, *Harvard Business Review*, January 11, 2019, https://hbr.org/2019/01/why-most-performance -evaluations-are-biased-and-how-to-fix-them. On assessments as imperfect, see Alison T. Wynn and Shelley J. Correll, "Combating Gender Bias in Modern Workplaces," in *Handbook of the Sociology of Gender*, ed. Barbara J. Risman, Carissa M. Froyum, and William J. Scarborough (Cham, Switzerland: Springer, 2018), 509–521, https://doi.org /10.1007/978-3-319-76333-0_37.

10. Bias Interrupters, *"Identifying and Interrupting Bias in Performance Evaluations,"* Center for WorkLife Law, 2016, http://biasinterrupters.org/wp-content/uploads/Iden tifying-Bias-in-Performance-Evaluations-Worksheet.pdf.

11. Marco Nink, "Many Employees Don't Know What's Expected of Them at Work," Business Journal, Gallup, October 13, 2015, https://news.gallup.com/businessjournal /186164/employees-don-know-expected-work.aspx.s

Chapter 8

1. Amy C. Edmondson, *The Fearless Organization: Creating Psychological Safety in the Workplace for Learning, Innovation, and Growth* (Hoboken, NJ: Wiley, 2018).

2. Erving Goffman, *The Presentation of Self in Everyday Life* (New York: Doubleday, 1959), https://books.google.com/books/about/The_Presentation_of_Self_in_Everyday _Lif.html?id=Sdt-cDkV8pQC.

3. Uché Blackstock, "Why Black Doctors Like Me Are Leaving Faculty Positions in Academic Medical Centers," First Opinion, *Stat*, January 16, 2020, https://www .statnews.com/2020/01/16/black-doctors-leaving-faculty-positions-academic -medical-centers/.

4. David Pedulla, "Diversity and Inclusion Efforts That Really Work," Gender, *Harvard Business Review*, May 12, 2020, https://hbr.org/2020/05/diversity-and-inclusion -efforts-that-really-work.

5. Lean In, *The State of Black Women in Corporate America*, LeanIn.org, 2020, https:// leanin.org/research/state-of-black-women-in-corporate-america.

6. Lean In, *The State of Black Women in Corporate America*.

7. Judy C. Casey, "Employee Resource Groups: A Strategic Business Resource for Today's Workplace," Executive Briefing Series, Boston College Center for Work and Family, https://www.bc.edu/content/dam/files/centers/cwf/research/publications3 /executivebriefingseries-2/ExecutiveBriefing_EmployeeResourceGroups.pdf.

8. Katherine Connor Martin, "New Words Notes March 2018," *Oxford English Dictionary* (blog), March 29, 2018, https://public.oed.com/blog/march-2018-new-words-notes.

9. Joe Chung, "Tenets Provide Essential Guidance on Your Cloud Journey," *AWS Cloud Enterprise Strategy Blog*, Amazon Web Services, March 8, 2017, https://aws.amazon.com/blogs/enterprise-strategy/tenets-provide-essential-guidance-on-your-cloud-journey.

Chapter 9

1. Stine Eckert and Jade Metzger-Riftkin, "Doxxing," *International Encyclopedia of Gender, Media, and Communication*, March 3, 2020, https://doi.org/10.1002/97811194 29128.iegmc009.

2. Paulina Villegas, "NDAs Have Long Been Used to Silence the Abused, Advocates Say. A New Law May Change That," Business, *Washington Post*, February 8, 2021, https://www.washingtonpost.com/business/2021/02/08/california-silenced-no-more-act.

3. GeekWire and KING 5, "UW Lecturer Defends 'Why Women Don't Code' Essay," Tech, KING 5, June 25, 2018, https://www.king5.com/article/tech/uw-lecturer-defends-why-women-dont-code-essay/281-567436719.

4. Buck Gee and Denise Peck, *The Illusion of Asian Success: Scant Progress for Minorities in Cracking the Glass Ceiling from 2007–2015*, Ascend Foundation, 2017, https://cdn.ymaws.com/www.ascendleadership.org/resource/resmgr/research/theillusionofasiansuccess.pdf.

5. National Center for Science and Engineering Statistics, *Women, Minorities, and Persons with Disabilities in Science and Engineering: 2017*, National Science Foundation, 2017, https://www.nsf.gov/statistics/2017/nsf17310/digest/about-this-report.

6. Stella Fayer, Alan Lacey, and Audrey Watson, "STEM Occupations: Past, Present, and Future," Spotlight on Statistics, US Bureau of Labor Statistics, January 2017, https://www.bls.gov/spotlight/2017/science-technology-engineering-and-mathematics-stem-occupations-past-present-and-future/pdf/science-technology-engineering-and-mathematics-stem-occupations-past-present-and-future.pdf.

7. Joy Buolamwini, "How I'm Fighting Bias in Algorithms," November 2016, TEDx Talks, 8:36, https://www.ted.com/talks/joy_buolamwini_how_i_m_fighting_bias_in_algorithms.

8. Buolamwini, "How I'm Fighting Bias in Algorithms."

9. "Coalition Letter to the Department of Justice Civil Rights Division Calling for an Investigation of the Disparate Impact of Face Recognition on Communities of Color,"

ACLU, October 18, 2016, https://www.aclu.org/letter/coalition-letter-department-jus
tice-civil-rights-division-calling-investigation-disparate.

10. Benjamin Wilson, Judy Hoffman, and Jamie Morgenstern, "Predictive Inequity in
Object Detection" (research study, Cornell University, February 21, 2019), https://arxiv
.org/pdf/1902.11097.pdf.

11. Caitlin Ring Carlson and Haley Witt, "Online Harassment of U.S. Women Journalists and Its Impact on Press Freedom," *First Monday* 25, no. 11 (November 2,
2020), https://doi.org/10.5210/fm.v25i11.11071.

12. Ellen K. Pao and Laura I. Gómez, "Dear @Jack: It's Time to Suspend Donald
Trump from Twitter," *Vox*, January 20, 2017, https://www.vox.com/2017/1/20/1433
6288/jack-dorsey-suspend-donald-trump-twitter-responsibility.

13. Ellen K. Pao, "Dear @Jack: Do the Right Thing for Democracy and Human-
kind . . . ," *Medium*, November 1, 2020, https://ekp.medium.com/dear-jack-do-the
-right-thing-for-democracy-and-humankind-632b94828381.

14. "Permanent Suspension of @realDonaldTrump," Company, Twitter Inc., January
8, 2021, https://blog.twitter.com/en_us/topics/company/2020/suspension.html.

15. Erin Carson, "Even after #MeToo, Women in Tech Say They're Still Getting
Harassed," CNET, September 16, 2020, https://www.cnet.com/news/even-after-metoo
-women-in-tech-say-theyre-still-getting-harassed.

16. Kapor Center, "Women and Girls of Color in Computing" (data brief, Center for
Gender Equity in Science and Technology, Arizona State University), https://www
.wocincomputing.org/wp-content/uploads/2018/08/WOCinComputingDataBrief.pdf.

17. Nina Zipkin, "Out of $85 Billion in VC Funding Last Year, Only 2.2 Percent
Went to Female Founders. And Every Year, Women of Color Get Less Than 1 Percent
of Total Funding," Venture Capital, *Entrepreneur*, December 12, 2018, https://www
.entrepreneur.com/article/324743.

18. Shonda Rhimes, *Year of Yes: How to Dance It Out, Stand in the Sun, and Be Your
Own Person* (New York: Simon and Schuster, 2016), 139.

19. "Stereotype Threat Widens Achievement Gap," American Psychological Association, July 15, 2006, https://www.apa.org/research/action/stereotype.

20. Black Girls Code, https://www.blackgirlscode.com; Girls Who Code, https://
girlswhocode.com.

21. Anil Dash, "The Year I Didn't Retweet Men," *Medium*, February 12, 2014,
https://medium.com/the-only-woman-in-the-room/the-year-i-didnt-retweet-men
-79403a7eade1.

Chapter 10

1. Sanjoy Chakravorty, "Viewpoint: How the British Reshaped India's Caste System," BBC, June 19, 2019, https://www.bbc.com/news/world-asia-india-48619734.

2. Oxfam India, *Mind the Gap: The State of Employment in India in 2019*, March 28, 2019, https://www.oxfamindia.org/Mind-Gap-State-of-Employment-in-India.

3. Nitasha Tiku, "India's Engineers Have Thrived in Silicon Valley. So Has Its Caste System," Technology, *Washington Post*, October 27, 2020, https://www.washingtonpost .com/technology/2020/10/27/indian-caste-bias-silicon-valley/.

4. Isabel Wilkerson, *Caste* (New York: Penguin Random House, 2020), https://www .penguinrandomhouse.com/books/653196/caste-oprahs-book-club-by-isabel -wilkerson.

5. Wilkerson, *Caste*.

6. Angela Saini, *Inferior: How Science Got Women Wrong—and the New Research That's Rewriting the Story* (Boston: Beacon Press, 2017), https://books.google.com/books /about/Inferior.html?id=U5DEDgAAQBAJ.

7. Angela Saini, *Superior: The Return of Race Science* (Boston: Beacon Press, 2019), https://www.google.com/books/edition/Superior/GFuUDwAAQBAJ.

8. Jane Coaston, "National Review's Weak Attack on Affirmative Action," *Vox*, March 21, 2018, https://www.vox.com/policy-and-politics/2018/3/21/17143150/conservative -scientific-racism-national-review; "David Starkey: Historian Apologises for 'Clumsy' Slavery Comments," Entertainment and Arts, BBC, July 6, 2020, https://www.bbc.com /news/entertainment-arts-53308061.

9. Melissa Tandiwe Myambo, "Being Darker Makes Being a Migrant Much Harder," Arts and Culture, *Conversation*, December 15, 2019, https://theconversation .com/being-darker-makes-being-a-migrant-much-harder-128340.

10. Cynthia Sims and Malar Hirudayaraj, "The Impact of Colorism on the Career Aspirations and Career Opportunities of Women in India," *Advances in Developing Human Resources* 18, no. 1 (February 2016): 38–53, https://doi.org/10.1177/152342231561 6339.

11. Doris Weichselbaumer, "Multiple Discrimination against Female Immigrants Wearing Headscarves." *ILR Review* 73, no. 3 (May 2020): 600–627. https://doi.org/10 .1177/0019793919875707.

12. Lori Nishiura Mackenzie, Lourdes V. Andrade, and Sarah A. Soule, "The Cost of Fitting In," *Fast Company*, October 19, 2020, https://www.fastcompany.com/90564479 /the-cost-of-fitting-in.

13. Division for the Advancement of Women, "Gender Mainstreaming," extract from *Report of the Economic and Social Council for 1997*, chapter 4, United Nations Department for Economic and Social Affairs, September 18, 1997, https://www.un.org/womenwatch/daw/csw/GMS.PDF.

14. "How Breaking Gender Barriers Can Increase Immunisation Coverage," Gavi, https://www.gavi.org/news/media-room/how-breaking-gender-barriers-can-increase-immunisation-coverage.

15. University of Liverpool, "Female Led Countries' COVID-19 Outcomes 'Systematically and Significantly Better,'" August 18, 2020, https://news.liverpool.ac.uk/2020/08/18/covid-19-outcomes-systematically-and-significantly-better-in-female-led-countries.

Index

data gathering and use, 33–34, 46,
123–124, 130, 135–136, 138,
181–183
exclusionary practices in, 30–31
"housework" in, 79, 90–92, 182
meetings, 81–84, 216
psychological safety in, 167–192
Workplace bias. *See also* Systemic bias
detrimental effects of, 8
examples of, 6
inherent, unconscious nature of, 10
as obstacle to DEI, 6
performance evaluations, 158–163
recognition of, 11
women of color's experience of, 7–8,
25, 32, 34, 37–39, 46, 48, 57, 60, 69,
103, 127, 140–141, 145, 246–247
Wu, Lilian Gomory, 124–125

Xerox, 186, 188

Yeo, Oswald, 30
Yousafzai, Malala, 55

Zaki, Jamil, 67, 73